Judaism Unbound (Bound)

Provocative Conversations
About the Jewish Future with
Visionary Thinkers
and Practitioners

Written and Edited by

Dan Libenson and Lex Rofeberg

Ben Yehuda Press
Teaneck, New Jersey

JUDAISM UNBOUND: BOUND ©2025 Institute for the Jewish Future. All rights reserved. No part of this book may be used or reproduced in any manner whatsoever without written permission except in the case of brief quotations embodied in critical articles and reviews.

Published by Ben Yehuda Press
122 Ayers Court #1B
Teaneck, NJ 07666
http://www.BenYehudaPress.com

To subscribe to our monthly book club and support independent Jewish publishing, visit https://www.patreon.com/BenYehudaPress

Ben Yehuda Press books may be purchased at a discount by synagogues, book clubs, and other institutions buying in bulk.

For information, please email markets@BenYehudaPress.com

Illustrated and designed by Katherine Kaestner

ISBN13 978-1-963475-66-1

Library of Congress Cataloging-in-Publication Data

Names: Libenson, Daniel, editor. | Rofeberg, Lex, editor.
Title: Judaism unbound (bound) : provocative conversations about the Jewish future with the most visionary thinkers and practitioners / written and edited by Dan Libenson, Lex Rofeberg.
Description: 1st. | Teaneck, New Jersey : Ben Yehuda Press, 2025. | Summary: "This book is for those of us who hunger for deep conversations about what Judaism is and what it is for, what Judaism has been and what it might become. Libenson and Rofeberg explore the landscape of the Jewish future in 26 discussions with Jewish thinkers and leaders transcribed from the wildly popular Jewish podcast Judaism Unbound. From April N. Baskin on audacious hospitality, to Brett Lockspeiser on the future of Torah, from Paul Golin on intermarriage to Miriam Terlinchamp on embracing the weird, these conversations touch on faith and community, on being a good Jew and being a bad Jew (but in a good way!)"-- Provided by publisher.
Identifiers: LCCN 2025018441 (print) | LCCN 2025018442 (ebook) | ISBN 9781963475661 (paperback) | ISBN 9781963475807 (ebook)
Subjects: LCSH: Judaism.
Classification: LCC BM562 .J836 2025 (print) | LCC BM562 (ebook) | DDC 296--dc23/eng/20250510
LC record available at https://lccn.loc.gov/2025018441
LC ebook record available at https://lccn.loc.gov/2025018442

25 26 27 / 10 9 8 7 6 5 4 3 2 1   20250530

To you, a dissatisfied optimist,
ready to co-create a new Jewish future.

Contents

Introduction 1

PART ONE
The Crash of Rabbinic Judaism and the Rise of the Third Era

A Time of Wandering 8
Benay Lappe / Exodus Part 1 10
Barbara Thiede / Not Your Rabbi's Judaism 25
Irving 'Yitz' Greenberg / The Third Era 39
Irwin Kula / Death and Rebirth & Judaism's Job 56

PART TWO
Mixed Multitudes

Mixed Multitudes 82
April Nichole Baskin / Audacious Hospitality 84
Joy Ladin / Judaism from a Transgender Perspective 100
Paul Golin / Intermarriage and the Future 115
Juan Mejia / Becoming Jewish on the Web 131

PART THREE
Reinventing Jewish Practice

Early Incarnations of Third Era Judaisms 150
Miriam Terlinchamp / Embrace the Weird 153
Shira Stutman / Spreading the Good (Jewish) News 163
Denise Handlarski / Secularsynagogue.com 180
Dan Horwitz / The Well 188

New Communal Structures

August Kahn and Tal Frieden / Judaism on Our Own Terms 198
David Cygielman / Moishe House 209
Sara Levy Linden and Shira Rutman / San Francisco Urban Kibbutz 217
Beth Finger / Jewish Without Walls (JWOW) 226

Artistic Re-Visions

Amichai Lau-Lavie / Lab/Shul 238
Adina Allen and Jeff Kasowitz / The Jewish Studio Project 247
Sarah Lefton / BimBam 258

Empowering 'Regular Jews'

Benay Lappe / A Traditionally Radical Yeshiva 268
Brett Lockspeiser / The Future of Torah 274
Aliza Kline / OneTable 284
Jenna Reback / Bad Jew Weekly 295

'Regular Jews' Experimenting

Eileen Levinson / Haggadot.com 304
Tiffany Shlain / Six Days a Week 313
Kristin Eriko Posner / Nourish Co. 323

Afterword 332
Steven Kaplin / Podcasting Judaism 333

Acknowledgments 356
Kickstarter Supporters 360
About the Authors 362

Introduction

Genesis

At this writing, the *Judaism Unbound* podcast has been listened to over two-and-a-half million times since we released the first episode on March 4, 2016. Because we had a sense that we were starting down a significant road, we titled that first episode "Genesis." And just as God destroyed the first Creation in a flood, we destroyed our first episode and re-recorded it. Even that early in the history of the podcast, it had already evolved.

In the months before we launched the podcast, we had been putting together an outline for a book we wanted to write about the future of Judaism. By that time, a bunch of relatively small organizations that made up what was being called the "Jewish innovation ecosystem" had been having some success for about a decade with initiatives aimed at engaging "unaffiliated" Jews. The science fiction writer William Gibson once said that "[t]he future is already here—it's just not very evenly distributed," and we wondered whether those organizations' work represented a Jewish future that was in fact already here. Perhaps a book that wove together a theory of the future based on what was gaining traction in the present would help accelerate a process of broader Jewish transformation. A new version of Judaism would emerge, built around a new ecosystem of institutions that would better resonate with what we have called "regular Jews."

The 2013 Pew Study of Jewish Americans had been published just about two years before we started work on the book. Its blockbuster finding was that 22% of Jewish Americans were what it called "Jews of no religion"—people who answered "none of the above" when asked what religion they were but who had Jewish parentage and/or otherwise considered themselves Jewish. While many Jewish communal professionals expressed concern that this number was so high, we believed it distracted from the much higher number of what might be called "Jews of low religion." Our hypothesis found substantial support years later in the second iteration of the study, released in 2020, in which additional questions were asked. While the proportion of Jews of no religion had risen to 27%, even more interesting was a finding that an additional 27% claimed that Judaism was their religion but replied "I'm not religious" to a question about why they didn't attend synagogue. Essentially, 54% of American Jews explicitly stated that they were "not religious," and most of the rest didn't seem interested in the offerings of the existing landscape of Jewish organizations.

While Pew's findings were consistent with our belief that conditions were right for a new version of Judaism to emerge, we decided we weren't ready to write the book we had envisioned. We knew how we'd frame the book—we were confident about the historical analogies we'd make and the traditional mythic stories from the Jewish tradition we'd invoke. For example, we felt like forty years of wandering in the wilderness was a powerful way to talk about the patience that we would need during a long transition from one version of Judaism to the next. But we had a nagging sense that we didn't know the details of the contemporary landscape well enough to make strong book-length assertions about whether the new Jewish future was already here yet or still en route.

We decided we needed to do more research, and we thought that if we did our research in the form of a podcast, perhaps scholars and practitioners would be more willing to talk to us. We could tempt them with the possibility that their ideas and projects would reach new audiences who would hear from them directly, in their own voice. We hoped that having these conversations out loud and in public could be a way to gather and catalyze others who were eager to engage in the grand experiment of re-inventing Jewish life in the 21st century.

As it turns out, we were on to something! March of 2016 was still the relatively early days of podcasting, and thanks to a surprising number of downloads in the first few days, Apple featured *Judaism Unbound* as a "New and Noteworthy" podcast, which helped us gain a substantial listenership right out of the gate. As we write this, we have released over 450 podcast episodes—we have never missed a Friday in over eight years and have also released quite a few bonus episodes—and people collectively spend nearly half a million hours with us every year. Pretty quickly, the podcast became its own thing, and we more or less forgot that it had started as research for a book. Our on-air conversations with the wise and creative guides who have shared their visions and stories have challenged and changed us.

In our first episode (both the original one and the re-recorded one), we talked about the many meanings of "unbound," including being untethered by geography, by the definitions of what and who is Jewish, and by what a Jewish life is "supposed to" look like. We pointed out that many Jews feel bound to Judaism by accident of birth, not choice. What would a Judaism look like that had the gravitational attraction to re-bind people through choice? The idea of an "unbound" Judaism breaks free from the notion of Judaism as an all-or-nothing bundle. What if some elements speak to you, but others don't? Does that make you a "bad Jew"? We asserted that, while no one knows what Judaism will look like in 100 years, it will be healthier and more compelling if many more people are involved in the creative process of re-thinking, re-imagining, and experimenting. The podcast was our invitation to "regular Jews" to become part of this new creative class, and now so is this book.

Who and what is this book for?

Though the original book we intended to write remains a project for a future time, we are delighted to offer this book as a fresh version of the journey we have taken together with our podcast listeners—a compilation of some of the highlights from our first 200 conversations. Our intention for this bound version of *Judaism Unbound* is that it extends the breadth of people reached by these voices, as there are still many people who don't listen to podcasts.

If you are in the non-listener group, welcome to *Judaism Unbound*! We think you will find these interview transcripts compelling and personally relevant, just as our listeners have over the past eight years.

For podcast listeners, we hope that the movement of words from the ear to the page gives a new depth of engagement with the ideas we have been exploring together. Being able to annotate the pages, re-read passages that are particularly striking to you, and flip back and forth between thematically connected interviews allows you to grapple with these ideas in a new, more tactile and tangible way.

We have arranged these transcripts in a new order—interviews that took place years apart are now on adjacent pages—that puts podcast guests into conversation with one another. As such, we believe this book is a profoundly new and different experience from the podcast.

How to engage with this book

We hope this this book will look pretty beat up in a year—dog-eared pages where you've found quotes to return to, exclamation points and question marks in the margins, coffee rings and wine stains throughout, the odd napkin tucked between the pages covered in doodles and ideas you wrote down during conversations with family and friends.

From the beginning, we meant for *Judaism Unbound* to empower people to learn what they want to know and experiment in their own Judaism. We wanted it to be an invitation to be part of a community of people grappling with the future of Judaism and their place in it. We always believed that our listeners—and now our readers—didn't need to or want to be told what to think. Now, with this volume, we are literally putting the future of Judaism in your hands.

You can read this book start to finish, in the order we've placed the transcripts, or you can choose your own adventure, reading one or two transcripts at random or because a certain topic came up in conversation at a Passover seder you attended. To spark your personal reflections and catalyze dialogues with others, we've included conversation-starter questions throughout the book (after each interview in Part 1 and Part 2, and after each grouping of interviews in Part 3). But if you have other questions, don't be locked into the ones we have provided.

Again, we mean for this book to facilitate your learning journey, not to be our guided tour.

Though we have made the editorial choices around structure and order, we have not attempted to make things linear, nor have we tidied things up to perfectly fit a pre-existing, singular narrative. The greatest joys of these conversations are often the unexpected side-trips, the personal quirks of voice and expression, and the ways in which each guest comes to common themes in their own idiosyncratic way. We've worked hard to ensure that these joys are retained in the text, even as we've trimmed the verbatim transcripts for readability and thematic foregrounding.

In the introductions to each section, we have provided a few framing ideas, many drawn from the episodes of the podcast where it was just the two of us processing what we were learning, but we have consciously held back from giving you too many of our opinions here. We certainly have opinions, but *Judaism Unbound* has always been about believing that people can think for themselves and come to their own conclusions, as long as they feel inspired and invited to do so. If you want to hear more of our opinions, check out the "Dan and Lex episodes" of the podcast, or stay tuned for books we may write in the future. We want to hear your opinions, so please email us any of your thoughts at hello@judaismunbound.com.

Having said all this, we must also acknowledge that the task of translating the podcast into book form presented us with a frustrating set of limitations. The editorial process of creating a coherent and readable book required both selection and reduction. Selection was challenging because it meant leaving many extraordinary guests out of this volume. We tried to choose a set of conversations that captured some of the big ideas that represent the arc of our journey of learning and re-thinking. In the name of readability, enjoyable bits of each interview had to be cut. The pain of these choices is eased by the knowledge that the full episodes of each interview are available on the *Judaism Unbound* website at www.judaismunbound.com or your favorite podcast app.

That said, welcome to *Judaism Unbound*!

—Dan and Lex

Fall 2024

PART ONE
The Crash of Rabbinic Judaism and the Rise of the Third Era

A Time of Wandering

We created the *Judaism Unbound* podcast out of a conviction that we are living in a momentous time in Jewish history. Informed by both our own experiences and our exposure to the thinkers you will meet in Part 1 of this book, we were convinced that something big and new was happening in Judaism. The innovations we were seeing were more than just marketing or window dressing, but rather signals of an emerging new era of Judaism—the Third Era according to Yitz Greenberg's accounting.

It seemed to us that the best way to understand our time in Jewish history was as a "time of wandering," an in-between time, a liminal space, a period of transition as one version of Judaism is ending and the next version is being born. We have been here before, whether in myth or history—whether in the forty years of wandering in the wilderness between Egypt and Canaan or the chaotic century-and-a-half between the destruction of the Second Temple and the composition of the Mishnah.

History reveals that Jews have a knack for reinventing Judaism during times of wandering. In what Barbara Thiede calls the "magic treasure box" of Jewish history, we see patterns of cross-cultural exploration and adaptation, disjuncture, and ongoing innovation that open up the possibility that the seemingly radical and discontinuous changes now unfolding are actually not at all untraditional. They are the tradition.

Our time of wandering began around two centuries ago, when the Enlightenment destabilized Rabbinic Judaism and, in Benay Lappe's parlance, Rabbinic Judaism began to "crash." For the past two centuries,

Jewish thinkers and leaders have responded to this crash with a variety of potential solutions, including Hasidism, Zionism, and the Reform Movement and its progeny. These efforts were significant and transformational, but they do not appear to have been sufficient, at least in terms of their appeal to more than half of American Jews today.

The people whose voices we have gathered into Part 1 of this book—Benay Lappe, Barbara Thiede, Yitz Greenberg, and Irwin Kula—brought foundational concepts and language to help us think about where we have been, where we are now, and what's over the horizon. While they use different terminology, they all share the sense that Judaism is undergoing a profound paradigm shift. Each asserts that Judaism as we have known it has ended—Kula says it most simply when he says that "Rabbinic Judaism died"—and yet all are fundamentally optimistic about Judaisms that are in the process of becoming.

Whether we greet our current transition with dismay, anxiety, denial, ambivalence, or optimism, we can all acknowledge that the experience of wandering is rife with ambiguity. It is hard to know how to live a Jewish life in a time when it is unclear what Judaism even is or ought to be. Each of us has questions about what it means for Judaism to be undergoing dramatic change. Are we breaking the unbroken chain of tradition? Repairing an already-broken chain? Or linking a new chain onto the old one? And what does it all mean for us?

Benay Lappe

> *"Every master story will ultimately, and inevitably, crash."*

Exodus Part 1

Benay Lappe is the founder and Rosh Yeshiva of SVARA: A Traditionally Radical Yeshiva. SVARA's mission is to empower queer and trans people to expand Torah and tradition through the spiritual practice of Talmud study. SVARA's method of Talmud study is intended to shape learners into the kinds of people who are moved to, equipped to, and courageous enough to bring about a more just and equitable world.

An award-winning educator specializing in the application of queer theory to Talmud study, Benay Lappe has served on the faculties of the University of Illinois at Urbana-Champaign, Temple University, the University of Judaism, the Reconstructionist Rabbinical College, the Graduate Theological Union's Center for Jewish Studies at UC-Berkeley, and The Wexner Institute. In 2016, she received the Covenant Award for excellence in Jewish education.

Benay Lappe was our very first guest on the podcast. Her "Crash Theory," which we discuss in our conversation, has been an important foundational idea for *Judaism Unbound*.

Dan Libenson: Lex and I are really interested in what's been called your "crash theory," and we thought this would be an interesting place to start thinking about the kinds of changes that we are seeing in the Jewish world today. Could you give us a summary of your way of thinking?

Benay Lappe: So, it basically goes like this: The idea is that we all inherit "master stories"—from our religious traditions, from our country, from our families, from the places we work—and these master stories come to answer our basic human questions. And these are questions that we all share: What's right? What's wrong? What does it mean to be a human being? How should I live my life? What's important? And so on.

And these master stories work until they don't work. It's just part of life—it's the way things are. And every master story will ultimately, and inevitably, crash. And what I mean by "crash" is that that master story will cease to work for you, or will stop answering those basic human questions for you, because of one of three things: either you found another master story whose answers you like better, or something will have happened out in the world that will make those old answers no longer work, or something inside of you has changed, and what used to seem true no longer seems true, and your story no longer works.

And there are three, and only three, possible responses to a crash, ever:

Option One, which is denying that a crash has occurred and reverting to your master story and hanging on for dear life. Building walls around that old master story to make sure that nothing interferes or threatens it again.

Option Two would be accepting that your master story has crashed, completely rejecting that master story, and jumping off into a completely new story.

And Option Three is to accept that the story has crashed, but instead of abandoning the story, you stay in it and retell it and make it better. This is kind of the remix/upgrade/retell option.

So that's the basic scheme.

Dan Libenson: And how do you see these three responses specifically happening in the area that you study the most, which is the Rabbinic period and the transition into the Rabbinic period from the Judaism that had come before?

Benay Lappe: If you want to throw "Jewish skin" on the theory, the master story is the biblical narrative. I'm going to locate the primary crash of Biblical Judaism at the crash of the Second Temple. And what crashed as a result of this historical event was that we needed a new way to be human if you were Jewish, a new way to organize meaning: How do we think about how to have a relationship with God? How do I know what's right and what's wrong? I think the truth of the matter is that that master story had been crashing for a long time even while the Temple was still standing.

And what I believe happens is that some group of people are, kind of, the canary in the coal mine for every crash—they're the people who are the "queerest," if you will, not necessarily because of their gender or sexual orientation, but because they are the people for whom the current master story is working the least. And there's going to be a "crumble" before every crash, and for some group of people—the queerest—that master story's going to be crashing first.

And I think the Rabbis, in my mind, were very queer. They were people for whom the story was working least. So, I think for 100 or 200 years before the destruction of the Second Temple, there was a small group of people, whom we now call the Rabbis, who were already creating a new form of Judaism. They were gathering in little "ashrams," that we now call synagogues, and doing this newfangled kind of ritual called prayer that they imagined was actually going to conjure up God's presence . . . when they could've gone to the Temple down the block.

Okay, so now you get to the year 70 or, let's say, 69, and it looks pretty bad for the Jews, and what are people going to do? Now you no longer have just the canaries in the coal mine experiencing the crash, but everyone's experiencing the crash.

So who goes Option One? It's just sort of a rule that if you're employed by the master story, you're going to be an Option One person. In other words, if you're part of the power structure, you're going to do whatever you can to make sure that master story stays. And you're going to revert to it. And you're going to build a wall around it, literal or figurative. And, of course, it was the priests who went Option One—the ones who couldn't imagine any other way to be a human being or to do God, or to do Jewish, to do community.

And who went Option Two? Well, it turns out that it's just a rule that when there's a crash, most people go Option Two. So, somewhere around 90% of Jews after the destruction of the Temple in the first century went Option Two. That's what we would call "assimilation"—at least, eventually, it becomes assimilation. In the beginning it isn't, and we'll come back to that, because I think people who go Option Two are very, very interesting—probably the most important, eventually, for this cycle. That is, if they come back. But we'll get there in a minute.

So, most Jews went Option Two, and they said there's just no way to be a Jew anymore. Obviously, God doesn't love us anymore. Everyone knew in the ancient Near East that, if your temple was destroyed, the deal between you and God was over. And they left. And, initially, they became pagan, and—if they stayed Option Two—eventually blended into non-Jewish society.

Option One and Option Two are actually opposite sides of the exact same coin. They share the same basic underlying wrong-headed notion that stories are fixed, eternal, unchanging, and immutable. If there's a crack in one, you either have to do whatever you can to pretend it didn't happen, or you throw the whole thing away.

And one small group of guys—this group of queer, fringy radical hippy guys, whom we call the Rabbis—went Option Three. And they said, "There are parts of our master story that we can actually change, that we can save, and there are parts about our new reality that are actually good, that we can bring in." And then, with Option Three, they retold the master story. They essentially invented—I believe—what we now call Rabbinic Judaism.

So, I think what's interesting is to ask ourselves: Why do people go Option One? Why do people go Option Two? Why do people go Option Three?

Dan Libenson: It's interesting in the context of where Judaism is today to think about the possibilities of, on the one hand, trying at all costs to preserve the system that we have inherited, and on the other hand, leaving it—or at least leaving its institutions.

What are the first generation of people that go Option Two like?

Benay Lappe: People who go Option Two have recognized something that is very true for them in some aspect of the world that is not part of their old master story. And if they eventually can become an Option Three person, they will bring back what it is that they found outside, and that will become Judaized—it will become incorporated into the tradition and enrich it.

I've often joked, what do you get when an Option Two person comes back to Judaism? You get yoga *minyans* [Jewish prayer groups]. But seriously, what you really get is an evolving Jewish tradition.

Dan Libenson: What do you think makes somebody choose the option that they choose? What makes somebody go Option One, Option Two, or Option Three?

Benay Lappe: I think it's a really interesting question. I think there are a number of components. First of all, there's a personality issue involved. I think we're somewhat hardwired, or grow up and become, or have a tendency to be, either Option One, Option Two, or Option Three people.

I don't know, if you're in a bad relationship for 10 years—let's say, an abusive relationship—and you're just staying, staying, staying, you're probably an Option One person. And you probably want to think about that. And if you're the kind of person who's in a relationship, and at the first fight, you're out of here, and that's a pattern for you, you're probably an Option Two kind of person. And you want to think about that. So, I think there's a personality piece.

And there's also an ability to tolerate dissonance. If you don't have much ability to tolerate dissonance, you're going to be an Option One or Option Two person, more likely.

Going Option One is an option that you take when you're not willing to lose your goodies. So, you've got to be willing to lose a lot of goodies to go both Option Two and Option Three. And I think the more experience you have with crashes in the past, the more likely you are to go Option Three. And that's why I think queer people tend to go Option Three.

And there are lots of kinds of queer people. There are queer people who are gender-nonconforming, they're queer about their gender or about their sexual orientation. But there are all sorts of queernesses. If you're queer—if you have a profoundly outsider experience of life—and you're surviving, you're an Option Three person, or at least you're going Option Three on that aspect of your life. And the more "crash-flex" you are, the more likely you are to go Option Three on any future crashes.

And people sometimes make these choices serially. When I first came out, or started to realize that I was gay, I went Option One. Back in the day, that's sort of what everybody did, because there weren't a lot of other great options, and it was very costly to do anything else. It meant losing your job, being kicked out of your home, and so on and so forth.

In my own personal story, at a certain point, I fell in love, realized, wow, it's okay to be gay, and went Option Two. I didn't think I could be gay and Jewish. And, eventually, I started realizing that I was giving up too much of myself, and that there might actually be a way to be gay and Jewish. And then comes queer rabbi, and that's an Option Three move.

So, you can make these choices serially, or you can make one and stick with it.

Dan Libenson: What you're saying makes me think about this puzzle that I've thought about in terms of the early Rabbis, which is, why does it seem that so many of them were either converts to Judaism, or the children of converts to Judaism, such as Rabbi Akiva, Rabbi Meir, and many others? And I wonder if it's related to this point that you're making, that people whose story is one where they've experienced other kinds of crashes and come through them, makes them particularly oriented to taking that Option Three path, no matter what might crash in their lives—in this case, it happened to be Judaism.

Benay Lappe: I think that's true. And I think another factor that makes Option Three stories attractive to outsiders—let's say converts, for example—is that they tend to be experimental.

The first thing we have to realize is that Option Three stories, and attempts at creating Option Threes, tend to be very, very thin. They don't feel authentic, they don't feel real, they certainly don't feel traditional, and very few people go for them. Very few people are willing to say,

"Yeah, this is how I'm going do Jewish." The ones who do have to live with that thinness . . .

Dan Libenson: And it's thin because it's so new, right? It's not that an Option Three is *necessarily* something thin; it's just that it's thin when it starts, because it just hasn't been around long enough to thicken up, right?

Benay Lappe: I think that's a part of it. Every Option Three is going to have three kinds of material in it. It's going to have some of the old story, which gives it thickness. It's going to have some new invented material, which is going to feel very inauthentic. And it's going to have some tweaks of the old stuff.

Each Option Three attempt is going to have a different proportion of old material that they bring in, invented material, and tweaked material. Some are going to be very close to the old master story, some are going to be far from it. Some will feel thinner because they're bringing down less of the old stuff. And some will feel thicker.

So, getting back to the issue of converts, if you look at any really successful cutting-edge Jewish Option Three community, you'll see a disproportionate number of converts and non-Jews who are attracted to it. And there are really successful communities that choose not to even use words like "Jewish community." This a community for people, and we're using Jewish stuff. The Kitchen in San Francisco is really mindful about doing that.

Dan Libenson: So, just to step back for a minute and compare, what are the advantages to Option One versus Option Three? I'm thinking of what we're seeing in the Jewish world today and people's resistance to some kind of Option Three that might be proposed today in Jewish life.

I feel like people who are actively involved in some kind of Jewish institution will say: "This provides the whole package for me. That new thing that may be going on—maybe it's really good at education, or maybe it's really good at Talmud study, or maybe it's really good at prayer, but it's not necessarily good at the other stuff. And that makes me feel unstable. I like the sense that I have a community to be part of and an organization to be part of that takes care of me systematically." It seems unlikely that some kind of new version, however good it might be, is going to be able to meet all of those needs early on.

But, when you think about somebody who may be an outsider—either because they are an actual outsider who converted, or maybe they haven't converted yet, or never will convert, or somebody who is an outsider in the sense that they are Jewish and their family has been Jewish for a long time, but they haven't been participating in the organized institutions—none of those "outsider" people is experiencing that same sense of loss of that stable Jewish system, because they never had it to begin with. So, in a certain sense, for them, this new thing is all gain, and they feel positive about the elements that have been added to their lives and don't have as much thought about the things that are being lost.

Benay Lappe: Option Threes tend to have a higher percentage of stuff that works, and they are, by definition, less burdened by the stuff that doesn't work anymore. So, they're going to be very attractive to people—just like you say, Dan—who are looking for something that works and aren't feeling the pain and the loss of this legitimacy, this whole "authenticity" stuff. They're not feeling that loss because, like you said, they never had it.

Lex Rofeberg: We talk so much about Option Two people—we don't call them that, we just call them "unengaged," we call them "uninterested," "uninvolved." I'm curious if there are strategies for taking people from a space of Option Two to a space of Option Three.

You talked about how that occurred in your own life. But how do we make that happen? Or does it have to just be organic?

Benay Lappe: Well, first let me crank back. I think we can connect the dots between the crash of the biblical era and the crash that we're experiencing now. And I think that we're in a crash as enormous as the crash of the Second Temple.

And what's crashing now is that new Option Three that the Rabbis came up with. And we've had a pretty good run of it, right? Two thousand years of that Option Three—not bad. And for the last, I don't know, 150 years or so, it's been crashing. We've been in a crumble, from Emancipation to Holocaust through modernity, and I think we're pretty close to the end. I don't know if we're at the beginning of this crash, or at the end of the crash, but we're in another similar crash.

So now, how do you get the Option Two people to come back? First of all, I think the Option Two people, as Dan said earlier, aren't really leaving Judaism—they're leaving our current forms of Jewish communal structure. They're leaving what they've been served up as Judaism, and they're very, very ready, and would be thrilled, to be presented with an Option Three that spoke to them. And it's happening more and more.

So, what does an Option Three have to have in order to appeal to Option Two people? Well, first, remember, it's got to do what stories are supposed to do, which is answer their basic human questions. And it's got to give them answers that make sense to them—people will no longer suppress their moral intuition, which the tradition calls "*svara*," in favor of a story that has answers that don't seem right to them.

What I think is really important is to uncover the native acknowledgement of the tradition that every human being has this moral intuition, which is what drives every change in Judaism, and what drives what we think of as Jewish.

I think that the Option Three that we've inherited, Rabbinic Judaism, was created and worked for a people that was oppressed and beleaguered, and relatively impoverished . . . and needed to have two challahs on the table on Friday night to feel a sense of self-esteem. And having two challahs has been really meaningful, because when you didn't feel that way six days out of the week, this ritual made you feel that way. Well, when you can have two challahs on the table any night of the week, maybe Shabbos has got to serve a different need.

Dan Libenson: I want to go back to a question of the perspective of the people who are going Option One today. People who are basically saying, "It is what it is." I feel like I hear this a lot: "Judaism is what it is—if you want to do something else, that's fine, but it wouldn't be Judaism. This is Judaism."

How do these Option One people perceive the people that are going Option Two, i.e., leaving altogether, or close to leaving, or going Option Three and inventing new forms? The basic attitude that I see, is that they say the people who are going Option Two are disloyal and not committed, and the people who are going Option Three are kind of doing something kooky that's not Judaism.

Benay Lappe: And, just to complicate things a little bit, the truth of the matter is any Option One that lasts for longer than a dozen years or so isn't really an Option One—it's an Option Three that is doing a really good job of selling itself as the real deal: "This is the way it's always been, this is authentic, this is the tradition."

But that isn't the way traditions work. Traditions really can't live very long if they actually are fixed and unchanging, because people change. So Option One is really more of a mindset and a myth than it actually is a viable choice.

What's unfortunate about Option One people is they wear the mantle of authenticity, and those who don't know any better—those who are not very familiar with how traditions work, or how stories work—believe them and become disempowered and inauthentic in relation to them, and, knowing that that option isn't attractive, think their only option is to leave.

But, as time goes by, you see the evolution of Option Threes. And, by the way, once you have a crash, you don't have a single Option Three, you have many Option Threes. And that's what you want. You want to nurture and allow as many Option Threes as you can, because each one is going to have a piece; this one's got the learning, this one's got the singing, this one's got the holiday piece. And there will be a kind of merger of incomplete Option Threes into something coherent. And then that will last for a while.

Dan Libenson: I'm thinking about the way that people who are perceived to have left haven't actually left, they have just chosen not to participate in the institutional approaches that we have. I'm really struck, for example, in the Pew Study [a 2013 demographic study of Jewish Americans], by the huge number of people who say that they're proud to be Jewish, or that being Jewish is important to them, but at the same time they're not participating in any institutional manifestations of Jewish life. Have those people gone Option Two? How do we characterize them?

I think that often the community characterizes them as having gone Option Two, when the reality is that if, let's say, there was a person who said, "Well, the only kind of Judaism that I would really love would be something that was full of singing and music," and they look around their city and they don't see anything like that, their only choice is to kind of stick with it as it is, and grin and bear the fact that it's not meeting their needs, or they can leave. Right?

But it's not because they've necessarily decided that the best thing is to leave. It's just because they don't really have another option.

So I'm struck by the question of how many people who seem to be going Option Two really would go Option Three if they could.

Benay Lappe: I think the vast majority of them. The vast majority of people want to be integrated—they want all their molecules to be living inside their body at the same time. They want their Jewishness, and their "queernesses," of whatever variety, all to have a place in their life. And I think you're absolutely right—most people go Option Two because there aren't enough alternatives.

And Option Three is really hard. It's uncomfortable, and you're never sure if you're getting it right, and it's never going to feel really, really good for you, it's never going to work for those of us going through the crash. It might work for our grandchildren, but it's never completely going to work for us, and it's hard.

Dan Libenson: I think about the immigrant experience—and I'm not sure if this relates more to Option Two or Option Three, maybe you have a thought—but when I think of first generation immigrants to a country, to America for example, it's very heroic to be that immigrant because you're never going to fully integrate into that society, but in theory you're setting it up that your kids will be able to.

I think that's probably true of people who go Option Two and who go Option Three. I think that if you just leave something that you were once part of, then you do feel this intense sense of loss, and you probably never feel fully comfortable and happy in that new reality even if you've chosen it.

And the other choice is to go Option Three, which is to try to create some kind of synthesis, and so maybe you feel a little bit less of a sense of loss because you haven't completely left it, but you're also integrating less into the other option. And you're also feeling sort of unstable and not fully comfortable, and yet perhaps you're setting something up that will be the only thing your children ever knew. And they'll feel just fine about it.

Benay Lappe: Also, I think there is loss—period—after a crash. No matter which way you go, there's going to be loss. And that's, kind of, part of the deal. I'm not trying to say that a crash is an unfortunate event—it's how life works, and it's really what initiates growth. We grow by realizing that something that was working before isn't working now. And that can be a really good thing.

Judaism is in a really big period of growth. Maybe it's a little bit adolescent right now, so it's got a lot of adolescent issues. But this is how people grow, and this is how traditions grow. They have growth spurts and then periods of stability. I think we're in one of these painful growth spurts when you have growing pains.

Dan Libenson: It reminds me of an experience that I had recently when I was in Israel, and I was trying to explain to people the kind of work that I do in the Jewish community. And a lot of people, whether they were religious or not, they would say, "So, you're working to stop assimilation." And I would say, "I don't feel great about the word, 'assimilation.' I don't think that's what's going on." And they would say, "Why?"

And I'd say, "Well, I see assimilation as something that people are actively trying to do—they're trying to become part of this other culture, and it's somehow bad, because they're leaving our culture. The reason why they're leaving is because they're trying to join this other culture. And what I see is something quite different, which is that people actually really would like to have a strong sense of themselves as Jews, if they only could."

But this is where I really like the language of "crash," because something has crashed in that story of Judaism, either for them personally or in some bigger way. They literally cannot just join the Reform Movement and feel great about that, because there's something that just would feel absolutely wrong to them about that.

And so they are, then, stuck in a situation where they are actually not trying to assimilate. They say, "I really would love to have a Jewish life if I could figure out what a Jewish life would look like that would make sense for me. And I've looked around and I don't see anything."

Benay Lappe: I think you're absolutely right, that most people who go Option Two aren't really rejecting anything. They're in this enormous holding pattern, which will probably last longer than their lifetime, during which they will hope for alternatives but won't find any. And what we're hoping for, I think, is that we can lay down enough Option Threes to attract them, or attract their children.

I think this is just what happens in a crash—you get very small numbers of people going Option Three, because most people aren't equipped to be Option Three leaders. And there aren't any Option Threes already in place for most people to grab onto, so they'll go Option Two.

And the new Option Three is going to be very, very small. And lots of people are going to scream, "We're dying, we're dying," but we're not. That's just the phase we're in post-crash. We've been here before. This is how it works.

Dan Libenson: Why do you think we're in a crash period today, and what is it that you think has crashed?

Benay Lappe: I think you can diagnose a crash by looking at how many people are going Option Three, how many people are going Option Two, and how many people are going Option One. And if you count the numbers of people going Option Two, you can see whether you're in a period that needs a little tweak or a period that's in a full-on crash.

The numbers seem to indicate that Judaism, as we're packaging it, as we're presenting it, as we're using it, as we're teaching it, isn't speaking to people. It isn't answering their basic human questions.

They're looking elsewhere for guidance, for a sense of meaning, for senses of community. And those are the needs that Judaism has traditionally tried to fill, and it's not filling those needs for people. So, that's why I think we're in a crash.

Dan Libenson: I think that's really interesting in light of something that Lex and I talked about in our first episode, the concept of *ipcha mistabra*—this idea of "opposite thinking": How can we look at the same data and look at it in a different way than most people look at it?

I'm thinking about the demographic surveys that tend to get interpreted by the Jewish community organizations as: our problem is that people are leaving Jewish life, and our solution needs to be to somehow figure out ways to attract them to the institutions of Jewish life.

And what you're saying, as I'm understanding it, is that the way to interpret those demographic surveys is to see those numbers as evidence that the institutions of Jewish life have crashed in such a way that those people will never join those institutions. By definition, numbers of that magnitude are a symptom that those ways of being Jewish have crashed. They indicate *not* that we need to do more to educate people or somehow change them so that they'll come back and join, but that we need to work to accelerate some kind of process of Option Three Judaisms being created that could attract those people, perhaps.

Benay Lappe: By definition, when you're in a crash, the Option Three that works will be something that would've been unrecognizable to those for whom the old story worked before the crash.

In other words, this is a model of a disruptive change, not a sustaining change.

When you have a crash, the new master story is one in which you're achieving the same goal—in other words, you're creating a certain kind of human being, and we have a very specific notion of what a Jewish human being should look like, and it actually is very different from the ideal notion of what a Christian human being or a Muslim human being should look like . . . we have a certain idea and that stays the same overall. What changes and what becomes unrecognizable is the way in which we get there.

And I think what Judaism will look like in 100 years will be unrecognizable to us. But that doesn't scare me. I feel very optimistic, because the Jewish world is so much more Option Three today than it was just a handful of years ago, and more and more Option Two people are showing up and going, "Wow, this is amazing."

QUESTIONS FOR REFLECTION

- Consider the three options that Benay Lappe identifies for responding to profound changes or crashes in our "master stories." Can you think of people in your own life who exemplify each of those three response strategies?
- Who do you know that tends to adopt Option 1—deny the change and work to shore up and preserve the master story?
- Who do you associate with Option 2—the strategy of accepting the change but leaving the old story completely behind?
- Can you think of anyone who has chosen Option 3—accepting the change and staying with the master story in order to make it better or transform it? What does that look like?
- Think of a time in your own life when you have experienced a major shift or change—how did you move through the three options? Where have you landed so far?
- Lappe suggests that for many people, Judaism as we've known it "isn't answering their basic human questions." Is this true for you? What is a question you have that you wish Judaism would answer for you?
- A key idea for Lappe is the importance of acknowledging each individual's innate moral intuition or "svara" even if it is different from an old story that they've been taught. Can you think of a time when your own svara has been in conflict with a tradition or belief you were taught? What did you do?

Barbara Thiede

> "All of modern Western Judaism lives in a place where every yardstick that is applied to what makes us Jewish becomes a Rabbinic yardstick—but that Rabbinic yardstick is relatively new to our history."

Not Your Rabbi's Judaism

Barbara Thiede is an assistant professor in the Department of Religious Studies at the University of North Carolina-Charlotte. She teaches a range of courses on the texts of Hebrew Bible, Jewish history, the history of European antisemitism, and Jewish magic.

In addition to being a professor, Barbara Thiede is also an ordained rabbi in the Jewish Renewal movement, where she is known as Rav Shulamit Thiede. When we had our interview, she was a member of the Vaad, which is the board that oversees rabbinical education through Jewish Renewal's Aleph Ordination Program.

Thiede's books include *Male Friendship, Homosociality, and Women in the Hebrew Bible: Malignant Fraternities* (2022) and *Rape Culture in the House of David: A Company of Men* (2022). She is currently at work on her next book, entitled *Yhwh's Emotional and Sexual Life in the Books of Samuel: How the Deity Acts the Man*.

In her rabbinic role, Thiede performed Lex's wedding, where Dan met her for the first time. Our conversations with her, on and off the air, helped flesh out our intuitions about the non-linearity of change throughout Jewish history.

Dan Libenson: We've been exploring a lot of thinking that comes from within the world of Rabbinic Judaism, and we've also talked a lot about the ideas that we've called "folk Judaism," suggesting that the people have a different perspective, potentially, than the Rabbis. It seems that even now, in the 21st century, we often are looking at a world that's set up within the context of Rabbinic Judaism. Your writing questions that, and I'd like to start with a snapshot of your perspective on how Rabbinic Judaism fits into Judaism.

Barbara Thiede: What I have to say about this is actually hardly new. What is new is to hear it in seminary settings, in congregational places, in places in Jewish life.

Scholars have known for decades that we have no objective proof that there was any group of rabbis who saved Judaism in the first century of this Common Era. We know, in fact, that the Rabbis later on created a series of myths that were so powerful and so amazingly compelling that once—and here's the scary moment for some of us—once the Rabbis are given their role in Jewish communities, in part, by a rising Christian empire, that becomes the narrative of what Judaism is, that becomes the identity of how Judaism is practiced.

All of modern Western Judaism lives in a place where every yardstick that is applied to what makes us Jewish becomes a Rabbinic yardstick—but that Rabbinic yardstick is relatively new to our history, relative to the extraordinary diversity of Judaisms throughout our history, it is rather a narrow yardstick to be using.

Dan Libenson: The basic story of the Rabbinic myth is that the Temple was destroyed in the year 70, and there was a period of instability during which a group of probably Pharisees, which was one of the sects back then, got together and became the Rabbis and reimagined Judaism, along a similar line to the way that the Pharisees were talking about it before the destruction of the Second Temple. Out of that emerged the Rabbinic Judaism that became the next version of

Judaism. Here and there are some isolated communities that wandered away before that Rabbinic Judaism took hold ... but basically, Rabbinic Judaism is Judaism.

Could you help us understand what really was going on historically? How should we understand what was going on before the destruction of the Second Temple and in the years after the destruction of the Second Temple?

Barbara Thiede: I'll do that with the historian's caveat—the one that I give all of my students—which is that in 20 years you could find out that I lied to you. Twenty years from now, we'll know differently than we know now. I will also do one other thing—and that is add to the mythology you've just described, Dan. Because if you go on Chabad's website, what you'll find is this idea that the Rabbinic project actually is not saving Judaism, but keeping an old, longstanding line going—that that's what they do, just by writing things down, by getting together. All of this actually well predates the first century.

You've got these two essential narratives—that the Rabbis saved Judaism by creating something cutting-edge and new, and that Chabad-world definition that they preserved what was already always there. Both these narratives are myths. They have little to nothing to do with any of the history of what I would call Judeans rather than Jews. In fact, a lot of our terminology is off. The word "Jews" is a word that doesn't really get used for our people until the Common Era, and the first locations for its use are the New Testament and the work of early Christian Patristic fathers. They're the ones using that term in the way that we then come to adopt it and use it for ourselves.

The reason that I emphasize this is because these Judeans have already been in diaspora for hundreds and hundreds of years. They've already been building synagogues across Asia Minor, across Europe, across the entire Roman Empire. They have already created communities in which they are defining and redefining what their practice is. They are an ethnos—a people group—and they have inherited a set of traditions, they have inherited ancestral narratives, and they have inherited, to some extent, an important identity marker in terms of the genetic sense of where they came from. Even if they've been living in

Alexandria for hundreds of years, they still may be marking themselves as Judean. They also may be protesting "being marked as 'Judean.'"

Start to finish, prior to the destruction of the Second Temple, these Judeans of Rome, of Alexandria, of all of these amazing different settings, have been living without the Temple as their central binding institution. They have been living with, around, and in company with Roman and Greek and various other cultures, Persian cultures. They freely adapt to the cultures that are keeping them company. They also, quite clearly, will defend things that are important to them—the right, for example, not to have to worship the emperor.

They're living lives that actually are so vibrant and attractive that we have a number of records of Roman writers getting a little worried about the amount of Romans who are adopting Judaic practices—Seneca and Juvenal both do this, both say, "Oy, we Romans are not observing our ancestral practices—we're doing things like those Judeans over there."

These lives are lived vibrantly, richly, mostly peacefully. Our ancient forefathers and foremothers were living pretty interesting lives . . . which, I will also say, include much more power, input, and activity from women than any of us would expect, including women in apparently important leadership roles in early synagogues. There was also a lot of very interesting interrelationship with people who are attending synagogues who are not Jews.

We have this incredibly vibrant life, and the literature of Second Temple times almost never mentions the Temple. The whole saga that, once the Temple is destroyed, everything falls apart—Jewish life is broken into pieces, there's this desperate longing and agonizing over the future—there's no evidence of that. It's a Rabbinic story, it's a Rabbinic myth. That myth, of course, exists in part as a foundation story—to explain how the Rabbis become important, and why they should have.

Insofar as we do have rabbis speaking to one another in little groups, discussing the law—yeah, they do that. But they are talking to *each other*, and they have absolutely no role—or almost no role—to play in the lives of the vast majority of Jews in the first centuries of the Common Era. People aren't consulting the Rabbis on legal issues; they're going to their local Roman legal officials. Their marriage contracts are not being written in Hebrew—they're being written in Greek. Children are being named with Greek names. Synagogues are not built according to Rabbinic strictures—they don't have things in the right direction, stored in the right place.

Jewish community life that is taking place in those synagogues is not taking shape according to a Rabbinic direction of any kind—instead, people are fundraising, people are manumitting their slaves, people are getting together for festivals and having fun—they're living Jewish lives, but they're not living Rabbinic lives.

Lex Rofeberg: Some of our listeners may have never heard anything about this history. Others might say, "I've heard of things like the Sadducees or the Essenes." There's certainly an awareness from certain communities of Jews that there were others out there—but I feel like many of them think, "Those folks were dissenters," or maybe they just think of those communities as having less authenticity. Could you say more about what this time was like, and how all of these groups were engaging with one another and with Judaism?

Barbara Thiede: The first thing I'd like to say is something that many of my students find really challenging. Frequently, when I've gone to churches for various interfaith moments, I've been asked, "Look at what happened with Christianity—how it spread throughout the world. What do you have to say to that?" We all know the subtext, right? "We won, and you didn't—so this is clearly an indication that God wanted this rather than that . . . you are the that, we are the this." My answer to that usually is, "The fastest growing religion today is Islam." Or, "Constantine could have converted to Judaism—there were about the same number of Jews as there were Christians in the Roman Empire." Accidents of history are interesting things—choices that are made are interesting things.

Now, the list—Sadducees, Essenes, Dead Sea Scrolls—is the classic list of, "Oh, there were Judaisms." It's a Jacob Neusner approach to this—Jacob Neusner, the great historian. But even those groupings are not representing 95% of Judeans of the Second Temple time, or the first centuries.

And here's how this gets back to that question I get asked by

Christian communities—when people do the, "Well, the Rabbis won..." I want to say, "Hmm . . . and had it not been for the emergence of Christianity, which created an incredible power base around Church and around clergy . . . and then also created a compelling need to know, 'Well, who are the leaders that look like us in that minority community? Ah, they are the Rabbis. . .'" In some respects, we can thank Christians for the Rabbinic power that we enjoyed, benefitted from, and which defined us.

I say all those words in positive terms because I want to make it clear that my intention is not to say this was all mythology, and therefore we don't have to pay attention to it. The Rabbinic narrative, and the Rabbinic frame, has been absolutely critical and formative to Western European Judaism. It is also, in many, many respects, an extraordinary, beautiful, rich tradition which deserves a lot more attention than we give it.

My concern is that in a world in which Judaism has been measuring itself by that yardstick—has been beating itself by that yardstick—we have the opportunity to instead look at this grand diversity of our history and tap a myriad of sources that are rich, variegated, and worth our time. Conforming to the Rabbinic one and reinvigorating the Rabbinic model is not our only choice for Jewish identity, Jewish life, Jewish community, and Jewish future.

The Western, Ashkenazi-dominated world needs to step back and take a little bit of a dose in humility and learn. It needs to learn a little bit about its own history so that it stops reading Rabbinic history as the history of Judaism. It also needs to explore deeply, and listen deeply, to Jews of other countries, other traditions, and other worlds.

Then we need to have a conversation—all of us.

What is it that none of us—I ask my students this—what is it that you would never give up about Judaism? What would that thing be that is so visceral to who you are, that you can't imagine yourself or any other Jew without it?

Start there. For some Jews in the world it is Rabbinic *halachah* [Rabbinic Jewish law]. For some Jews, like the Kaifeng Jews, it might be the books of Torah mixed in with a little Confucian wisdom.

Dan Libenson: Is it right to say that there are at least two traditions that have been in play, even in the Eastern European Ashkenazi world, for the last thousand years? One is the Rabbinic "elite" tradition that has gone in different directions—it's gone in the direction of having more focus on law; it's gone in the direction of Hasidism, which is more focused on the spirit; it's gone in the direction of Reform Judaism with more of a focus on social justice; and in various other directions—but it's all versions of that elite Rabbinic tradition. But at the same time, in parallel, there's another tradition—and it's the tradition of the "regular Jews," who sometimes follow what their rabbis suggest, and sometimes don't.

I was talking to a group of rabbis recently about the idea that it's really important for rabbis to have a vision of their own role—but it's also important for rabbis to understand that the people also have a vision for what Judaism is *for them*. They may not always know how to articulate it, but it's wrong to say that they're just ignorant and don't care. It's often that they *do* have a real deeply felt sense of what it means to them, or what they want Judaism to be—and they're feeling just as let down by the rabbis as the rabbis are feeling let down by them.

Could you help us think that part through?

Barbara Thiede: The first thing I want to do is add that there's more than two, and the third piece that we need to be thinking about is the extent to which Jews of any world—Western or otherwise—are also integrally involved in surrounding cultures.

If you just take a look at Joshua Trachtenberg's old classic on Jewish magic—of course he says it's all about folk practice, and then he quotes one rabbi after another as his sources, which is its own kind of commentary on what you just said. But still, one of the cute little pieces in there is how women of the Medieval period would want to have some iron in the room when they were giving birth; this was really important—to get a key to the synagogue and have it in the room of a birthing woman. But if there was no key to the synagogue available, you could ask for the key to the local church. We need to think about that.

Understanding the complexities of our history is actually like opening up a magic treasure box—there's so much there sparkling for us to look at, and it goes beyond, "Here are the elite rabbis in their various forms, and here are the people doing whatever they're doing." Interaction with cultures, peoples, music, art, experience, economies around us also has played a role in how we create and re-create ourselves.

One thing I do want to come back to, though, which is really important, is the notion of the people being "ignorant." One of the things that drives me personally most into the corners of my room to bang my head against the wall is when rabbis talk about the ignorance and the apathy of Jews. First of all—nu, what's new? When were rabbis not complaining about the ignorance and the apathy of Jews? You're saying something new for us? Don't think so. The other thing about this is—according to whose model are these Jews ignorant and apathetic? According to which yardstick are they uninterested?

I look at people of Lex's generation, of my son's generation. Those Jews—yes, many intermarried—are definitively still describing themselves as Jewish because it's important to them. And maybe they don't know what they're saying when they say "traditions," but they do know this—they do know that there's a people group they belong to. They do know that that people group owns traditions, ideas, texts, ways, folk practices. And they are often much more literate about what that really means in defining Judaism than we give them credit for. It's just that they may not necessarily be primarily interested in what we think we have to teach—which is the Rabbinic model as the be-all end-all form that we will preserve Judaism in.

In a thousand years, Dan—maybe even in 500 years—I really wonder whether Rabbinic Judaism will look to Jews at that time very much like how we now see Second Temple times. "Oh, that's interesting—that's how they were."

Lex Rofeberg: As a rabbinic student, I wrestle with the role of rabbi—both historically and today. It seems that, even though you are a rabbi, you're able to step outside that perspective and question what the role of a rabbi is. I'd love to hear a little bit about how you, while critiquing all of these historical and contemporary manifestations of Rabbinic authority, are also a rabbi. How do you wrestle with all of that?

Barbara Thiede: You are right—I do wrestle with that. I find myself sometimes frustrated with colleagues because of the tendency, which we all have—this is going to happen at any profession—but there's a kind of self-congratulatory process that I find is dangerous if we want to be the kinds of paradigm shifters we keep saying we want to be.

But what if you sit down to Hanukkah, and instead of telling that narrative of Hellenism versus Judaism—which tends to very much reinforce a rabbinic narrative around the dangers of assimilation—what if you turn it on its head? In a congregational setting, you have everybody sit down to a table, and on the table you have different things on everybody's plate. A couple of them are mock coins—the ones with the goddesses and gods on one side and the menorah on the other. Maybe there's a *shtickle* Philo [a little piece of Philo]. That will give you a different sense of what Judaism could have looked like in the first century. You do this in your own private home, in your communal home, and on every single plate you have evidence of the way these things were being lived together. You have everybody get their Jewish names for the day and if they're living in Alexandria, those names might be "Philo," or "Alexander," not "Judah," not "Joshua."

Then, after you do this, you look around the room—you look at the art in the room, and the furniture in the room—is all of that Jewish? What happens when you walk through the house? Do you see some Jewish things? You surely do. Do you see a lot of things from all over the world? You might. What kinds of Jewish lives are the Jews who own that house, who are living in that house, living? In what way are they, just like those of the second century BCE, integrating, joining together—exploiting, even—the riches of the cultural worlds that are at their fingertips, and still remaining Jewish? What kind of Hanukkah would we be celebrating?

And then at the close of that night, everybody brings their *hannukiah* [Hanukkah menorah] to the table, and we light the candles—because some things are eternal, and they last forever. One of those things is how incredible a light looks in the darkness. I want to make it real for my community that Jews, and Judaism, is that treasure box. I don't want to do it in a way that measures their practice—they have more practice than they know.

I think that the history that we have gives us that opportunity to think as rabbis in those settings, Lex, as people who can encourage everyone in the room—even ourselves—to ask, "What is Judaism? What do I love here? What makes me feel at home?" We can do it almost as friends, because we ourselves—you and I—will be continuously asking that question of ourselves too, as we should—rabbis or not.

Dan Libenson: I have a question for both of you that comes out of this conversation. I think we're seeking a Judaism that is, let's say, primarily emergent from the needs and perspectives of regular Jews. At least you and I, Barbara, have been "regular Jews" for a long time before going on to a Jewish professional course, whereas Lex went on to that Jewish professional course at a younger age.

I've tried very hard to resist the idea that I should become a rabbi, because I acknowledge the Rabbinic story is a myth as you've explained to us. Wouldn't it be important for those of us who are saying we want to explore the Judaism that comes from that other line to create our own set of understandings of what our leadership looks like, and what we call it?

If I were to become a rabbi, I would almost be pushed over to the first line—and there's nothing wrong with it, it's just a different line than the one that I'm trying to live within. It strikes me that you're also trying to live within that line—and yet, you pursued and wanted to have the role of rabbi. I'm wondering—and you too, Lex—how do you think about all that?

Barbara Thiede: Every year in Jewish Renewal, when we ordain our people, we read a lineage. The lineage is a fairly traditional lineage—except that, God bless him, Reb Daniel Siegel added women into the lineage. You just inspired me to think about the lineage of Rufina—Rufina, the *Rosh* [head] of a synagogue in the second century CE. The lineage of these human beings, the lineage of the God-fearers, the lineage of the elders of Alexandria who had to navigate the horrible violence of first century CE. The lineage of the Jew in Alexandria, the young Jewish man who describes himself as an Alexandrian when the local authorities described him as a Judean—he says, "No, I'm an Alexandrian." We've got that.

Lex Rofeberg: "I'm a Polish Jew"—Bernie Sanders.

Barbara Thiede: Amen—right.

Lex Rofeberg: "I'm a Polish-descended American Jew."

Barbara Thiede: Exactly. There is a lineage here that needs to be claimed—and I think, actually, that there's part of me that wants to run out and find all the Daniel Libensons out there and say, "Not only claim it—name it for yourselves. Look for it, identify it, and lift this lineage up."

When I made the decision to enter rabbinical school, I felt that I needed that world to establish the credentials. If I were doing this now, I might feel differently—but at that time, there was a credentialing issue. I suppose that, to some extent, I walked into that world, loved that world, and do love that world—and have walked out inspired to credential your lineage, Daniel. That's what I want to do. I want to, from the Rabbinic space, say, "Guess what? We needed you. We need you now," and to do what I can from that space to say, "You are authentic in ways you don't even know yet—let me support that."

Lex Rofeberg: I love what you just framed, and I love citing the lineage of Rufina. My lineage is the lineage of Korach—I love the lineage of the heretics, and I think of Korach in the Bible as one of our first obvious heretics, who is understood by his own leadership—and by God, and by later eras of Jews—as being other, and being different from the ideal. It's not that I am doing nothing that would be deemed ideal by Jewish authorities—but I actively want to shift what it means to be a Jew, and the ideals of Judaism, so I need to be in the conversation where that's happening. At a certain point, I decided that going to rabbinical school would help me to do that.

I will be ordained, God-willing . . . and I'll want to *not* use the title "rabbi" a lot of the time. But I also want to use it sometimes. By becoming ordained, I have both options.

Barbara Thiede: I have to say that I almost never introduce myself as "Rabbi." People do respond differently to me when I put my hand out and say, "It's nice to meet you—I'm Barbara Thiede," than if I say, "I'm Rabbi Thiede." If I have earned the right to be a teacher for our people, they give me that right. And I have to re-earn it every single day, I have to earn it every single week. No title grants me that right—it is my fellow Jews who grant me that right.

Dan Libenson: The way we're talking about rabbis and

non-rabbis—we're setting this up as almost a binary and two lines that should somehow be at odds with one another. But what I think we all really want is some moving forward where we say, "Can we sit together as equals and hash out a new path forward?" I think it's interesting to ask rabbis and non-rabbis what that path forward might look like.

Barbara Thiede: You're putting me in mind of this moment in which *The Forward* [a newspaper that cover the Jewish community] published rabbis' comments on, essentially, "What is the greatest threat to Judaism?" A high number responded with "apathy" and "ignorance" and all of this.

In order to have that conversation, one of the things that's most important is to get rabbis—forgive me—to be quiet, to listen a little more. They're used to doing a lot of talking—I'm used to doing a lot of talking. We could listen a little bit more. I'd love to sit rabbis down in a room, and I'd say, "Okay, now your task is just to listen. You're going to listen to the educated, articulate, interesting, creative Jews that walk through this door. You're going to take, for a moment, your expectations about what you think Jews need to do to be Jews—and you're just going to listen to what they are already doing. In what way is their existing practice fulfilling the expectations of ritual that you think have to start by opening the *siddur* [prayer book]?"

Dan Libenson: I'm thinking back to where we started this conversation, in terms of the discussion about diaspora. You've spoken about and questioned whether "diaspora" is even the right way to look at it. So much of what goes on now is Judaism as relationship to Israel—as relation to people, state, and land of Israel—both for people who live in Israel, and more importantly, for our context in the United States, as people outside of Israel.

I'm speaking politically, but I'm not *just* speaking politically. We seem to have built up for ourselves this idea that nothing we do outside of the land of Israel can ever really be as deeply or authentically Jewish as those who are doing it in closer proximity to Jerusalem or to the Western Wall or to whatever ideas of history that are located there.

Barbara Thiede: I don't know that the term "diaspora" can be divorced from the idea of grief, of longing, and of exile by most Jews today. That, I think, is hard for them to do—because the mythology has put "diaspora" together with a set of emotional conditions. It's in our liturgy, it's in our prayers, it's in our narratives, it's in our stories.

But if I look at the history, I'm not seeing that set of emotional conditions applying to the life that people are living in the diaspora. What would happen if diaspora was for us, now, not associated with the grief, the sorrow, the longing that we should feel, or guilt—but rather, part of a self-conscious and confident choice to expand the reach of Judaism all over the world, and to do so with enthusiasm, with joy, with creativity, with life? What would happen if that's what we meant when we said "diaspora"? I think that that's important for us to acknowledge and to think about, because we live in a world that needs our attention to the world, and to conditions in the world.

I've had colleagues who have said, "When I went to Israel, I felt like I was standing on holy ground—it's holier there than any place else for me." I deeply respect that they felt transformed by something—but I live in a world where there is no ground that is holier than any other, and I need to be conscious of that to be the best Jew I can be for the world.

I am not the Jew who thinks, "Oy, we're assimilating, we're dying out, we're at risk." I see, instead, when I look at our history, an extraordinary capacity to re-create and reinvent ourselves. I think Judaism will do very well in the future, and I have no fear for us—because we have great gifts that we possess, and we have great learning to explore, and we have great creativity we have yet to tap.

QUESTIONS FOR REFLECTION

- Barbara Thiede asks her students *What is it that you would never give up about Judaism? What would that thing be that is so visceral to who you are, that you can't imagine yourself or any other Jew without it?* How would you answer this question?
- Thiede speaks to a disconnect that she observes between how rabbis perceive "regular Jews" and the real complexities within the practice and thinking of everyday Jews. She suggests that the practices and choices of "regular Jews" might not always be valued, understood, or even visible to people who are solidly within the Rabbinic tradition. What is your experience of this? What do you think would change if we shifted perspective to seeing "regular Jews" as having important questions, concerns, and practices to learn from (rather than seeing their choices as evidence of "apathy" or "ignorance")?
- In this episode, Barbara Thiede, Dan, and Lex each shared their way of thinking about what it means to be a rabbi. They consider what kinds of knowledge and perspectives Rabbinic authority supports and limits, and what it might mean to be part of a different lineage of leadership within Judaism. What is your relationship to Rabbinic leadership? How have you embodied or experienced other forms of leadership within your Jewish life?
- Another question Thiede offers involves a re-thinking of the emotions we associate with the word "diaspora." She asks us to consider: *What would happen if diaspora was for us, now, not associated with the grief, the sorrow, the longing that we should feel, or guilt—but rather, part of a self-conscious and confident choice to expand the reach of Judaism all over the world, and to do so with enthusiasm, with joy, with creativity, with life?* How have you thought about "diaspora" in the past? What does Thiede's question open up for you? What role could you envision playing in a diaspora conceived of in this new way?

Irving 'Yitz' Greenberg

> "...those gifts which we have, says Judaism, ought to be recruited—are recruited—by God to get everybody to participate in this process of repairing the world."

The Third Era

Irving "Yitz" Greenberg was the founding president of Clal: The National Jewish Center for Learning and Leadership. He currently serves as president of the J.J. Greenberg Institute for the Advancement of Jewish Life and as Senior Scholar in Residence at Hadar, an organization dedicated to engaging a diverse range of people in serious Jewish learning. His thinking has been foundational for generations of Jewish leaders, both within and outside the mainstream, including us.

Yitz Greenberg started his career as a scholar and theologian, especially interested in the meaning of the Holocaust for Judaism and Jewish theology. He was an influential figure in Jewish-Christian dialogue in the latter part of the 20th century. He served as director of the President's Commission on the Holocaust from 1979 to 1980. The Commission conceived of and supervised the creation of the United States Holocaust Museum.

In the 1990s, Greenberg worked with the philanthropist Michael Steinhardt to create the Steinhardt Foundation for Jewish

Life—formerly called Steinhardt Foundation/Jewish Life Network—which was an early philanthropic project with an innovative approach to funding entrepreneurial projects in the Jewish community.

Yitz Greenberg received rabbinical ordination from Beth Joseph Rabbinical Seminary (Yeshivas Beis Yosef) and holds a Ph.D. in American Studies from Harvard. He has published many books and articles, including *The Jewish Way: Living the Holidays* (1988).

In the 1980s, Yitz Greenberg introduced the idea that we are living in the third "great cycle," or the Third Era, of Jewish history, the first two being the Biblical era and the Rabbinic era. This idea felt very resonant with our own sense that we were living in a time of revolutionary change, and we were excited to have him as the guest on our 100th episode.

Dan Libenson: I first heard the ideas about what you call the "Third Era" at a talk you gave at the Hartman Institute about five years ago. It has become the background music for a lot of the thinking that Lex and I have been doing about ways that Judaism can be reimagined, and the more central role that what we call "regular Jews" might play.

I was hoping that you could begin by laying out the basic ideas of what you call the three eras of Judaism, and where we are in Jewish history.

Yitz Greenberg: The first era of Jewish history, you might say, is the Bible. And in the Bible, you have a very powerful central message of the Jewish religion: that the world will be redeemed, that the world will be perfected, that humanity is in a partnership with God to do so. But all the characteristics—the institutions, the worship, and so on—very much grow out of a picture of a dominant God who is the dominant partner and who really controls everything that humans do.

I came to the conclusion that, after the destruction of the [Second] Temple, the Rabbis—the new leadership—and new institutions emerged because God gives up control because God wants humans to take on more responsibility, and more authority. Thus, no more revelation from Heaven: the Rabbis have to figure out what God wants of us at this very moment. And one could go further and say that in the Temple people were much more passive; in the synagogue, people are much more participatory and active, and so on.

Now, I've come to the conclusion that the Holocaust and Israel show that God has again self-limited. One might say we are living in the age when God is totally hidden, when the intervention—the control—of history is not seen, but rather God acts through humans. That is to say, in this Third Era, God has asked humans to take full responsibility for the outcome of the Covenant.

To put it in the simplest fashion possible: we're living in the Third Age, the age when the humans are fully responsible, when God is totally present, but hidden. My guess is that in the future, a thousand years from now, this will be called "Lay Judaism," or the "Lay Era of Judaism." Just as we have Biblical Judaism, with priests and prophets, and Rabbinic Judaism, with rabbis and teachers, this Third Era will be the era of the lay leadership and of the hidden God and human responsibility.

Dan Libenson: When I heard you speak, you articulated an idea that I thought was really beautiful and empowering. It is this idea that, in each of these eras, as God withdraws further back, two things happen. The first is that, although withdrawing, God is also coming closer; and the other is that, as God withdraws, more responsibility falls on the shoulders of human beings and therefore more human beings are needed to shoulder the responsibility.

Could you explain how we get to that third stage? What does it look like when human beings shoulder all of that responsibility?

Yitz Greenberg: First of all, thank you for noticing that point because people are confused sometimes. When I speak of God giving up control, or God becoming more hidden, I don't believe God is withdrawing. That's historically one of the ways it's interpreted—God is turning away from people, or, of course, in the secular version, God is distancing because God isn't there. But my point is—and this is the Rabbis' point, but I think it applies today also—God is more hidden, but God is actually more present. When God was more visible, more transcendent—more dramatic control, intervention, miracles, visible miracles, and so on—God was also very unapproachable. One could not see God without dying, one could not touch sacred places without being killed, as it were.

So, the Rabbis said God had become more hidden, but God is actually present. Because God is hidden, the lay people needed to be educated in order to see where God is, and this is what Rabbinic teaching was about. And it turned out, according to the Rabbis, God was found now not just in the Temple, or behind all kinds of protective walls, but God was in the home, God was at the head of the sickbed, God was in the bed making love where people are doing this properly, God was in learning Torah, and having a family conversation around the table.

Projecting that trend, my argument is now God is totally hidden. I mean by "totally hidden" that we have a secular culture in which one can develop an understanding as if there is no God—or one can only see God not in some dramatic overriding of natural law, but in the natural law.

So, that means that God, I believe, is available not just in a synagogue or in a so-called holy place, but literally in every place. But, you have to look, you have to dig, you have to become sensitized.

The logic of what I'm saying is that—just as the Rabbis said people must become educated so they will encounter God and know how to relate to God in the hidden place—today, the average lay person will have to become as knowledgeable, as participatory, as aware, as religiously active, as the rabbis or the leadership was in the Second Era. So, therefore, we're talking about a democratization that's finally complete. We're living in an age where—at least in capacity and potential—everybody can be a religious equivalent of a prophet or rabbi. And that is, of course, the opportunity, and maybe the challenge.

Lex Rofeberg: When you talk about every human being capable of being a prophet it implies that human beings are something pretty special. I know that core to your thought is the idea of *tzelem elohim*—the idea of human beings in the image of God—and related to that, the infinite value of human beings as a fractal of God. I'd love to hear more from you about how those concepts interweave with what we're talking about, and the increased role of human beings in the era that we're in.

Yitz Greenberg: Very important point you're raising—and I still think this is the central value, or idea, of Judaism. In particular, the central teaching that the human being is in the image of God means that the human being is such an amazing creature, such an amazing capacity of life.

The Talmud's interpretation of humans being the image of God is that they have three inherent dignities. The way I like to put it is,

"We hold these truths to be self-evident: that all human beings are created in the image of God, and they are endowed by their Creator with three inalienable dignities." And those dignities are infinite value, equality, and uniqueness.

Infinite value means that human life is worth everything. It's worth spending millions to save a life, it's worth spending millions to heal and cure a person; in other words, money should be no object—and in principle, every human being should be treated and given whatever they need, whatever it costs, to keep them alive and healthy. (I leave it to you to decide whether taking away medical insurance from millions of people, which will threaten their life and health and ability, is compatible with a value system that says human beings are worth infinite value.)

Now, take equality. Again, the idea of the image of God means that, unlike human images, in which a Van Gogh is worth more than a Greenberg painting because it's a better quality, in human beings white skin or black skin should not make any—it does not make any difference, in terms of value. Or male or female. In other words, all images of God, by definition, are equal, says the Talmud.

And the third is all images of God are unique.

Now that's dignity. And therefore the Jewish dream—and this is the central teaching of Judaism—is that this world must be repaired and improved so that it fully supports and respects and honors these dignities. In other words, you have to make a world so wealthy that it can spend an infinite amount of money to save a life. You need a world that is so democratic that everybody is treated equal, and there is no oppression, there is no tyranny, there is no discrimination, there is no degrading. And a world that so respects uniqueness that stereotyping is broken, that discriminatory rejections or lumping of people together are overridden.

And Judaism is a revolutionary religion, because it said not only, "This is what should be," but it claimed that God has recruited humans to join in a partnership to make the world that way.

So, "image of God" has a double meaning: on the one hand, the three dignities that everybody's entitled to; on the other hand, it means we have godlike powers—powers of mind to analyze consciousness, to analyze the universe, and figure out the code of DNA, and figure out the power of the atom so that we can turn it into a force and into power and to light, and figure out technology. So, those gifts which we have, says Judaism, ought to be recruited—are recruited—by God to get everybody to participate in this process of repairing the world.

And the goal is, at the end, what I call "the triumph of life"—namely, we believe that life itself can win out, and should win out, over all the enemies of life.

Not just of human life, by the way. I mean things like poverty or hunger or oppression or degradation or war—these are all things that Judaism teaches can and should be overcome. It will take a tremendous effort. And that's what humans are supposed to do.

Dan Libenson: As I was looking at some of the things that you've written, and listening to you, I was finding myself struggling with the idea of image of God as the underlying foundational concept.

For many of our listeners, and for myself, who struggle or don't believe in God, how do we think about the God language? For those of us who grew up in a religious environment, it's the natural way to talk. But I wonder if—especially when we talk about a God that's withdrawing, and a God that's in all sorts of unusual relationships with human beings—are there other ways that we could be thinking about this, or ways you've had success translating these ideas to make them just as powerful?

Yitz Greenberg: The fact that God gives humans total responsibility, it seems to me another way of God saying, "What's important is perfecting the world—not worshipping God. What's important is not how you please me or impress me or worship me, but what you do for my creatures, for my world."

The way I like to put it is, it is now intellectually easier to be atheist than to be a believer. I think that if you see this as God's will, then I see it as God, in effect, saying, "Atheist or religious is not important—what's really important is how you treat the *image of God*, a fellow human being." If you don't want to use the language "image of God," my answer is, you don't have to. I think, in a sense, there is a conscious choice here—religiously speaking now—to downplay the formal structure of belief in God, statements about God, worship of God, toward the human worldly consequences of such ideas.

I want to add one thing—I moved in this direction before I even saw the Third Era idea for another reason. It really was the impact of the Holocaust on me. One of the most stunning and striking things about the Holocaust—I mean, total degradation, total killing, not just wiping out the Jews, but humiliating, making them suffer first, trying to make them into garbage and into nothing before you kill them—the more I thought of it, the more I felt the following profound and very shocking truth: Some of the people who carried this out were deeply religious. They believed in God.

One of the most shattering scenes I read about in the war crime trials was the trial of the Einsatzgruppen—the people that shot men, women and children daily. They killed a million and a half or more Jews, face to face, shooting them down and massacring, day after day for 18 months. One of the people put on trial as a leader, as a captain, as an important officer, was himself a minister, a religious minister; and others—18 out of 25—were highly educated, etc. The story goes, in Simferopol, which is in the Crimea, they were shooting the Jews and killing the Jews in the Crimea, and it was the day before Christmas, and the commander said to them, "We've got to finish this job because we want to celebrate Christmas tomorrow." At the trial they asked, "What'd you do?" The minister said, "We got up early that morning, and we took out the last Jews, and we shot them all. We got back just in time for the religious celebration."

Himmler said to his confidante—Kersten reports it in his diaries—"We insisted every SS man must believe in God; otherwise we'd be no better than the atheistic Marxists."

I said to myself, "Take that, and now let me take the reverse." Albert

Camus, who was an atheist—a self-proclaimed atheist, on the index of the Catholic Church for being an atheist—Camus says that in France he joined the underground when he saw what was going on with the Nazis. Now, in a speech to a group of Christians—Christian monks, no less—after the war, he said, "I want you to understand . . . when I joined, one of the biggest shocks that I learned was that people—Catholics, who I thought were old regime, reactionary idiots—gave their lives to stop this. Then, no less shocking to me, was to meet Marxist Communists, my fellow travelers, who sold out and joined." He said, "At one point, I, who was an atheist—I want to tell you, I began to pray, 'If only the Pope would say something—maybe he could help us fight the Nazis.'" He said, "I don't want to tell you bluntly—you want to call yourself Christian? Be my guest. It means nothing. I learned calling yourself a Marxist means nothing. To me, it's: Are you for or against what's going on here?"

My conclusion from that was—don't tell me you believe in God and then go out and shoot men, women, and children. Don't tell me you're an atheist and then give your life to prevent that from being done. My answer is—the atheists will forgive me—if a person is willing to give their life to save the image of God, if a person consistently shows reverence for the image of God, no matter what, then they show, as it were, a recognition of the fundamental sacred reality that's behind the image of God.

I'm not God's PR agent who demands membership. That's not the division point anymore.

Lex Rofeberg: If the differences between atheists and believers are really not the core debate of our time, and it's about aligning around belief in the infinite value and sacred dignity of human beings—what does that mean for another duality that we think about often in Jewish life, which is Jew and other? As we enter an era where, in your view, the role of God is changing, how does that also affect the ideas of Jewish chosenness, or the unique role of Jews?

Yitz Greenberg: I do believe in the chosenness of Jews. The only point I make is that I think God is a God of multiple choice—by which I mean to say that I don't think we're the only chosen ones. In fact, what "chosen" is really trying to say is: Do they have an experience of being singled out—which, by the way, is another way of saying, "Are they loved?" When I've been loved—when someone loves me—I feel very much singled out, and I think that's what the tradition was trying to say.

I believe that God has reached out in the same way through Christianity. I believe God has reached out through secular, as well as other religions, to human beings—and they have to respond. The Jews should feel the same way as everybody else—namely, that they are chosen, that they're important, that they have God's love. It's meant to be not a source of superiority, but of inspiration to respect, and do that to others. To imitate God, and do unto others, so to speak, what God has done unto them.

Let me rephrase that . . . I believe pluralism is just as essential as religion. We see when you have an absolute claim, an absolute authority in the name of God, it leads to the same process—killing, mass killing, the cheapening of other people's lives, anybody but your own, etc. That's a challenge for all of us. If every religion and every group would say, "I want to achieve part of the achievement of the perfect world, but I can't do it alone. I have to know my own limitations. Even if I have a special relationship to God, I can't do it alone."

I say this to the Jews—12, 14 million people are not going to lift a whole world. If we try, we're going to get a hernia.

The way to do it is to, if you can work with a billion, 900 million Christians, a billion Muslims, 800 million, 900 million, whatever, Buddhists, Hindus—and if each of those groups will roll up their sleeves and join in this process, we've got a shot. That's why I pointed out pluralism. I'm not a relativist—I'm not saying you have to have a belief in God or an absolute of any sort—but you have to know the limits of that belief and absolute. You may have a truth in God, but you don't have all the truth that God has given. Your own truth may have elements of mistake and weakness and error which you can correct—or which you can learn from others to correct.

That is the future I see. Again, just as I say being a believer is no longer an absolute line as the defining point of the person—so is

Jewish/non-Jewish not the absolute line.

Dan Libenson: Can we talk a little bit more about the substance of Judaism in the Third Era, as you see it? Because I think that when a lot of our listeners think about why they're not drawn to Judaism as we know it . . . in your language, we're looking at a Second Era of Judaism, and we're living in the Third Era.

How do you see some of the specific dimensions of Judaism changing in the Third Era, such as prayer or Jewish law or various practices, holidays? It would seem that the Judaism of the Third Era would need to be as different from Rabbinic Judaism as Rabbinic Judaism was from the Second Temple Judaism, with its sacrifices and priests and all these dimensions that I think most Jews today would fail to recognize as Judaism.

Yitz Greenberg: It's a very telling point—and, of course, part of the answer I'm going to give is I don't know. I'm as interested as you are to see what happens—I'm looking forward. I don't know if I'll live long enough to see it all, but I'm making some guesses in my [forthcoming] book, and I'll make some guesses now. I think some of it will be new and will not be recognized—or at least not be recognized when it starts. I believe there will be whole phenomena that will be very different. Or, there will be a continuation of past phenomena with new value and new understanding and new direction or focus—and there will be some improvements or changes in the same way.

For example, Shabbat for me is a day totally other from the rest of my week. It's a day in which I'm totally focused on being—even though I'm a workaholic and a hard driving doing type and so on, and even though I celebrate human creativity and human productivity—I think it's made possible a tremendous upgrading of life and life dignity. Shabbat is a day where I totally transform.

I remember a friend, Haskell Bernat, who's a Reform rabbi, said to me, "I keep Shabbat—not like you, meaning, for example, I listen to music on Shabbat, which means playing an instrument or turning on radios, which you don't do. Why? Because I feel that music deepens my spirituality, it deepens my sense of the beauty of life, it enriches my emotional and personal relationships, and so on." I said to him,

"Number one, I consider that a valid ... it's a pluralist Shabbat—it's a different expression of the same value."

I think Shabbat will be a feature of the Third Era. I think it's even more needed now, when there's totally saturated, 24-hour cycles of news, etc., and when we are all internet-addicted. Whether it will be a total cessation of electronic activity, or whether it will be partial—or, as in the case of Bernat's suggestion, that some of the activity will be using what is classically considered *melakhaha*—or work that's prohibited on Shabbat—but doing so for spiritual and personal growth, and to carry out the deeper meaning that Shabbat is about—I'm open. Let's find out.

Maybe in the Second Era, the rabbis said, "Since God is hidden, let me help you—You're eating a fruit; stop and appreciate the beauty of the fruit, the flavor. And you know what? Realize this was created by God." So they made a *berakhah* [a blessing]. The blessing gave you the insight that what seems to be a secular experience—eating a fruit—is really a religious connection to the depth of Creation.

What will happen in the Third Era? Will there be a new *berakhah*? Certainly we'll need one. When I'm a doctor about to operate to remove a pathology, a cancer that would kill this person, when as a doctor I'm developing a genetic improvement that is going to change the quality of life of a person for a lifetime—will that be a berakhah? Maybe it won't be a berakhah—maybe it will be a meditation. Maybe it won't be a meditation—maybe it will just be an attitude.

My point is, in the Third Era a lot of the religious activity is seven days a week—not just on Shabbat—because in the activity you have a sense of depth, of religious and sacred, and the value in the life of the other person.

I go down the line—if I'm a businessman, can I get a sense that I'm part of *tikkun olam* [repairing the world]? That means not creating a product that improves life, but how about that I pay the workers who make it for me a living wage? How about I give them work circumstances that respect their dignity? How about I'm not, as a farmer, taking people and sweat labor, or sweatshop labor, or migrant labor, and exploiting them? Again, will I make a blessing over that?

How will I express it? I remain fascinated.

I think of my wife's old joke, "If rabbis were women, we would have had a humdinger of a *berakhah*, a blessing, for giving birth—now we have none." Okay, so maybe some of it will be women or other people, newcomers to the experience, will create a new blessing—or, as I said, maybe it will be an attitudinal, a meditational, a spiritual expression of this sense of, "Wow."

Those are some of the new phenomena—and I think there will be new institutions. They will be secular institutions—I believe that. And I think one of the reasons the synagogue is less effective is that the language of the prayers, or the expectations of the rabbis, or the claims of the teaching assume a God-in-control that isn't there anymore—and not because I'm an atheist, but because that's the way God is operating right now.

I think learning will be more important than ever—intellectual learning, understanding, getting the past, getting the past precedents, getting the past values down. Because I play off them—they enrich my repertoire, so then I can either apply them directly or modify or develop a parallel new one from them.

Even if I'm uneducated, I'll have access through the internet and be trained to have access to every tradition. It's the old joke—the greatest rabbinic decisor of the past generation was Rav Moshe Feinstein, and he had a tremendous memory—but the truth is, not a total photographic one. A young student with a good computer and access to the Bar Ilan registry of past rulings has access to more information than Rav Moshe Feinstein. Now, if we can train him how to apply that information—this is my dream—every person can be their own decisor, every person has the strength and insight to know what to do at this moment, based on past records and based on, obviously, my judgment as to how you apply them today.

Dan Libenson: It struck me as you were talking that there are questions of how to reckon with the overwhelming amount of material that Second Era Judaism represents, both by people who are currently engaged in it, and by the people who aren't.

Business advice books often suggest you should have a "stop doing" list. The idea is that we have limited capacity, and it's very hard to take on new things when your time is already completely occupied with the existing things. Somehow you have to make room for the new things by stopping to do a certain set of things that you've been doing.

In your own experience—as an Orthodox Jew and a practicing Jew—how do you think about ways that people might reimagine Judaism in these fundamental ways, and is that additive to what is already expected of Orthodox Jews? And if it's going to ultimately replace some of it—as Rabbinic Judaism did to the sacrifices, for example—how can people on the inside think about that without somehow feeling that they're engaging in some kind of betrayal of the past?

And on the flipside, when we say that this is the Lay Era, and that all these folks who have not been immersed in the world of Jewish practice are now invited to shoulder the responsibility of leadership—is it realistic and necessary to say, "And the ideal is that they will somehow master the knowledge of all of what's come before?"

How do we really make this transition when we have 2,000 years of accumulated Second Era Judaism?

Yitz Greenberg: My answer is: let many flowers bloom, and let's find out—in other words, let's see what works. Let's see which works, [which] I can't control. And thank God, we are living in a society which is so without centralized control that no one can stop the experiments. One of the advantages of living in a society like that is that you have a lot more religious experimentation, and a lot more ethical activity than you would have when it needs approval and control from the center.

There will be experiments, conscious or unconscious, about how much of the past you bring with you and how much of the past you drop.

How much of the new stuff do you sacralize, and how much do you simply do without sacralizing? I welcome all of the above, and I think we should learn from all of the above . . . and then if it turns out that one really works a lot better than the others, then I think we would move in that direction. But let's for the moment try it on, see what works.

Rav Kook, the Chief Rabbi of Israel before Israel became a state, once said, "Our task, as religious leaders, is that the old shall be renewed, and the new shall be made sacred." I think that's exactly what a vital, living religion does—valuing the intensity of life.

We have the double task of taking from the past what vitalizes and intensifies life, what enriches it—and where it doesn't, correcting it or improving it—and we have to take the new and bring it into the sacred ground.

There will be new holidays, and there will be new a lot of things—but I hope in the spirit of people understanding that life is a cycle, that a conscious life is richer.

That's step one.

Step two is—the more your responsibility, the more you should know. And if you are responsible and carry out your responsibility, you want to try to know. Yes, I think we have to try to upgrade Jewish education—so the average person should have a higher level... I joke about this, but it's not a joke at all—I think the average layperson, someday, should have the same access or mastery that the greatest specialized scholars in the Second Era did. How is that possible? Probably not possible—but you gave me the answer, I hope. We'll teach them how to use the internet and how to use access, and we'll do more work, literally, classifying and working out the past records and the angles of understanding of them so that people will have tools to ask good questions and to explore and to apply. Again, all the past traditions—even from an Orthodox perspective—don't have the answer for a totally changed environment. You have to apply it and use your judgment. It's going to be all of the above.

If you live totally without tradition, you're living in one century. The beauty of Jewish tradition, I think, is you're living in multiple centuries. Just like stereophonic music is a lot richer than monophonic, I think these traditions give us a depth of living, and these visions give us an intensity of living. I think that's what Judaism is trying to give the world. I hope the whole world joins in this process of living more intensely, embracing life more fully, and working to improve the conditions so that everybody in the world enjoys this opportunity.

My final point on that would be that individuals will become more specialized. When I give this talk on Third Era, sometimes a rabbi will get up and say, "But you say I have no future. What will the rabbi do in the Third Era? I'll be out a job." I tell him, "No. You know what you can become? In the Third Era, the laymen are going to be the rabbis—but you can become a rabbi's rabbi." Meaning—educate them, enable them, be a resource for them. I believe there will be both rabbinic and lay resource people—people who have put more time into learning, and who have a special feeling for it, a special knowledge, a special sensitivity and intelligence and intuition as to how to apply it. Such people will emerge as natural guides or leaders in this process.

Dan Libenson: I think that the distinction is one of authority. In the Second Era, the rabbis had authority over the Jews, and in the Third Era, that authority is not there for most Jews in the same way. I think what's interesting to those rabbis who ask, "Do I have a job in the future?" is that if your vision of that job is that it's one where you are an authority that dictates to Jews what they must do—you may be out of a job. If you're willing to accept a job that says, "How do I be a guide, how do I be a scholarly advisor or whatever, but I embrace and accept the idea that people may not go in the direction that I think is the best," that will be a new definition of the job.

In the Second Era, Judaism was something that was presented as, "This is what you must do." And in the Third Era, it's likely to be one that will be defined out of the choices that Jews, and perhaps others, make.

Yitz Greenberg: I say amen to everything that you said here. Again, it's part of the creativity—it's alive, it grows, it develops. I think this is going to be a real opportunity, and a real challenge. Can I participate in this process? I think it's a privilege to be alive at such a time, because you can contribute to the process, too.

What you said about authority is so correct, but—speaking now in God language—that, to me, is the point of the Third Era from God's perspective. By becoming totally hidden, by asking people to take human responsibility, God is saying we're now living in the age of voluntary covenant. People don't keep it because God is punishing them, or because God imposed it, or because they once accepted it. They're keeping it voluntarily, because—despite the risks, despite the setbacks—they really believe in the vision and the goal. Does that mean

God has no authority, no influence? Quite the contrary.

The authority is no longer imposed—it's earned. The authority is no longer automatic—it is chosen by those who follow.

I think this kind of authority will be more modest and more credible and more influential—and I think, at the end, a majority will end up with a more committed, more substantive, more voluntary, more loving relationship both with tradition and to God or whatever that they believe in—and that this is part of the long-term upgrade of human dignity. I hope so.

QUESTIONS FOR REFLECTION

- Yitz Greenberg says that Judaism teaches of *each human being's infinite value, equality, and uniqueness and that we must repair and improve the world so that it fully supports and respects and honors these dignities.* What aspects of your work in the world and your quest for social justice embody and express these three "inalienable dignities"? In what ways does your Judaism and Jewish practice align with Yitz's charge to "repair and improve the world?"
- In our conversation, Yitz Greenberg described a dual challenge that faces us in the Third Era: *We have the double task of taking from the past what vitalizes and intensifies life, what enriches it—and where it doesn't, correcting it or improving it—and we have to take the new and bring it into the sacred ground.* What is one element from the traditions of Judaism that ["vitalizes and intensifies"] your life? And what is something that has been considered secular, or perhaps simply new to the Jewish traditions, that you feel is worthy of bringing ["into the sacred ground"]?
- Yitz Greenberg suggests that in the Third Era, we will find that religious activities—activities undertaken with depth and a sense of the sacred—are not reserved for Shabbat, but are happening every day of the week. How does this connect to your experience? Where do you see the sacred in everyday life? How are your experiences of the everyday sacred different from or similar to your personal practice and experience of Shabbat?

Irwin Kula

> "Either Judaism in the next iteration was going to be a wisdom and practice that could help all human beings flourish—and therefore had to be taught and offered in accessible and usable ways—or I was out of this game."

Death and Rebirth & Judaism's Job

When we interviewed him, Irwin Kula was the co-president of Clal: The National Jewish Center for Learning and Leadership, a think tank, leadership training institute, and resource center founded by Yitz Greenberg and Elie Wiesel. He is now president emeritus.

Irwin Kula is the author of the book *Yearnings: Embracing the Sacred Messiness of Life*, and also the co-founder and executive editor of *The Wisdom Daily*. An eighth-generation rabbi, Kula has appeared numerous times on *Newsweek*'s list of America's most influential rabbis.

Our conversation with Kula includes discussion of *The Innovator's Dilemma*, a book by the late Harvard Business School professor Clayton Christensen, which has deeply influenced Kula's thinking and ours. Christensen's work asserts that paradigm shifts generally come about through what he calls "disruptive" or "non-linear" innovation, rather than incremental evolutionary change. While Christensen's ideas were developed in the arena of business, we agree with Irwin Kula that they have great relevance to the future of Judaism.

PART TWO

Mixed Multitudes

Mixed Multitudes

In Part 2, we take up the question of who exactly is standing with us at this creative edge. Who has already embarked on this journey of wandering? If leadership and authority in Jewish life are no longer embodied in rabbis alone, but are seated in a diverse array of individuals and communities willing to assume the responsibility for keeping Jewish wisdom and practice alive and relevant, who is stepping up to lead the way? And, if there are new multitudes of people to invite and include, who might be in that mix?

Irwin Kula helped us crystallize our thinking about "who" with the concept of disruptive innovation, a business theory of change developed by Harvard professor Clayton Christensen. Christensen points out that paradigm-shifting disruptive innovation in business rarely comes from within an established company or institution—think of the game-changing shift from film photography (Kodak) to digital photography (Apple). The change almost always starts outside the sphere of the current players and is first adopted by customers peripheral to the old product. After a time of iterative development, the new product may become more broadly popular.

Applied to Judaism, we can see how the response to the First Era crash aligns with Christensen's theory. The architects of Rabbinic Judaism were rabbis outside of the structures of priestly Judaism who worked over centuries to create something that might stick. We think the "makers" of the Third Era will also be people and organizations primarily outside the mainstream Jewish institutional landscape. Its early adherents are likely to be those who are not connected with (or even disenchanted by) mainstream Jewish institutions.

We know that in Exodus, the Israelites were accompanied by a mixed multitude comprised of "miscellaneous hangers-on," including Egyptians intermarried with Israelites, slaves, mercenaries, and others not of pure blood. We can imagine this least invited group of fellow travelers as a motley collection of riffraff whose presence at the margins of the wanderers was largely incidental to the story. If anything, their presence served to amplify by contrast the importance of the "pure and true" Israelites at the center of the narrative.

Now, in this new era, the metaphor of the mixed multitude takes on a different meaning and a new importance. The Third Era challenges us not only to "broaden the tent"—welcoming and including those who have historically been at the margins—but also to rethink the entire construct of center and margins.

The adventurers, experimenters, and spiritual entrepreneurs at the creative edge of contemporary unbound Judaism are the people least embraced by the Judaisms of the Rabbinic era. These former "outsiders" include Jews of Color, women, Queer and Trans Jews, intermarried Jews, disaffected American suburban Jews, new converts to Judaism, Spanish-speaking American Jews, and emerging communities of Jews in South America, Africa, and online. Without coordination or self-concept as leaders of a singular "movement," each group is, in its own way, upending old perspectives of what "inside" and "outside" mean. They are "inside-outing" Judaism, going far beyond "tagging along" or pleas for inclusion in an agreed-upon Jewish center. In the new era, they are instead creating their own centers in which multiple and diverse perspectives, especially those of people who have felt excluded from the mainstream, are not merely tolerated or accepted, but privileged as fresh starting points for apprehending a fuller understanding of Jewish wisdom and practice.

In this collection of interviews, you will find guests who are thinking deeply about the diverse people who are among the new multitudes of wanderers. Each of them is committed to creating Judaisms that speak to and from the perspectives of "least invited" groups, and each is working to make space for a profound shift in which individuals and communities who have historically been rejected or actively unwelcomed—or at best tolerated as "miscellaneous hangers-on"—are welcomed and empowered as leaders of the emerging new age.

April Nichole Baskin

> "...normative practice has left 60% of our community not engaging in Jewish communal life, which to me is a call to action for us to reconsider our practices."

Audacious Hospitality

At the time of our interview, April Baskin was serving as the Vice President of Audacious Hospitality at the Union for Reform Judaism (URJ). Before joining the URJ, she was the national director of Resources and Training at InterfaithFamily (now 18 Doors) and, before that, president of the Jewish Multiracial Network.

Following our conversation, Baskin undertook a new role as the first Racial Justice Director for the Jewish Social Justice Roundtable, a position she held from 2019 to 2021. In addition to this, she was a founding steering committee member of the Jewish Liberation Fund, a community-funded Jewish foundation dedicated to sustaining and growing the Jewish movement for justice and liberation. At the time of publication, Baskin serves on the philanthropic leadership team of Rise Up: Nurturing the Soul of Jewish Justice.

In August 2023, April Baskin was ordained as a Kohenet, a feminist, Earth-based Jewish/Hebrew priestess. During her four-year residence in Dakar, Senegal, from 2019 to 2023, she launched Joyous Justice, a social justice and spiritual transformation company focusing on strategic leadership consulting, coaching, and education aimed at fostering deeper healing, belonging, shared power, and justice in service of collective liberation. This period also involved an extensive Afro-Indigenous ancestral "coming home" body of work, which was supported and contained within Baskin's journey toward her Kohenet ordination. Recognized as a Faith Leader to Watch by Center for American Progress, Baskin currently is the lead coach of Grounded & Growing, a trauma-agile social justice leadership program and community, and hosts the Joyous Justice Podcast.

Dan Libenson: I'm interested in the difference between hospitality and *audacious* hospitality. Could you share how you think about that?

April Baskin: Within a Jewish context, audacious hospitality is about welcoming all. I think of our community as existing within a tent. Audacious hospitality is thinking about how we push out the tent poles to make room for more people. It's also thinking about how the tent is designed, who it was originally designed for, and whether that design speaks to the needs and identities of Jews today.

For me, audacious is about moving beyond simply welcoming in the other person. It is about doing work on a deeper level that says, "I am so committed—we as a community are so committed to this, that if we are really doing hospitality well, it's actually going to shift how we are as a people. When we invite those people to the table, it's going to shift what we have on the table and when we're meeting."

To me, it's a shoutout to Rabbi Abraham Joshua Heschel and his speaking of moral grandeur and spiritual audacity. It's about courage. It's a way of thinking of inclusion and hospitality and diversity as a *tekiah* moment—a wakeup call—to really be bold and courageous and step outside of normative practice to function beyond it. That normative practice has left 60% of our community not engaging in Jewish communal life, which to me is a call to action for us to reconsider our practices.

We tend to perceive ourselves as being more welcoming than we actually are in practice.

There was an informal study done almost 10 years ago in North America involving a secret shul shopper—a secret synagogue shopper.

The findings that were relayed to me by a former leader were that none of the secret synagogue shoppers received any welcome. Most of these communities would say that they're welcoming—so to me, there's a disconnect somewhere between the way the community perceives itself and what they're actually doing and how other people are receiving it.

One part of changing that is just around having greater awareness and training around how to be welcoming. And I think that there's also a deeper element there that is connected to the anti-Semitism and Christian hegemony that Jewish community has to navigate. White Christian communities don't have to have a security guard at the front of their community, and I think that that takes its toll—but that also isn't an excuse for us [not to] raise the bar and do better.

Lex Rofeberg: It's funny you mention that secret shul shopper study. I remember hearing about it, and I decided to do the experiment for myself. My mom had moved to a new city, and I was visiting her for the High Holidays.

I decided I was going to go to tashlich—the service that's often done in conjunction with Rosh Hashanah, where you cast your sins and bread into the water—and not instigate any conversations. I'm naturally pretty outgoing, I start a lot of conversations with people, but I was going to see what happens if I don't.

This was a very big Reform congregation, there were probably 100 people, and we met at the congregation, and we walked from there to a body of water that was close by. I was right next to people the entire half-mile walk and nobody said anything to me. No words, zero. It was a strange experience, that helped me empathize with people who aren't as comfortable in those spaces. I know what *tashlich* is, I know how to drop the right lingo and do the right things, but a lot of people don't have that. It was an important moment for me, but it was also kind of tragic and devastating to see.

April Baskin: Thanks for sharing that—and I'm sorry that that happened. I'm glad that you have a really solid grounding—because a number of people don't. They have a variety of experiences with similar elements to the story that you shared. It happens too often.

When I work with congregations I try to function from a place of non-judgment, but also with a real attempt at honesty and assessment.

Let's see what's actually happening here and analyze it and change our behavior so that we can get different results. We need this information so that we can properly analyze and diagnosis the situation and take a different course of action.

There are decades of hurt, of repeated experiences, ranging from the silences that you experienced to stories like that of the interfaith family who found out a week before their child's bar or bat mitzvah that one of their parents was not allowed to join them on the *bimah* [the podium or platform in a synagogue from which the Torah and Prophets are read] and were deeply hurt. They'd been involved for a number of years, but they left and didn't come back. There are many versions of that story.

So there's the real-time issues, and there's also a backlog of real hurt that we need to find ways of addressing.

Dan Libenson: When we're talking about this idea of being more welcoming, I'm curious who you think are the people that we're trying to be audaciously hospitable *to*? As I'm thinking about that, my mind is, of course, starting with Jews of Color and intermarried people, and LGBT people. We get the whole list going.

But I also wonder, "Who actually is comfortable?" In response to our podcast, we've heard from all different kinds of people who write to us telling us how meaningful it was to listen to this podcast. I've realized that only a minority feels included, and the majority of people feel excluded. Because they don't speak to each other, the majority don't recognize that they're actually the majority. If this is true, then maybe the whole project of welcoming is a lot more interesting and different than we thought. If it turns out that it really is a very small minority that feels included, that seems to be a major topic of concern and opportunity.

April Baskin: That's a great question! Audacious hospitality is about welcoming all for that very reason.

I think of the work of audacious hospitality as having three primary contexts. The first is within the congregation, which is really important. Then there's threshold work—both physical thresholds as well as threshold moments, where people are first encountering a community and trying out a tashlich or other High Holiday service. And then there's the external outside context, both on land and online.

The first piece of outreach is always ensuring that the congregation has meaningful and inclusive policies to begin with because, I feel accountable to the people who I am welcoming into communal spaces. If those spaces aren't ready for them then we need to pre-pave a path.

When congregations really want to do more effective work around, say, gender inclusion in terms of transgender individuals and gender nonconforming people, I often pause and say, "Is this congregation or congregational conference ready to host them? Are we prepared to accommodate them? Have we thought through some of the basics around having an all-gender bathroom? Have we done the work that's necessary before they get there, to ensure, when they show up, that it's a validating experience—that they feel seen and accounted for?"

Of course, one of the challenges with this work is that audacious hospitality is not about being all things to all people all the time. It is about a baseline accountability and greater cultural awareness and social capacity and ability to navigate challenge and difference.

To return to those three contexts, if a congregation is losing members, we need to stop that trend. If it's not working for those people, I don't even want us to get to the other people yet—because we haven't dealt with the problem to begin with. There are so many people who are just barely in the tent—and I want that to change. I want our communities to shift, to be more relational, to be more agile, to be able to have conversations with people.

It isn't quite this simple, but I think because of our analysis and our funding in the Jewish community, we often miss the fact that if you ask people good questions and you just listen, they will tell you what they need and what they want. If you deliver that, they will show up.

I agree with you, Dan, that there is a silent majority of people who don't feel fully included, and there are many different elements there which I try to parse out a little bit. All of it is significant and is worthy of being addressed, but I place a different level of priority around people who have chronically not been allowed into the space, who are not able to participate in lifecycle events, who aren't getting a religious school education or an informal education because of financial or cultural barriers, or because their parents are consistently confused as hired help when they walk in.

Those examples, to me, feel quantitatively and qualitatively different than someone whose views are being challenged but who still has access to all of the resources that the community has to offer.

Lex Rofeberg: I'd love to hear more about how we can work with people who have historically or are now barred explicitly or implicitly from Jewish spaces.

What is the audacious hospitality strategy with respect to them?

April Baskin: There was a study—I believe this came out of Pew—a study that demonstrated that 60% of Jews are not currently affiliated with Jewish institutional life. In other studies I've seen, as well as anecdotal information from the thesis I wrote about Jews of Color and from tracking what I've seen around the country in terms of who's showing up, that 60% includes, disproportionately, Jews of Color, LGBTQ Jews, Jews with disabilities, Jews from interfaith families, and Jews who are poor or working class.

I want to bring in more of those voices. One, because I think it's just the right thing to do. And also because I notice that these groups are great sources of change. I love the disability advocacy movement saying, "Nothing about us without us." I use it all the time—it's one of the core tenets of audacious hospitality. It says that we have to center the voices of the people who are most directly affected.

Recently, I heard about the concept of universal design which also came out of the disability advocacy movement. Universal design is this concept that if we are to include everyone, including those on the margins, and take that into account for everyone, that it's going to improve the experience of everyone. I bring a more intersectional approach to this and I think audacious hospitality builds on it and makes it better, but there are a variety of examples of that I can talk about.

Think of *mezuzot*—if we have mezuzahs, the posting that goes on the doorframe—at a level that people in wheelchairs can reach, that just made that mezuzah accessible to every kid and every small person in your synagogue. And, if our synagogues are better at welcoming people of other faith backgrounds, and provide a lot more English and opportunities to learn that are approachable—your synagogue [has] just gotten easier to approach for a whole bunch of Jews who have been disconnected or who never went to religious school.

Dan Libenson: I'm interested in thinking that through a bit further. We're going to have one category of people saying: "I would love to join this synagogue, except for the ways in which it's not designed well for me, both physically and maybe in other dimensions of it." We can change that—we can move where the mezuzahs are, we can find ways of coming to the Torah without having to walk around—whatever the barriers may be.

And for every group it's different—like you were saying earlier, for trans people it would be that the bathrooms aren't the right bathrooms. So we could be as nice and welcoming as we want—but if people ultimately come in and the space isn't really open to them, then we haven't really done what we've pretended in our own minds that we've done, that we wish to have done. We didn't really do it because we didn't get deeply enough into it. So for this category, the question becomes how can we really do it? How can we be truly welcoming?

I think there is also, though, a category two, which requires us to acknowledge the privilege question. I think a lot of the people within Jewish institutions—synagogues and all sorts of other institutions—don't fully realize that welcoming alone is not enough. They are not recognizing that the way that we're doing things today—the basic fundamental things that we're doing Jewishly—wouldn't be done this way had a wider array of people been involved from the beginning.

The issue is not only how to help this thing that was created by cis white people become more open.

For this category we have to ask: "What if these folks had been part of the design of this enterprise from the beginning? How many things that are going on here today would be different—profoundly—because it had been created by this collective in the first place?" The question, in a sense, is how do we get there—is that part of the aspiration?

April Baskin: I'm in the throes of trying to navigate both of those categories. At the Union for Reform Judaism, my team has developed six guiding principles of audacious hospitality that are based around *middot* [virtuous actions]. A number are connected to *Mussar* [Jewish practice focused on ethics and character development] and the intensive study of Jewish values.

It starts with welcome. It starts with *hachnasat orchim*—of welcoming guests—and *ohel patuach*—an open tent. I think that's often what people think audacious hospitality is. But there are six other values that this work entails.

Where it lands—to cut to the chase—is around leadership and justice. It's this concept that our leadership and justice work in the world is going to look very different if we go through a process of truly having an open tent, of doing watchfulness and assessment, of taking time to do a lot of self-reflection to be aware of where we think we are versus where we actually land.

The work continues through knowledge and self-awareness. Once we do an assessment around what we need, there's likely going to be collective learning that needs to take place in a community to begin to shift understanding. We need to honor diversity—this concept of *kavod*, which I love—I loved it as a Hebrew school teacher, I love it now. This idea of not only respect, but honor.

So, it's not just about welcoming. That's the common phrase but it includes the questions of who's actually already here who we're just not seeing? And who we could begin to have different conversations with if we just noticed and acknowledged them and engaged their talents and insights?

The principles continue on through courage and compassion in the "do" area, the places where "the rubber meets the road." There are very few concepts associated with the work of audacious hospitality that are new. It's just that we are trying to find ways of getting past the obstruction and the challenges that have prevented communities who wanted to make these changes before from doing them.

The work requires asking, "What's happening here? We had a young person on the board, we had this initiative take place—and then it fell through, it didn't work out. Okay, so in this community what do we need to work on? Young people's voices aren't being listened to. They're actually leading, but that leadership isn't being met with *kavod* and trust and a willingness with experimentation. Let's figure that out—let's pinpoint exactly what is getting in the way of us moving forward and finding ways of addressing it."

In terms of your second category, though, where would we be if Jews of Color had been involved from the beginning? It's hard for me to even imagine—my reality as a Jewish woman of color is so not that—but I can tell you what it looks like now, in terms of how my leadership is beginning to shift the nature of the way we talk about it. It is new to say, when we have these conversations, "Yes, we are still a predominately white Ashkenazi Jewish community—but I want our community to begin to see and understand itself as a multiracial Jewish community." That is a very different place to enter a whole variety of conversations.

Lex Rofeberg: I live in Providence, Rhode Island. I can draw a line around one square mile in an upper middle-class area in Providence, and it encloses virtually all of the Jewish infrastructure: the Jewish buildings, the synagogue, the Federation, et cetera. I look at the calendar of all of the institutions here, and I think, "If I were one of those people who didn't have access to a car, or who lived in a less affluent area, would I be able to participate in Jewish life at all in Providence?" It would be very hard.

Can you talk about how economics and geography play into the issue of hospitality?

April Baskin: Socioeconomics is huge and is something that is challenging for us to talk about. I've chosen not to focus primarily on that to start, because it's interwoven into all the other ways that we group people. I take that into account whenever thinking about race and ethnicity and LGBTQ identity and interfaith families—I weave socioeconomic concerns throughout.

As challenging as that is for some, in some ways it's also easier. It's very concrete whether or not you're inclusive of those different groups. As we begin to account for issues like chronic unemployment and employment discrimination—whether it's around race or disability or gender or sexuality—we have a backdoor way to account for socioeconomic differences. And by getting some of those populations who have more socioeconomic diversity through the door, we can begin to have that conversation.

On my office's dry erase whiteboard, I have drawn these satchels of different categories. I have the diversity satchel and the lifecycle one and the generational one ... and socioeconomics is really big. A colleague of mine, Gila, said it very well. She once said to me, "April, you have mild, medium, and spicy issues here." Socioeconomics, to me, is a spicy issue.

Dan Libenson: I like that mild, medium, and spicy metaphor. I think it gives a good sense of different ways to approach this stuff. I would imagine—tell me if I'm right about this—that most synagogues, of all denominations these days, are probably more or less in the category where, really, it would be a big achievement if they took the mild sauce.

Give us some concrete sense of what mild looks like, with regard to various important populations. What does mild look like in regards to Jews of Color? What does mild look like as regards intermarried families? What does mild look like with regard to people with disabilities, or LGBT people, et cetera?

April Baskin: Great question—what does this look like in practice? It starts by a congregation identifying that they're interested in doing this work, and that they think their community has something to gain by it. And/or that it's a fundamental part of their understanding of Jewish values—a range of Jewish values—whether it's *b'tzelem elohim*, the concept that we're all made in the image of the divine, or a range of other values. And that they're willing to put some resource and time and support behind taking time to do this.

When someone from a congregation downloads the Union for Reform Judaism Audacious Hospitality toolkit, it starts with all of these welcome resources—because many Jews are ready to take action. They need to know enough about process in order to understand—but once they get that, they just want to dive in. We're letting them scratch that itch, so here's a greeter training, here are 10 practices you can do to help make your synagogue more welcoming on Shabbat. And then it goes into a deep dive.

There is an overarching checklist for congregational self-reflection, which provides a broad sense of, "Do you have something on your website? Are there resources in your library? If you look at your calendar of programming over the year, does it reflect racial and ethnic diversity?"

If we begin to think of these things, not as ancillary, but as part of who we are, then it's really about who we are as a people. If we are in relationship with our people and we are proximate, how does that accountability and that relationship get reflected in who's on the bimah, in how we lead board meetings, in all the different ways that we might express our commitment?

Dan Libenson: Maybe this goes to spicy, but I'm thinking about how LGBT Jews over the last decades have, not by choice, created their own synagogues. I think that gave them a certain amount of cohesion and power and gave them a way to come into non-LGBT synagogues—regular synagogues that have been around for a long time—with some sense of power and confidence.

As I'm thinking about audacious hospitality versus hospitality, it's like hospitality is "You're welcome in my space," while audacious hospitality is, "I'm giving you the keys—it's your space. I hope that you'll welcome me." The super spicy version of that is, "Somehow can I empower you to come in with an agenda, and tell me what it would look like for this place to be the way it should be?"

I'm wondering whether maybe there are potentially other tools that would allow those folks who are scattered in all sorts of congregations around the country, in ones or twos to find one another, and potentially to build something new together. It's going to take time—but eventually they might be able to do the work that essentially the LGBT Jewish community did over all those years in exile. I'm wondering if some of that's going on, if some of that's on the agenda, and how you think about it?

April Baskin: I love that question. It takes me back to some of the misguided ideas that I find our community has. One of them is around an aversion to affinity groups. I think a part of that has to do with the legacy that this country has around segregation. I think about pivotal moments for me in my leadership as a woman of color within the Jewish community and how I benefited immensely from the visionary and liberatory leadership of Yavilah McCoy when she first founded (in 2000) and started Ayecha [an organization providing diversity education and advocacy for Jews of Color] more than 10 years ago. It completely enhanced and shifted my understanding of self and what Judaism could look like.

When you're in a room with just Jews of Color—all of a sudden, you realize, "Oh! All that stuff—that's not just me. That ain't just me! Oh, wow—I'm not the only person with bodaciously large hair. I'm not the only person—I'm not the only Jew who dances with my tush. Apparently, this is a Black Jewish thing—and wow." I got to see that the observance of *halachah*—of traditional Jewish law—looks different with women of color. It looks like dancing to KRS-One and to Parliament. For me this was a world-opening experience.

But I also remember when Yavilah was first coordinating events for only Jews of Color thinking, somewhat irrationally, that my mother couldn't go. I was going to be in New York, my mother lives in California—that makes no sense. She was never going to go anyway, but I was aware of the theoretical possibility of my white Jewish mother—and that she couldn't go. I had some stuff come up around that, right? But when I was in that space, I got to have an experience that had been missing my whole life.

Lex Rofeberg: As a white guy with two Jewish parents whose Jewish identity has never been questioned, I have all sorts of privileges. But I am now in an interfaith relationship.

So my Yavilah McCoy moment is from the TV show *New Girl*. There is a Jewish guy character named Schmidt on the show who marries a Hindu woman. It's this beautiful, incredible ceremony and there is nothing at all about parents being upset about it. It's just happy, and it's just great.

For me, that's the closest thing to what I imagine it would feel like to experience your perspective being validated. But when I look at the interfaith program we're doing, we don't seem to have yet fully internalized "Nothing about us without us."

It would be really cool if the sequel to this incredible Jews of Color fellowship that you're describing is some fellowship specifically for people who are in interfaith relationships, not just to be welcomed, but to lead—to be the ones at the front of the table, setting the agenda.

What do you think about that? How do we take those next steps where interfaith folks are not just welcomees, but welcomers?

April Baskin: I think that's a phenomenal idea. Supporting, normalizing, and celebrating diverse interfaith couples and families is central. It's so central, in some ways, that it's almost invisible.

When we created the fellowship, it was at a particular time period and cultural moment for our community—and now, two years later, the conversation around interfaith couples and families has been pushed to the fore in a more dramatic way.

This is an issue that affects me personally. My parents were turned away from two Jewish communities as a (then) interfaith and interracial couple with young children looking to engage in Jewish community in Northern California. In retrospect, I can see that the work of the URJ's outreach department most likely had an impact on the kindness and welcoming that my parents were met with when they finally reached out to a Reform synagogue. But if my parents hadn't continued looking—if the pain had been too much, after getting rejected outright twice—I wouldn't be here, doing this work.

Despite all the progress that's been made, there are still barriers, and we still see a disproportionate number of people who are in interfaith relationships or families on the margins. This is long-term work.

Dan Libenson: We have wanted to probe at the question of whether the kind of radical innovation that we're looking for can only happen outside of the world of institutions and in the startup space, or in people's own homes—or whether it can also happen within institutions. We've been surprised, over the course of doing this show, to find that there are a number of institutions that have more capacity than we might have thought to do some of this work within themselves, but they do have to accept a certain set of self-limitations. The idea of *tzimtzum*—the idea of God making Godself smaller in order to make space for human begins—also applies to institutions. They have to make themselves smaller, or the people who have been in them smaller, so as to make space for others.

It strikes me that the Reform Movement—because of ideological openness, demographic realities, and leadership—may be in a position to say, "We can be one of those institutions."

In the business world, an example might be the department store chain the Dayton-Hudson company. Seeing the threat that places like Walmart and Kmart posed to them, they incubated Target. They had the foresight to say, "We can incubate some things that don't look a lot like what we are today. If it works—then that is another exciting direction. We're not going to get there through small changes—we're only going to get there if we can incubate some of these new ideas in a powerful way."

I'd love to know what you think about that.

April Baskin: I'm not someone who's discounting the role of synagogues and Jewish institutional life. The conclusion that the synagogue is not the place of innovation—one, I don't think that's true, and two, that's just not enough. What that means to me is a bunch of people I love don't have a place in Jewish life—in a core part of Jewish life—and that's not acceptable to me. I came into this role as a leader and a dreamer—and someone who grew up within the Reform Movement and saw the capacity for this movement to lead on some key issues. If we're really able to convene conversations that can be productive and honest and transparent, I'm hopeful about what's possible.

It may be easier for someone who has had access to synagogue life and to institutional Jewish life to dismiss it. But an important part of my work is being a voice for people who have not had that opportunity, and who find meaning in it. Through those individuals, I think that there is an opportunity for—it sounds over the top, but I'm just going to say it—I think that there is room and opportunity for there to be a renaissance in Jewish institutional life.

A number of people who are now on the fringes are vibrant and interesting and brilliant and have a tremendous amount of grit—and there's a number of things that we should change so that they don't have to keep tolerating it. I have spent tens of hours crying and processing the pain and racism and different things I have encountered—and I am still here.

There are literally thousands of Jews with all different kinds of identities all over the country. My hope is that as we build momentum, and as we build more infrastructure in this work, we can connect with more and more inspired and directly-impacted individuals and allies to move these important issues forward together.

QUESTIONS FOR REFLECTION

- When in your life have you experienced audacious hospitality? What difference did it make?
- Dan and April share the sense that the group of potential participants in Jewish life who are feeling unwelcome may be larger than the group who currently feel welcome and included. Does this observation match your own experience? What opportunities excite you most when you think about the diverse array of people who could be brought under the "tent" of Judaism?
- Envision a world in which every spouse of a Jewish person, regardless of the faith tradition in which they were raised, were welcomed with audacious hospitality into Jewish life. What kinds of practices might be part of that audacious welcome? What kinds of things do you think might happen as a result?
- April observed that historically, synagogues have not embraced "affinity groups." What do you see as the benefits and potential challenges of groups like Jews of Color or LGBTQ Jews?
- When Dan raised the question of whether the disruptive innovations of Third Era Judaism are most likely to emerge outside of existing Jewish institutions or whether it is possible that they will also emerge from within, April responded with a strong argument for the potential of disruptive change from within, saying "there is room and opportunity for there to be a renaissance in Jewish institutional life." Do you agree? Where do you see real innovation emerging?

Joy Ladin

> "Many people say, 'How can you reconcile being trans and being Jewish?' At first, I didn't even understand the question—they had never been apart for me."

Judaism from a Transgender Perspective

When we interviewed her, Joy Ladin held the David and Ruth Gottesman Chair in English at Stern College for Women of Yeshiva University, where she taught from 2003 until her retirement in 2021. She was the first openly transgender professor to work at an Orthodox Jewish institution. At the time of our conversation, Ladin had recently published *The Soul of the Stranger: Reading God and Torah from a Transgender Perspective*, a book of theological ideas and textual commentary, which was published in 2018.

Ladin's memoir, *Through the Door of Life: A Jewish Journey Between Genders*, tells the story of her gender transition and describes how she built a new life for herself as a woman. Ladin's published poetry includes *Transmigration, Coming to Life, Impersonation*, and *The Future is Trying to Tell us Something*.

In 2021, Ladin's *The Book of Anna* won the National Jewish Book Award in the category of poetry. Her most recent book of poetry, *Shekhinah Speaks*, was published in 2022, and many of its poems were first read publicly on *Containing Multitudes*, a weekly video program Ladin hosted during the COVID-19 lockdown period on jewishLIVE, the live-streaming video platform *Judaism Unbound* created.

Dan Libenson: Could we start off by hearing a little bit about your story, for our listeners who are not familiar with it?

Joy Ladin: I grew up in the 1960s, and, like many of what we would now call transgender children at that time, I grew up in hiding and without an awareness that there were other people like me. From a very early age—this doesn't always happen with trans kids—but from a very early age, I had a sense of female gender identity, but I picked up quite quickly that my sense of myself was not like other people's sense of me. Because there was no acknowledgement that somebody like me could exist, I assumed that this was something that shouldn't be spoken about, that it was a bad thing, that it was a shameful thing, and that I had to hide the fact that I didn't identify as the male that everybody saw and knew me as.

Although I did find out that there were other people like me, I remained afraid for most of my life to live my female gender identity. For me, the root of that fear was that I would be unlovable if people knew me as I was. This was the assumption that I made as a child—don't let your parents know who you really are, because if they know then they won't love you, they'll see you as something monstrous. I kept making the same decision, which was I would rather be loved, even though I didn't feel people were loving *me*, than be myself and be seen as unlovable.

That continued until my mid-40s, when I started breaking down physically and emotionally. I had struggled with suicidal depression all my life—that's also common for trans people. But at this point, I realized I simply couldn't go on living as a man, and I had to decide whether killing myself or gender transition was the better option. Strange as it may seem, that was a really tough choice for me—it wasn't obvious. Other people seem to feel like that was a no-brainer, but I felt like, "Really, there are benefits and drawbacks to both options here."

I'd come out to my college girlfriend, who I then married, when we were sophomores. She had said at the time that as a heterosexual woman she couldn't be with somebody who didn't look like and act like a man, which I think is reasonable. I knew that if I couldn't keep living as a man, that would be the end of my marriage, and at that point, we had three small children. I would lose my home, and I thought I would lose everything else also. I certainly didn't think I would be able to go back and teach at Yeshiva University, which is where I was.

I was hanging on until I could receive tenure. My marriage had fallen apart. It was clear that I couldn't hold on very much longer. More or less the moment I got tenure I sent out a coming out letter to my dean. To my surprise—although it's common practice for organizations that are dealing with their first gender transition—they didn't fire me. They put me on what they called "involuntary research leave," which was a brilliant invention—I don't think anybody had thought of forcing an academic to do research on full salary before. The only condition for me continuing on full salary and benefits with my job title was that I could not have anything to do with students.

For many academics, this would be a dream come true, but I had never experienced discrimination before.

I really hadn't been an object of antisemitism, I was mostly seen as a heterosexual white man. I didn't know the kind of pain that feeling discriminated against causes.

I loved teaching at Stern College for Women [Yeshiva University's women's college], so this really hurt. As a poet, I'd always seen jobs as just a way to make money to support writing. Given the opportunity to spend the rest of my life making money and writing, it was very strange to me that it hurt.

Miraculously—and for reasons that I suspect literally no one knows—after a year, Yeshiva University responded to my attorney's demand letter by saying, "Of course you can come back and teach. We always meant you to come back and teach." They had said over and over again, "You'll never come back and teach," but no, actually, that was a misunderstanding. So I got to teach comp and do all the other kinds of work that I loved at the school.

I've been there ever since. But of course, it is different to be there as someone seen as a heterosexual man—highly valued by the culture—versus somebody seen as a transgender person, which I think is something that Orthodox culture simply does not have any slots for. For most of my students, they either, I think, see me as other, or they see me as somebody with a serious sexual fetish that I'm trying to drag other people into, or they see me as mentally ill. One creative person opined that I was really a gay man who was transitioning because looking like a woman is a better way to pick up men. This person doesn't understand gay men either. It's a great example in that culture . . . it's a very homophobic yeshiva culture, for obvious reasons. If you've got men with these intense relationships, that's something you need to be thinking about. He was trying to use that category to understand me.

That's just what people do—we take the templates that our cultures offer us, and we try to understand the messiness of humanity, including our own messiness, in terms of those categories, which are always limited.

As I said, I think queer cultures also have limitations in their understanding of somebody like me. Religious queer people often feel like, "Well, when I go to a queer conference, some parts of me are understood, and other parts of me are looked down on. In religious contexts, it's the reverse."

Dan Libenson: What you're talking about opens up so many questions. Could you start by explaining what you mean when you say, "I didn't transition to make myself happy, but I did it in order to live?"

Joy Ladin: Yes. I said in the memoir and in the book that I just published that when my best friend suggested my name should be Joy, I just laughed in her face because I was so miserable. This is a bad joke, to say, "Hi, I'm the most miserable person you've met. My name is Joy."

But one of the ways that American culture tries to understand big decisions that human beings make is we try to understand them in terms of happiness. Individual happiness is one of the highest values in the culture. We hold individuals responsible for their level of happiness. We judge, and we expect them to judge, their success in terms of whether or not they're happy. We ask "Are you happy in your job?" Not, "Is your job enabling you to contribute to the world in important and meaningful ways?" but, "Are you happy?" I'm not saying these are bad questions, but that's often a way that people think about gender transition and trans identities. Why would you make a decision that changes everything in your life if it's not going to make you happy?

There are many different kinds of people we now gather under the term "transgender." I really only know one of them well—and that's me. I'm not trying to speak for everybody. I've heard many times from the kind of trans person that I am—which is people born into and assigned one gender on the basis of their bodies, but who strongly identify with the other gender—that many of us hold off on gender transition until it's a matter of life or death, partly because there has simply been no way to explain why I would be making this change that would make sense to anybody that I cared about. There was no moral code where you could say, "Look, morally, I need to do this." If you say, "I need to be true to myself and honest with other people," most people are like, "No, really, we don't need to know this about you—this is TMI. We would much prefer you to act like a gender we understand than do whatever the heck it is you are telling us you need to do."

I kept considering this myself—should I do this, should I not do it? My culture is saying, "Will it make you happy?" Clearly, it was not going to make me happy. The first thing my gender therapist asked me, actually, when I started to talk with her about this, was, "Did anyone ever teach you to be true to yourself?" It's striking to me that, no, my family didn't teach me to be true to myself. All of us are virtuosos at denial. Like many families, they wanted me to be who I needed to be in terms of other people.

Judaism provides the idea of *pikuach nefesh*, which is that if it's a matter of saving your life, there are very few commandments that you shouldn't violate—because you can't actually do any of the other commandments if you're a dead person. The other moral guidance I got was that people kept telling me, "If you kill yourself, your kids are going to be really messed up, and they will be likely to kill themselves."

In fact, I called the therapist in crisis and I said, "I just can't go on anymore," and instead of comforting me and encouraging me the way I had been looking for, she said, "Look, you can't kill yourself, because you have to stay alive long enough for your children to reject you. If you kill yourself, they will be frozen in their anger at you and their rage. They'll basically spend the rest of their lives stuck at your grave raging at you, and that will damage them permanently." She gave some scary statistics about how much more likely the children of people who kill themselves are to kill themselves.

Lex Rofeberg: Thank you for your honesty about your considerations of suicide. We can't avoid the topic of suicide in conversations like this—it looms very large, and we avoid it at our own societal peril.

Could you share about how your book—*The Soul of the Stranger*—helps us understand the queer and the Jewish experience in our tradition?

Joy Ladin: When I started living as myself, the attention that I got really was mostly because of the strange quality of having a trans person at an Orthodox Jewish university. A huge proportion of my thinking about my trans experience has been done has been in Jewish contexts, and often centers on the relation between trans and Jewish identities.

I found that people found this a really strange idea. Many people would say, "How can you reconcile these, or put these together?" At first, I didn't even understand the question—they had never been apart for me.

One thing is that I was so lonely that I had a strong personal motivation to develop an experience, no matter how strange, of connection with God. God is not a very good playmate, if you're six or seven years old, really not a good playmate. But nonetheless, if God's the only person you have to pal around with, that is what you do.

The other thing is the trans experience of being different, which gave me this motivation not to discount my perception of God's presence.

And the third thing was, although my parents weren't religious, my mother has a very strong sense that being Jewish means something. And because being Jewish meant something to my mother, she connected our family to a synagogue, sent me to a Hebrew school, and when I was in synagogue, I had texts that referred to God. I immediately said, "Oh, other people have perceived God."

But I was really doing this without religious guidance. I read prayers, and I'm like, "Oh yeah, God. Got that." I read the Torah, and I immediately thought, "Wow, fantastic—there's a book that is all about a character who, like me, doesn't have a body to make them physical and intelligible to the people that they want to have relationships with and that they love." As a young child, I think we are blessed with boundless narcissism. It never occurred to me to say, "You can't analogize yourself to God." As I mention in the book, it's a good thing that Moses Maimonides wasn't hanging around my synagogue and warning me against the kind of naive identification that I was making.

For me, it was the Jewish tradition that offered stories and texts that helped me give shape to this and see what other people made of God. These different elements of my life and self, to me, fit together seamlessly, and they literally kept me alive. If I had not felt that I had that relationship with God, and that that was something that I shared, at least theoretically, with other people, I don't see how I would have made it out of childhood. As it was, I tried to kill myself a couple of times.

I would read these passages, and I would see God, and I would relate to the difficulties God was having in relating to human beings. I think many other people come from religious traditions that are like, "God's good at everything. God's great at everything." It's very puzzling when you read the Torah and you see God screwing up, or not being able to communicate clearly, or decreeing things that don't happen. These create huge theological problems. To me, those were not theological problems.

I also didn't struggle with the idea that God was all good, and that everything God did was good, because I did feel created by God. That was a really incredible feeling.

I was so different from people that I was pretty sure I was handmade. There was no assembly line rolling off people like me. But I was made in a way that was excruciatingly painful, and that was part of the package. If I wanted to feel created by God, I had to accept that I was created in ways that hurt and that were difficult and that involved suffering. I didn't have this ideology of an all-good, all-everything God.

This book came about because I got two awards—a Hadassah-Brandeis award, and an NEA grant—to write a book of nonfiction. And because of the NEA, it couldn't be an academic book—it had to be creative nonfiction. It was like, "Okay, I got to write this book—and it can't just be an academic book, so I'll draw on the stuff that I've read. It will be about reading Torah from a transgender perspective. That should be easy for me, because I've always read the Torah from a transgender perspective."

This was a really evolving process. Rabbi Burton Visotzky, who teaches at the Jewish Theological Seminary, had been encouraging me to write a book like this, so I asked him, "How do you think I should write it?" He said, "Write it so that the widest possible audience can read it." When I thought about that, I was like, "Oh, no. The 'widest possible audience' means that I can't use all of the devices academics use to protect ourselves. I can't armor myself with quotations from other people, or pretend I'm not saying what I'm saying by ventriloquizing through other sources."

If I wanted to write to as many people as possible, I had to strip all that away and try to tell the truth in the most direct way that I could. And I had to find the aspects of *my* truth, because I'm the only person that I really know about this. I had to try to ferret out the parts of my experience that also related to other readers of biblical text's experience, other trans people's experience. But I couldn't base that claim of commonality on what anybody else had said.

The sense of differentness that made it easy for me to read the Torah and relate to God made it really, really hard and scary to say, "Yeah, this thing, I think, is something that I have in common with other people."

As I rewrote the book, I was really revising my whole life, my whole understanding of myself. That's why the book ends up in a place of critiquing my own childhood ideas of distinctiveness in my relationship with God. I had to realize that, yeah, actually, when you're relating to God, the differences that seem so big to us—they certainly had defined my whole life, that sense of difference—they're nothing.

Dan Libenson: I was struck by the moment in your memoir when you are raging at God, and you say, "You don't know what it is to be rejected by your children." Then you pause for a minute, say, "Oh. Now I actually get it."

In your books, you act as kind of a mediator for many of us who are not trans to understand God in a better way, in a different way. Specifically, in *The Soul of the Stranger* you talk about how in Jewish tradition we're very comfortable with the idea that God is not a physical being like we usually are—but nevertheless, we'll use gendered language to talk about God, and we have metaphors and images of God that are human.

We understand that we have to do that because we are human, and it's the only way we can access God. You present that as a version of what's been happening to trans people throughout history, and suggest that in some ways we're doing a terrible injustice to God by not allowing God to be who God is. You talk about how it's actually not fair of humans to not accept God's own understanding of God's self.

I would love to hear a little bit more about how you think your experience and your perspective shapes an understanding of God that's deeper than is perhaps available to many others, and how you've tried to translate that for those of us that haven't had the experiences that you've had.

Joy Ladin: I think it's a common thing for trans people—my hunch is most trans people, but I've never done a survey—to say, "Wow, the people that I love and am relating to can't really understand me, because the culture, the language, the categories that we have available for ways of understanding people, the roles that are based on gender and assumptions about it—they just don't work for someone like me." I think it does feel unfair. Why isn't society set up to understand me? I think that would be lovely, if cultures were, in fact, individually tailored to the needs of individual people.

As a trans person, I felt peculiarly poorly served by my culture, and that I was always having to choose between being in relation to people and being who I was, which would render me incomprehensible. Those were in tension with each other, and it was constant tradeoffs. For God, those tradeoffs are absolute.

It sucks that we can't understand God on God's own terms, but that is the definition of being human.

That's where Maimonides comes into the book—because Maimonides thinks in an incredibly sustained way about what it means to have a being at the center of your tradition, of your religion, of your life, that any time you try to understand that being in any way, you have done a terrible injustice to God.

One of the things that I realized when I was writing this work was that I didn't want to just talk about being a transsexual of my generation—male to female. I wanted my audience to be anybody who is something more complex, anybody who can recognize parts of themselves that don't fit into the cultural categories that are available.

Then I realized I don't know what this means when it says God creates human beings in God's own image—no idea what that means. That is a Jewish koan, as far as I'm concerned—you have a being that has no image and say you're created in that image ... that is the sound of one hand clapping Jewishly. But I nonetheless believe that this is true. So there must be some part of human beings—despite how different we are from God—there must be some part of us that is really like God. I don't believe it's human reason—human reason has been taken down many pegs, thanks to things like the Holocaust and corporate efficiency, monstrous misuses of reason.

As I was working on this, I thought, "Oh, the part of us that must be akin to God must be the part that, like God, doesn't fit into human categories."

We have that incomprehensibility, which is why nobody is going to seamlessly fit inside human categories. That means that, at a root level, every human being has this incomprehensible vastness. Trans people and other people who are queer are forced to recognize that—because the categories fit us so badly. For me to identify as trans is saying, "There's a huge part of me that doesn't fit into these categories, and it's so big I've got to wreck my life and relationships in order to live that, and then see what happens." But I do believe that there is just no human being that is so simplistic that we fit into human categories.

That is why I ended up feeling like I did want to make a bridge between trans and non-trans people, because I was hoping everybody would recognize that we're always making this choice about, is it more important for us to be absolutely who we are? Because if you're with other people, relating to them is going to cost you some measure of your individuality and spontaneity and impulse. But if you love people, and if you want to be loved, if you want to be understood, if you want to be part of community and intimate relationships and friendships, it's a tradeoff we make all the time.

Lex Rofeberg: I really appreciate what you're saying about the defining tradeoff between the individual identity and the belonging in a group. I've found, in Judaism, a beautiful tradition that has been entirely out of style for a few thousand years, but it's a ritual that you talked about in your book, which is the Nazirite vow. What is this Nazirite vow, and how does it connect to questions of being trans, Jewish and otherwise?

Joy Ladin: Part of the Nazirite vows is you abstain from any contact with any part of the grape plant, and any kind of grape product. No raisins, no wine, no stems. Now, grapes are a central agricultural product in the Jewish culture—in fact, part of the Jewish vision of messianic days is everybody sitting under their own vine. Saying you can't have that, and you not only can't have that, but you can't be anywhere near it, or have any contact with it, is going to really disrupt a lot of social relations.

If you come from a grape growing family, your family is really screwed—suddenly they've lost a worker. You can't market the stuff, you can't be involved in cooking the stuff if you're a woman—that's going to mess things up. But even if your family doesn't have those kinds of relationships with grapes, you can't go over to people's houses and have wine or grape juice. You can't make *Kiddush* [the blessing, over wine, that opens Shabbat and festival meals].

Fundamentally, the Nazarite vows are designed to say, "It's more important for me to relate to God than it is for me to relate to human beings." When I learned about that, I went, "Huh. That sounds a lot like what I was seen as saying by my wife, when I said I need to live my female gender identity, and she said, 'You're willing to disrupt our entire lives in order to do what you call being true to yourself.'" She wasn't wrong—that is what I was doing. I understood it in a different way than she did. That's also what I think Nazirites would have been doing.

With regard to individual self-determination, I didn't see the Torah saying anywhere people just need to be true to themselves—it doesn't say that. But the Torah does often say that people need to be true to themselves for the sake of their relationships with God.

Abraham is not a Nazirite—he couldn't have been, because those laws didn't exist. But he completely disrupts his family and violates all of his obligations to his elderly father and to other people by following God into the wilderness. There's no human justification for that behavior—but clearly, that is the truth that Abraham felt he needed to pursue.

Your relationship with God is sometimes going to need you to do things that seem crazy and wrong—or at least massively inconvenient—to the human beings around you. You're going to have to violate their roles and categories and expectations, and they're not going to understand why you're doing it, because you're doing it for the sake of a relationship with a being who doesn't make any sense.

Dan Libenson: As I have been reading your work that helps us look at the material of the Jewish past in a new way through a trans perspective, it got me thinking about the Jewish present. What wisdom is there in your experience, in the trans experience, that helps us think about Judaism itself as being in a time of transition, and the struggle of not knowing what you're supposed to do in that kind of situation?

Joy Ladin: That moment in the Jewish present has been recurring in different forms at least since the Enlightenment. If you look at the post-Temple days, there were various places and points where you can see lots of Jews saying, "Huh, this isn't working anymore."

There are many people who have said to me: "Oh, I'm a Jew—that means I must be able to understand and express myself in terms of whatever being a Jew means." Then they look at what being a Jew means in their local context, and are like, "Huh, that's funny—this isn't meeting my needs at all."

For example, there are many forms of Judaism that do a terrible job at addressing individual suffering. I think that that's one reason that a lot of the best American Buddhists are Jews. There was a 19th century rabbi I've been quoting for years, but have no idea what the name of this rabbi is. The quote that I saw that I've long gone to was, "Everybody who doesn't feel that they're in exile is not really awake." For that rabbi, that sense of, "I'm here, I'm supposed to be able to make a life here, but it just doesn't feel right—I don't have what I need to make sense of myself and my life," for him that was a basic condition of humanity, of spiritual awakeness. You have to have that sense of dissatisfaction.

I was certainly never taught—and I think a lot of Jews are never taught in America—that you're allowed to do something with that. That Judaism has been around for 3,000 years—literally nobody knows everything that has been Jewish. That means that nobody knows everything that could be Jewish. Any version of Jewishness we've been taught is just a teeny little edited selection. If you don't like it, you're just scratching the surface.

None of the categories for trans people—and there are 64 or 128, whatever it is, however many Facebook comes up with—they will never be enough.

Maybe what we will all end up with is a long list of nouns. But it will be like, "If you really want to know about me and my gender, you need to sit still while I tell you a story."

I think that that is what this sense of dissatisfaction with what it means to be a Jew is summoning us to do. It's saying, "You should be dissatisfied, because whatever you're thinking of as Jewish right now—it's just a moment in your story. And it's not just your story—Jewishness, Jewish civilization, Jewishness as a spiritual practice, Jews as a people, Jews as an essential part of the spiritual DNA of humanity—we need your dissatisfaction to keep leading you from one point to another, because it is your dissatisfaction that gives meaning to these different forms of Jewishness."

Lex Rofeberg: Whoa. I think you've encapsulated what this project of *Judaism Unbound* is trying to do, in terms of stoking this dissatisfaction and acting on the dissatisfaction. Thank you. Are there any other insights you'd like to share?

Joy Ladin: The book that I wrote is really meant to be the starting point, because all I have to work with is this one person's set of experiences and readings. My hope is that, by the end of the book, many people will say, "Oh—being trans is one of the flavors of being human. Being a trans Jew is one of the flavors of being a Jew. Like every other way of being human or being Jewish, it has perspectives and insights to offer. Once we recognize the humanity of trans people, those insights don't only belong to trans people.

Because we recognize you as human—that means your insights are actually available to us.

As long as we're willing to stretch our definition of humanity so that we don't other you, we get to have the benefit of whatever trans experience offers, as Jews, as religious people, as human beings."

I felt like that was your premise from the beginning of this conversation, and I'm deeply grateful for that.

QUESTIONS FOR REFLECTION

- In her story of coming out as trans in her workplace, Joy Ladin describes experiencing, for the first time, the pain of discrimination. Has your life experience brought you to moments when some aspect of privilege that you had taken for granted was suddenly lost, or just made visible to you in a new way?
- Ladin says that her trans experience helped her to grasp that the defining experience that connects human beings and God is the experience of being beyond categories, an "incomprehensible vastness" that makes it impossible for us to ever fit perfectly into the categories we create to make sense of the world. When have you experienced feeling bigger than or at odds with human-made categories? How do you resonate with the idea that the vastness and unknowability in your own being might be akin to the vastness and mystery of God? Can you remember any moments when you've particularly glimpsed that connection for yourself?
- Ladin suggests that a sense of dissatisfaction is a basic condition of humanity and of spiritual awakeness. She calls us to engage with what we are dissatisfied with in our Jewish experience and see those points of frustration as actually summoning us forward toward something better. What are some of your own dissatisfactions with the forms of Judaism you were raised with? What do you imagine these dissatisfactions might be leading you (or us) toward?

Paul Golin

> "It's a chicken-and-egg question about which happened first—this search for meaning in Jewish community and Jewish life, or the rise in intermarriage. I think they went hand in hand."

Intermarriage and the Future

Paul Golin is now the executive director of the Society for Humanistic Judaism, the congregational and community-organizing arm of the non-theistic Secular Humanistic Jewish movement. At the time of this interview, he worked as the Associate Executive Director of Big Tent Judaism (formerly known as the Jewish Outreach Institute), an organization that specialized in helping intermarried people connect to the Jewish community.

Golin describes himself as the white Ashkenazi half of a "Jewpanese"—Jewish and Japanese—multiracial household. With Rabbi Kerry Olitzky, Golin co-authored two books, *20 Things for Grandparents of Interfaith Grandchildren to Do (And Not Do) to Nurture Jewish Identity In Their Grandchildren* and *How To Raise Jewish Children… Even When You're Not Jewish Yourself*.

Our interview with Paul Golin—Episode 16—was one of the first we conducted after the public launch of the podcast, so Golin was our first guest who had already listened to an episode of *Judaism Unbound*.

As such, our conversation begins with his reflections on how ideas Benay Lappe articulated in our interview with her (found in Part One of this volume) connected to his thinking about intermarriage.

Dan Libenson: As we were setting up, you mentioned that you've been listening to the podcast. Are there any ideas that we have laid out already that particularly connected with you?

Paul Golin: I was really interested in Rabbi Benay Lappe's crash theory. Applying that to intermarriage has been very interesting. Through that lens I can recognize that people go through those same three responses to a crash, which is either to insist that the narrative is still correct, or leave altogether—which is what the majority do, which is how you know it was a crash—or pick up the pieces and build something new.

And when I think about the Jewish communal approach to intermarriage, even today, I feel that it's dictated by the folks who are following Option 1 which is to retain the master story that, ultimately, intermarriage is not the preference. A lot of what's happening in the Jewish community around intermarriage is ultimately indoctrination to be more like us—and I think that that agenda ultimately is not going to engage the large segment of intermarried households.

Lex Rofeberg: I'm really interested to hear you make that application from Rabbi Lappe's crash theory—because part of our master story has been that the Jewish community is made up of Jews, and especially the set of people who are Jews *and* involved in particular institutions. What does it mean that the Jewish community, due to intermarriage, is now made up of a lot of people who aren't Jews?

Paul Golin: Your question leads me, in a very concrete way, to explain what I mean when I say that intermarriage is not the thing to focus on. The thing to focus on is Jewish meaning and purpose and why be Jewish? Why do it at all?

Those of us in intermarriages have to explain why we would do any of this to folks who did not grow up with it.

This is what, in a lot of ways, forced the issue for the Jewish community. We have to articulate: What's the benefit? What's the value in doing it? And if we find the benefit and the value of doing Jewish, then why is it only limited to Jews?

And I understand the answer from an Orthodox perspective, which is chosenness, or the need to ensure that you are Jewish in order to form a *minyan*. But if the activities happening in the organized Jewish community in America are about creating meaning and value for people, and they *do* create meaning for people, why would we want to limit it just to Jews? Why would we want to privilege Jews with it, or hold it back only for Jews? And my answer is we don't—or I don't—even as I do understand why certain folks do.

So you can see that this is a much larger question than just intermarriage. I think it's a chicken-and-egg question about which happened first—this search for meaning in Jewish community and Jewish life, or the rise in intermarriage. Because I think they went hand in hand.

I think that intermarriage is really a byproduct of a lot of different things that happened in American society in general and to American Jews.

But the organized Jewish community got real fixated on the marriage itself—and that was simply the wrong thing to fixate on.

Just as an illustration, my own personal crash in relation to Judaism happened when I was 11 years old at Jewish summer camp, where besides realizing that I liked girls more than they liked me, I also recognized that the universe is infinite. I grew up in New York City—we don't get to see a lot of stars. Then I was at camp in upstate New York and I saw all these stars, and it just really brought forward the concept of God and infinity. I was thinking all of these big things, and I realized I don't believe this. I then had the joy of explaining my realization that this religion doesn't work for me to the people who run Jewish summer camps.

When the Jewish community looks at me today as an intermarried Jew—and I got married when I was 36—some people (less people than used to, but still many) still see the moment of my marriage as the moment when I was lost to the Jewish people.

But if you're going to say I was lost to the Jewish people, it actually happened when I was 11. That's when my crash happened, and that's when I took Option 2 in a lot of ways. Or perhaps I would say I'm both Option 2 and Option 3.

The other problem with the conversation about intermarriage is the incredible diversity. Think about the difficulty of talking about "the Jews." You don't know anything, really, about someone you meet just by knowing that they're Jewish. You don't know how they vote—you may know, percentage-wise, that they're more likely to vote one way or another, but you don't really *know* that. You don't know what they believe, you don't know whether they are supportive of Israel . . . there's a huge diversity among Jews.

And the diversity among intermarried households is even greater because you have a sliver of intermarried households that are practicing the non-Jewish spouse's religion. At the other end of the spectrum, you have a segment of the intermarried that are Reform or even Conservative households that are deeply involved in the organized Jewish community. And then you've got incredible diversity in the middle.

So, intermarriage as a trend is something that can open doorways into a lot of complicated and nuanced conversations about what's happening, like tribalism and privilege within the Jewish community, and power and authenticity. But talking about "The Intermarried" is really problematic, even though the Jewish community seems to do it a lot.

These are all topics I'd love to get into around intermarriage—but to go back to this crash theory, one of the things I do is I'm the administrator on Facebook of the Jewpanese web page because my wife is from Japan. On this webpage I just throw up any article that's of interest to me where there's a convergence between Jewish and Japanese.

Now, is this a new religion, a new form of religion? Of course not. It's just an interest of mine—and there are a thousand people who like this page who feel some kind of connection to both Jewish and Japanese. And that's not a lot, but that's certainly more than at any other time in history.

And that kind of synthesizing is, I think, happening more and more—and it's something that the organized Jewish community, I feel, is mostly ill-equipped to handle because so many people are stuck with the founding master story and can't get away from it.

They feel very threatened on these levels that the community is not conversing about, like privilege and tribalism and so on.

Lex Rofeberg: So this seems to open up another set of questions that are in the Jewish communal discussion and worth elevating. There is this notion of "Ashkenormativity," or the assumption that Jews are Caucasian. What are the roles of race, ethnicity, and multiculturalism in your own personal narrative?

Paul Golin: This is a huge part of intermarriage. Now, right off the bat, I have to acknowledge I am a white male Ashkenazi Jew with both parents who were Jewish. So that puts me at the top of the privilege ladder—and so I am speaking now as an ally, and not as somebody who's experienced it. But I've done a lot of listening to folks who have, and I am part of a multiracial household in that my wife is Japanese and my children are mixed.

And this is hugely important to me—because the notion of "looking Jewish" is something that's very hard to break for people, myself included. I live in New York City, and I like thinking that I can tell who's Jewish when I walk around on the street.

And it's a stupid thing that I don't like about myself, but I also feel this kind of weird tribal positive thing of just being able to tell that somebody is Jewish by looking at them.

I know it is a bad thing moving forward, because it alienates people, and it puts people off—and it's never been true. This is the first thing that the Jewish community really needs to understand. It's never been true, but it's much less true now that there's a certain way to look Jewish—a certain Woody Allen, Jon Stewart Jewish look.

You want to help people get past this without having them feel this sense of loss. And I think that that speaks to the whole notion of privilege, and that people first have to understand what white privilege is—because that's the most important thing that's happening in the United States today. And when you start to understand that and acknowledge that you have it—if you have it—you also start to see privilege operating in many other ways.

I wrote a piece many years ago called "Born Jewish Privilege"—that there is a privilege to having a Jewish mother. Lots of Jews may know nothing else, really, about being Jewish, but the one thing they know with certainty is that if your mom's not Jewish, then you're not Jewish. And they feel very comfortable telling that to people who identify as Jewish and are Jewish patrilineally—it's their father that's Jewish. And those patrilineal Jews may be deeply involved in the Jewish community—they may be very well educated Jewishly, and Jewishly knowledgeable. But somebody who really has none of that, but has this privilege of having been born to a Jewish mother, can come up and say, "Well, then, you're not really Jewish."

When I step back, that, to me, is just completely absurd—the whole notion of being anything because that's what your parents are is something I just want to push back on very hard. It is, I think, an American ethos that it doesn't matter what your parents did. You are your own man or woman; you can make or break your life however you want, and you're not judged on who your parents are. Whether that happens in practice or not is a different question—but that notion that we should be judged as individuals is something that I bought into at a very young age, and flies in the face of this notion of Jewish by birth, and the requirement that you should marry another Jew.

Those were two clashing narratives when I was growing up—that we should judge everybody as an individual, not based on race or religion or creed or color, etc. Except when it comes time to get married—and then only marry a Jew.

And I heard that from my folks, I heard that from my rabbi and community and so on. But from a very young age, 10 or 11, I knew that this doesn't make sense to me. This is hypocritical.

Dan Libenson: I once heard Yehuda Kurtzer, from the Hartman Institute, describe a distinction between Genesis Jews and Exodus Jews. Genesis Jews have a sense of what Jewishness is that is connected to the stories of Genesis—which is fundamentally the story of a family and its special relationship with God. While Exodus Jews sense that what it is to be Jewish is not so much about a family, but about a set of ideas—whether those are beliefs or practices or laws, or a civilization. And when Yehuda teaches about that concept, he tends to say, "But it's a continuum, and most of us are both Genesis and Exodus Jews."

But I'm thinking, as I'm listening to you, that intermarriage is a primary driver of another enormous change, a fundamentally new notion of who the Jews are that seems to inevitably force a major reconceptualization of what Judaism is. If Judaism is not something that is passed down genetically (or certainly not exclusively so), and we start to think about the non-Jewish spouses of Jews as being fellow travelers, then why limit it to the spouses of Jews? Why couldn't anybody say, "I want to be part of this," and understand themselves to be part of this group—the pursuers of Judaism.

Do you think this really is the leading edge of a profoundly different understanding of what Judaism fundamentally is?

Paul Golin: Sure. I think that many different Judaisms will—first of all, *already* exist—but that many different kinds of Judaisms will exist, and that this might be one of them. On this podcast, Rabbi Irwin Kula spoke about Judaism as a technology.

And I thought that was an elegant expression of this notion that Jewishness has to *do* something.

The reason I would be involved in an organized Jewish community is either because it helps me personally, or it benefits my family in some way, or it helps me make the world a better place. Those are the three motivating factors for me. And I often share that lens with the folks I consult with, and ask them, "How do you articulate—for people who are not engaging with your Jewish communal organization—how it will benefit either them or their family or help them benefit the world?" And there's an understanding that, oh, well, that's a given, and everyone knows that that's what synagogues do.

But we're at a point where *not* everyone just knows that—and we need to have some explicit messaging about what's the point here, what are we trying to do with this? What does it do for you, what does it mean to do a particular Jewish ritual? Because if it doesn't mean anything, people aren't going to do it anymore. And people aren't as held to it by guilt or obligation anymore, so now it actually has to be working for people.

I often use Jewish prayer as an example. I think that a lot of people understand the benefits of meditation and have been reading all of these amazing scientific studies about meditation. So, can Jewish prayer work in that same way for people? If so, why does nobody ever spin it that way? It reflects this tension between those Option 1 folks who are clinging to this master story about why we have to pray, and everyone else. And the Option 1 folks are the ones who are, for the most part, running the prayer services—so if you turn them off, nobody's going to be running the prayer service. It's almost a catch-22.

Another example is synagogues. For folks like me who are on the outside it seems like that's where Judaism happens, that's where prayer happens, that's where religion happens. But, when you talk to the folks on the inside, that's often the least most important thing that they're doing there. I once had an amazing experience consulting with a rabbi and her board members, and I asked them, "What happens to you when you pray?" And it was a devastating silence, because nobody had ever asked them this question before. And then, finally, the board president kind of sheepishly said, "I have to admit, sometimes my mind wanders." And the rabbi turned to her and said, "You know what, me too." And it was like a weight lifted. They were actually able to talk about the fact that prayer was not the thing keeping them together as a community. It was just part of the trappings, when there was something deeper or different or more meaningful happening around other things like community or friendship or social justice.

The problem is, for folks on the outside, how could they possibly know that's what happens at synagogue when the only time they've been to synagogue is either the High Holidays or someone's bar mitzvah, and they're bored out of their skull by a prayer service that's inaccessible to them?

We are thinking about how we can tweak these things, so we put out there what we called "Open Tashlich." *Tashlich* is that service during the High Holidays when you cast away your sins by throwing breadcrumbs into a living body of water. And it's often the synagogue community who physically gets up out of their seats and goes to the water. We were just thinking—this is happening in public, so why not just open it up to everybody? So, we created a little one-pager handout about what tashlich means, why we're doing this—and opened it up to the whole community. It doesn't add any additional cost to the synagogue (unless they want to spring for the bagels, which we do encourage). But other than that, this is something that I think most Jews—and many other people as well—would find meaningful and profound.

Lex Rofeberg: I love that example. And I think tashlich is a really interesting point—because Rosh Hashanah is one of the more difficult Jewish holidays for me. But tashlich is the part of it that I find most resonant, time after time, year after year. It's so simple, but I think it's also very deep.

And as you spoke about it, I realized I kind of wish the High Holiday Jews—the people who only go once or twice a year during High Holidays—just didn't go to Rosh Hashanah services. There seems to be this sense that, "Oh, it's High Holidays—I still should be there. I still have to be there, even if I am twiddling my thumbs, not much is happening in my head or heart while I'm praying—I still got to go."

It seems more important to think about what's happening. That question you asked the board—what are you doing in your head? in your heart?—thinking about those questions over and over. What is the function of this institution? What is the function of this holiday? What is the function of individual prayers? When we ask those questions, we get at that broader "Why be Jewish?" question that you seem to be inviting us to talk about.

Paul Golin: Yes. And to bring it back to intermarriage, it is horrifying to me that the High Holidays are often the first exposure to the Jewish community for the partner that isn't Jewish. The service is so inaccessible and first-time people are not going to get any questions answered, even as they're flooded with questions about what's going on here. There's so much that we could be telling folks about what's going on.

And I wonder, where's the alternative? Perhaps just a class that is happening at the same time as service, that is simply talking about sin and repentance, for example. Let's just have a conversation about sin and repentance, and have a knowledgeable person leading that interesting conversation. Because the three hours of prayer service—there's no way somebody new to Judaism is going to be able to find resonance in that. But the meaning behind it, for those who have dug into it, could be very powerful.

Now, I think the Kol Nidre service is very powerful and meaningful, and yet I still won't subject myself to it. There are moments during the prayer service where I absolutely get goose bumps. The Shema gives me goose bumps when everyone sings it, because I know that those are the words that the Holocaust victims carried on their lips into the gas chamber. The Mourner's Kaddish has power, because I think of the people in my life that I've personally lost. Those moments of connection and power, though, are just not enough to get me into the door week after week or even year after year. I haven't been to a service in 25 years, because it doesn't do it for me enough.

Dan Libenson: I've been thinking a lot lately about an article that you wrote about Bernie Sanders. This was at a time when Bernie Sanders' Jewish identity was being questioned.

The idea you shared is that Bernie Sanders really is practicing a different form of Judaism than the form that is recognized by the organized Jewish community as *the* authentic form of Judaism. His Judaism is a Judaism that is more focused on more recent Jewish historical experiences than ancient ones. He's talking about the Holocaust, and how that caused him to take politics seriously, and he's connected to the American social movement tradition.

Ultimately, the question is whether this Bernie Sanders Judaism can be passed along to the next generation—and I'm not talking about genetically. It is not about whether Bernie Sanders' Judaism is a success or failure on the basis of whether his children are Jewish, or whether my children are Jewish. The question is how can we retain the potential power that Judaism has, planted in a new soil? How can the Judaism that we've inherited be the soil out of which a new tree grows that looks different from the old tree, but is nevertheless rooted in the deep Jewish wisdom, the deep Jewish technology? Could you reflect on that a little? Where does that lead you?

Paul Golin: One of the mistakes that the Jewish community makes is in not recognizing what's happening outside of itself. In reference to intermarriage, the mistake was in thinking that the way to prevent intermarriage would be to tell the Jews, "Don't intermarry."

In reality, I would argue, the single most important factor behind the great rise in intermarriage in America is that the rest of America wanted to marry us.

It used to be an absolute disaster for a white Anglo-Saxon Protestant family to bring a Jew into the family. And this is in our grandparents' lifetime—this isn't ancient history. But over time, Jews became an equal, if not sought-after, group of people as marriage partners. It was no longer a tragedy for a white Anglo-Saxon Protestant family to have their daughter marry a Jew. When you're only two or four percent of the overall population, it's more about what the rest of the people want to do than what you want to do.

So, we have to recognize that there are things beyond the Jewish community that are going to have an impact on the Jewish community. Technology is another one of those things. I wrote a piece a couple of years ago for the journal of Jewish communal professionals called "Judaism and the Singularity," in which I consider the impact that technology and virtual reality are going to have on humanity.

I opened that article by asking what would happen if you were able to deeply experience a moving, meaningful Jewish experience like standing at Sinai when we received the Torah, and have it feel real? And then what would happen if you could also experience the warmth of Jesus's hand on your forehead as he heals you? Or if you could meditate in the deepest way with the Buddha? Would you only choose to pick from the Jewish menu—or would you want to experience all of those things? And why wouldn't those things be open to everybody? I know why there's a segment of our community that says, "No, that's not how it works"—but I think that's how it's going to work moving forward.

I have been to Israel five times, but I've been to Japan eleven times, and I love it as much as I love Israel. I feel a connection, I have great admiration for the people there, and I'll never be Japanese; I can't convert into it. I can become a Japanese citizen, but no one there will ever consider me Japanese. But my kids are half-Japanese, and I feel a connection to that story as well. I hope that in their lives they will feel connection to the Jewish story and to the Japanese story.

To the folks who say, "No, you can't do both"—I say that people do more than both all the time. You have many different identities contained within you at any given time—and at different times, some are more powerful than others. There are certain times where my identity as an alum of the University of Michigan is absolutely the most overriding part of my identity—particularly when their teams are playing well—and at other times, being Jewish is the most important thing. And this idea that Jews need to have, as their primary or sole identity, being Jewish all the time—again, I don't think that works now, but it really is not going to work in the future when you've got every single possible option open to you.

So, it comes back to that question of why should they do Jewish? My personal answer is about connection to that history. And when you talked about Yehuda Kurtzer, who I'm a fan of, talking about Genesis Jews or Exodus Jews—I would describe myself as a Book of Maccabees Jew. Because first of all, [the Book of Maccabees] is not even included in the Jewish canon, right—so it's outside of that. But it's also the one that doesn't have the word "God" in it at all, and it's based on real history, and it's cool. So that's the one I'm most connected to, and that's how I connect as a Jew. But there's got to be 40 other answers as well, and they can all exist at the same time.

Dan Libenson: In your mind, what do you think Judaism looks like in 100 years?

Paul Golin: I don't think there's one answer. I would propose a number of different answers. And one of them is this notion of "this is something I feel connected to, this is something that I want to declare for myself"—in the way that people today say, "I'm a gamer." It's an identity that people have. So I think it's a way of identifying with a group of other people who share this common interest.

Another facet is this idea of Judaism as a technology—that it does something for you—it's this wisdom system. A very simple example is the answer of how much should I give to charity—what percentage of my income should I give to charity? There's an answer for it in Judaism. Or how do I give charity? There are beautiful conversations in Judaism about how to give charity.

That's not to say that those conversations aren't in other wisdom traditions—because they are—but Judaism is compelling. And if presented in a compelling way, people will pull from that wisdom tradition. And again, it may be that somebody is pulling from the wisdom tradition who identifies with a different religion more than with Judaism—but who cares? I don't care that that's the case. I think the folks that are most concerned about what is lost are the folks who are stuck in this tribal notion of, the world is divided by people—and personally, I think tribalism is a bad thing.

I think the real challenge for the Jewish community is universalism versus particularism. I am much more a universalist human than a particularist Jew, and I have this vision for humanity that is one where people are mixed. And though there are some folks having this conversation on a somewhat high level—I don't think it's happening regularly on the ground at Jewish organizations.

What the Jewish community does as an industry is create more particularist Jews.

We don't talk about it, but I would say that's really the ultimate goal of many—if not most—Jewish organizations. We're working on this particularist idea that Jews are a tribe—we use the phrase "member of the tribe" jokingly. But for universalists, it's off-putting—because first of all, most of us are already part of two different tribes, but more importantly, we have this vision which never gets any airplay inside the organized Jewish community: Wouldn't it be great if there was more mixing, more mashups, more choices that people can make?

To see where you stand on these kinds of things, ask yourself which charity is more important to give to? There are hungry elderly Holocaust survivors in Brighton Beach, Brooklyn, and then there are children who are starving to death in South Sudan. From the particularist point of view, which I understand, you think "If we don't take care of our own people, who will?" And from the universalist view, it's, "Well, these people are about to die. They are in much more dire need, so I want to support them." And this kind of conversation, of course, has been happening at a high level in Judaism forever: "If I am not for myself, who will be for me, and if I'm not for others, what am I?"

So the question has been there—but it's not happening on the ground. What I hear and see from many intermarried households is a different narrative from the persistent underlying notion in the Jewish community that it's not ideal.

For many of the intermarried themselves, it's not just ideal, it's better. Because we're contributing to this great mixing of people that's going to make the world a better place.

I also think that there are other benefits to the amount of intermarriage that has happened in the US that get no airtime in the organized Jewish community because they clash with the narrative that folks have bought into about intermarriage being bad. There is an unbelievably low amount of anti-Semitism in the United States—a historically low amount of anti-Semitism—and I believe a big part of that is because there's a Jew at almost every Thanksgiving table. It used to be much easier to dehumanize the Jews when you didn't actually know any—and at this point, almost every American works with a Jew or knows a Jew or has a Jew in their family. I feel that that's a very important part of the explanation of how come there's so little anti-Semitism in the United States [relative to other countries]—but that's not going to be celebrated by the organized Jewish community, of course.

Dan Libenson: Lex and I were talking recently about Jews that are criticized for giving philanthropically to "non-Jewish" causes such as education, hunger relief, the arts, et cetera. It's perverse that the value system of late 20th century American Judaism seems to be that to be a "real Jew" is to prioritize being Jewish in every aspect of life—to give primarily to Jewish organizations, to spend most of your time doing Jewish particularistic kind of things—as opposed to understanding Judaism as fundamentally about cultivating a certain kind of person who cares about the world and contributes to the world.

This leads me to my last question—which is that I'd love to hear you reflect a bit further about universalism versus particularism. Because even though we may criticize examples of an overly particularistic turn, at the same time, there is also a fair critique that it's not really possible to be a general universalist. The argument can be made that there's a real value in particularism, because particularism potentially gives you access to a deep wisdom tradition, to a deep value system, that ultimately allows you to be the best possible contributor to the larger society. From this view, to be a universalist is to lack a value system, a tradition that pushes you to contribute to the world.

And if the benefits of particularism are not happening because of how the Jewish institutionalized world has evolved in America, the solution would be to reboot the particularism of Judaism so that it is oriented towards pushing us to contribute to the world at large. But that's not an argument that we should give up on a particularistic Judaism.

Paul Golin: I do think that there is something profoundly powerful to being Jewish—it's why I do what I do. And I also think that there is something tremendous and amazing about being Japanese, and I am proud to have family members who are Japanese—and so on. And I think that the best of all of that will be retained—and lots of people can experience it, and lots of people will say, "This is me more than that is me."

I think this is very similar to what happened with intermarriage and Judaism in the United States. The fear of intermarriage in the 60s and 70s, through the 80s and, unfortunately, the 90s and 'til today, is that the Jews that intermarry are going to "assimilate" away from even being recognizably Jewish, and just meld into the general US culture. But that didn't happen—and it's because we're not a melting pot where everyone just becomes this grey blah nothing.

We are like a gumbo—we're a multicultural country, and we celebrate our differences. In New York City we just had a St. Patrick's Day parade all over the city, and many of those folks don't have both parents who are from Ireland, but there's a huge turnout for that kind of a celebration—and that didn't melt away after three or four or five or six generations in the United States. And I don't think that's going to happen for Judaism, either. But folks have to recognize that there's an opportunity for growth or for loss—and if you want to grow, and you want more people to experience Judaism, then you've got to recognize what is the universe that you're existing in, and how do you empower people to participate and benefit from it?

QUESTIONS FOR REFLECTION

- Golin describes two different ways of thinking about intermarriage between Jews and non-Jews. The first sees intermarriage as bad, or at least "not ideal," because it pulls Jews away from Judaism and diminishes the "tribe." The second sees intermarriage as positive because it has the potential to increase understanding between cultures and enlarge the community of Jewish "fellow travelers." Which understanding about intermarriage is closest to what you were raised with? What aspects of Golin's discussion of the benefits of intermarriage ring true for you today?
- Golin calls for the Jewish community to be more thoughtful about ways to invite non-Jewish spouses into Jewish services and wisdom traditions. If you were going to design a "welcome to Judaism—here's what you're going to love" program for non-Jewish spouses and partners, what would you include?
- At the end of this conversation, Dan and Paul have a dialogue about "particularism vs universalism" in which they articulate arguments both for and against each of these fundamental orientations. What value do you see in particularism? In universalism? What might it look like to hold both orientations?

Juan Mejia

"Judaism is resonating in places that we don't imagine, and in places that we can't control."

Becoming Jewish on the Web

Rabbi Juan Mejia is rabbi-in-residence for Be'chol Lashon, an organization that "grows and strengthens the Jewish people through ethnic, cultural, and racial inclusiveness." Mejia is an innovator in international Judaism who has been on the front lines of exploring how internet technologies can support geographically and culturally isolated people in learning about Judaism, forming Jewish communities, and becoming Jewish.

An exemplar of Jewish diversity in his own life, Juan grew up Catholic in Colombia but became curious about Judaism when he learned of his father's Sephardic Jewish lineage. His spiritual curiosity led him to convert to Judaism and eventually become a rabbi. He was ordained by the Jewish Theological Seminary in 2009.

Today, Juan is an activist and educator on behalf of emergent Jewish communities in Latin America. He lives in Oklahoma City with his spouse, who is also a rabbi, and their three children.

Dan Libenson: I think that the best place to get started is for you to tell a little bit about your story, because it's an extremely uncommon and interesting one.

Juan Mejia: I was born in Colombia 39 years ago to a middle-class Catholic family. My father's a doctor, my mother was an artist. I grew up with the benefits of that class in a Latin American country, which included an elite private Catholic School run by American monks. I always was very spiritually curious—for a while I even considered a Catholic vocation.

But when I was 15 years old, I discovered that my father's family had Jewish origins. They were very distant, going back to Spain, but some measure of it had survived until the latest generations. My grandfather remembered that his grandfather self-identified as a Jew and had some odd practices that he really couldn't explain. And that really got me curious.

I started to read about Jewish history, about Sephardic history, the story of the Jews of Spain where my family apparently came from. And when I graduated high school, I started studying philosophy at the National University of Colombia, and that gave me exposure to Maimonides and Spinoza and Hermann Cohen, and the wealth of Jewish philosophical tradition, which only deepened my interest.

In 1998 I took a little break from college to travel through Europe and ended up spending two or three months in Israel. And for me it was a great revelation, because in Colombia there's very little Jewish visibility and culture. There's no Yiddish in the television, there's no Hanukkah portrayed in the local [TV] series. People know that that building with the copper dome is a synagogue, but there's no representation in the outside culture. There are about 3,000 to 5,000 Jews in the entire country of 40 million.

Seeing Jewish life in Israel really being lived as a vibrant culture—religious and linguistic—was a game-changer and really led me to a lot of soul-searching. So, when I returned to Colombia I started to research Judaism quite diligently, and in the end I said, "This is my spiritual home. This is the wisdom that I can really get behind. This is a way of life that I could endorse. It pleases my reason, it connects to my heart." And—back then it was much more important—"It connects to my own personal family history."

I decided to convert to Judaism when I was 19 or 20 years old, and that's when a lot of the challenges that I am now addressing as a rabbi started to manifest. In Colombian culture, where Jews are not participating openly in the national discourse, and there is a complicated security situation—most Latin American countries have similar issues of urban violence and kidnappings—the Jewish community is not very open toward outsiders. Unlike in America, it's very hard for an outsider in Colombia to, for example, enter a synagogue and see a Jewish worship service. So, I had to develop my own Jewish observance and my own Jewish life on the margins of the community. I had to find other like-minded people, both Jewish and seekers, who would lend me books, and allow me to participate in their Passover seders. And I realized that that was kind of an untenable situation if I really wanted to make this a part of my life.

So, when I finished college I decided to do my master's degree work in a place where conversion was a thing. And there were only two places where that was a possibility. One was America and the other was Israel. And I applied to American and Israeli universities, and the first place that actually gave me a positive answer was the Hebrew University in Jerusalem. So, I did a Master's Degree in Jewish Civilization and was able to attend services and go to classes, see what a yeshiva looks from the inside.

I did my conversion and enrolled in the Conservative Yeshiva, which is a center for lay leader Torah development in Jerusalem. There I met my wife, who's from America, and that is kind of like the first chapter of my Jewish story. I never expected to become a rabbi. I wanted to keep working in academia—very devoted to philosophy, especially Jewish philosophy—but something kind of woke me up from that complacency and led me to the work that I do now as a rabbi.

Dan Libenson: How did you get from the master's degree at Hebrew University to becoming a Conservative-ordained rabbi?

Juan Mejia: It is all because of my landlady. When I married my wife, we decided to stay in the Conservative Yeshiva for another year of learning—not very different from the philosophical life. And we rented a little apartment in Katamon, and my landlady was American. I go to pay my rent, and she sits me down, she gives me tea.

The opening question is, "How come your English is so good? You don't sound Colombian."

"Oh, I went to this elite Catholic school where monks from North Dakota taught us English…"

She said, "Really? How come a nice Jewish boy like you went to Catholic school?"

And I tell her I was not always Jewish. So, I tell her my story, and she says, "That's a really good story. I want to interview you."

And she does this interview for the Sokhnut—kind of a PR piece. They feature students in different academic institutions in Israel in the yeshivot.

And the next month that I go to pay my rent, she says, "I got some emails for you."

"What do you mean?"

"You got fan mail."

This is because these stories are published in Hebrew, English, French, Russian, and Spanish on the website of the Sokhnut. So, my story about finding my Jewish roots and going back to them and engaging in Torah learning in Jerusalem apparently hit the internet pretty hard in Latin America.

And the emails that I was being forwarded were all the same, like:

"My name is Mario, I like to be called Moshe, I love Torah, I love Israel, I love the Jewish people. But I'm in Guatemala, nobody gives me the time of day."

"My name is Maria, my ancestors lit candles in the closet, and I really want to come back to my ancestral knowledge, but I live in a place with no Jews."

Those were the two scenarios that would repeat themselves. Either people were in complete isolation—"I'm living in the middle of a little town up in the Andes in Peru, and there's no Jews, I can't learn, I can't go to a community." Or, the more common case was people from the big cities with access to the internet. These were people who were a little bit learned, who could find the website of the Jewish Agency and find the story, said, "Look, I am really interested in Judaism," either because "I just love it, I think it's true, I think it's beautiful," or "I think my ancestors were Jewish, and I can't get the local Jewish community to engage with me."

And my wife, who is a very, very smart rabbi—but she wasn't a rabbi back then—she said, "Look, we've studied *Pirkei Avot* together," [The Ethics of the Fathers] "and 'In a place where there is no mensch, you be the mensch. In a place where is not a man, you be that man.'" It's a great saying from Hillel [the sage]. And I really took that to heart.

She said, "Look, this is a rabbinic problem—the communities, the rabbis down there can't or won't engage with these people, so you become the rabbi that engages with them, and you can get your Ph.D. in Rambam [Maimonides] later in life, but right now I think there's this calling for you to be a liaison between the established Jewish mainstream and this periphery that is being created by the web."

I cannot stress enough how much of this spiritual revolution is web-based. When I decided that I had a real deep interest in Judaism, I went to my university's library, and I checked out all the books they had on Judaism. This is the biggest university library in Colombia, the largest university in my country, and they had seven books about Judaism. And it was only through the internet, which was then in its infancy—we're talking late 90s—that I was able to live Judaism on my own, which is what I had to do while I was still in Colombia. It was all web-based.

And right now this is what is creating this global interest in Judaism—people find Judaism on the web. There's a need to create resources for them to learn. But most importantly, the internet is also allowing these lonely people to find community. I still have people in the middle of the Andes whose Judaism is exclusively lived online—or through Facebook, through Yahoo! Groups. Through whatever tool they have, they find other like-minded people in their proximity, and they create communities.

I have a running map of communities—what I call emergent communities—in Latin America. I have about 100 communities documented. Every single one of those started online. The internet is a key player on what is happening with conversion, in general, and conversion to Judaism, in particular. Because it's not just conversion to Judaism.

Religious migration is one of the key elements of contemporary spirituality. The Pew report of a couple of years ago says that 50% of Americans die in a different religion or denomination than the one that they were born into—one in two.

Latin America's always a little behind the curve in social and spiritual phenomena. But I see it in my own graduating class. I keep in touch with my high school classmates. There's 108 of us. And I see who has become evangelical, and I see who has become secular—like atheist, like militantly secular. I know who's dabbling in Buddhism and in Transcendental Meditation. And there's me, and there's another guy who's now also saying, "Maybe this is a path for me." Conversion to Islam is also on the rise, to Buddhism, to Hinduism.

Can the Jewish community reach out to these people who are seeking from the outside?

Dan Libenson: Juan, that is so fascinating. We have a million questions to ask you, but first tell us what are you doing now?

Juan Mejia: I was ordained in 2009. My wife went to school with me. She was ordained 20 seconds before I was, so she is my senior, and I need to listen to everything she says. It's alphabetical. She's Jacobson, I'm Mejia—there's only so much we can do. She got a job [in] the Oklahoma City community, so we moved here in 2009. I'm now the education director in her synagogue, but I've also been engaged since then in outreach work at night, during the weekends, and during the summers. This is mostly online, through Be'chol Lashon. I also travel quite a lot to these communities, visit them, bring them rabbinic services. So that is what I've been doing for the past eight years.

Dan Libenson: Please tell us a little more—who are these folks that are reaching you, what is it that they're trying to achieve, and what do you do for them?

Juan Mejia: I think the conversation has changed a little bit. In the beginning, in 2009, 2008, I heard overwhelmingly from people who thought they had Jewish roots. It's what's called *anusim*—other names for that is *marranos* (although that's a derogatory term), *conversos*. That was kind of like the hot narrative for these communities in Latin America when I was ordained and at the beginning of my work.

How did they find me? They found me online. I had a piece written about me in *Ha'aretz* [an Israeli newspaper]. I had a piece written about me in the *Jewish Week*, in one of the Latino Jewish newspapers in Uruguay. And when you put "rabbi," "*marrano*," and "*anusim*," [in a search engine] my name would come up.

So, when I opened up a website in 2009 to teach Torah, I said "I'm going to be teaching *parashat hashavua* [the weekly portion of the Torah read in synagogues on Shabbat] and Mishnah. I'm a rabbinical student. And this is going to be in Spanish." Because I saw that there was a need. A lot of these people have decent English, they can access Torah learning in English, but for people who don't have the linguistic ability, there is a huge handicap.

So, my goal then—and it's the only goal that I have continued to uphold from my early rabbinate—was I want to create good Torah in Spanish. I wanted it to be out there and available and accessible, and to take into account the reality of where people are.

A lot of the Torah online is put there from the perspective of the community that produces it. If I'm a rabbi in Long Island, and I have a blog, who is my expected audience? The people in Long Island who are my congregants. And if I'm a little bit more entrepreneurial, maybe I want to take this nationally. The same thing happens with stuff in Spanish. The main centers of Torah-teaching Spanish Jews are, on one hand, Argentina, and on the other hand, Mexico, and Jerusalem—mostly coming from the Orthodox world, mostly from the ultra-Orthodox world, and reflecting these values.

What I saw a need for was a Torah that is able to speak to people who don't have access to a synagogue, who don't have access to Jewish institutions. It's not just that I am teaching in Spanish, but I'm always cognizant of this do-it-yourself aspect of the Torah that they need to embody if they are going to eventually become Jews and join the Jewish people.

I had this great conversation in 2007 with one of my early students—a guy from Colombia. I'm texting with this guy *motzei* Shabbat [on Saturday night, after the end of Shabbat], "*Shavua tov* [wishes for a good week ahead], how was Shabbat?"

He said, "Oh, Shabbat was terrible."

"What do you mean Shabbat was terrible?"

The president of the little *havurah* [prayer group] that this guy went to in a city in Colombia took the *siddur* [prayer book].

"What do you mean *the* siddur?"

"Yeah, we only have one."

"What do you mean you only have one? It's ridiculous. I can send you a box of full of siddurim. I work at the library of the Jewish Theological Seminary—I have tons of stuff that is going to get *genizahed* otherwise" [is going to get put in the closet for books of sacred writings that are no longer being used but cannot be thrown away or destroyed under Jewish law because they contain the name of God].

He said, "Yeah, you know what, that's great, thank you for your offer, but the book that you're offering me—it's in Hebrew. We don't read Hebrew yet. The translation's in English, which doesn't help us, and it's Ashkenazi [using the approach of Jews with Eastern European origins], and we're a Sephardic congregation [using the approach of Jewish with Spanish origins]."

I go, "Oy! What do I need to do?" So, the first idea, the root that I've been developing for the past decade, is that I needed to create a siddur that was in Spanish, with transliteration, that followed the Sephardic tradition, and that could go anywhere.

So, for the next year and a half, I developed the siddur that I decided to call *Kol Tuv Sefarad* [all the wealth, or the goodness, of Spain]. I thought it was a cute name, and I created a PDF of a siddur—transliterated, translated, commented Sephardic siddur for Friday night, because that was the service that I saw that most of these emerging *havurut* [prayer groups] were really focused on. And I posted it online, and I said, "You are free to download it; you are free to make as many copies as you want. Just don't change it, and don't sell it."

And through that, people started to reach out, said, "We love the siddur, thank you, it really helped us out." And people started saying, "We really want to learn with you." So, I started teaching—every Sunday—basic Judaism, and more people started to come. Once social media started to kick in in 2008, 2009, the word spread, and I created a group of people who regularly study with me.

And among those people, there was a group from a city in Colombia by the beach in Santa Marta. They said, "We really love your Torah, we really think that you are the rabbi for us. Would you work with us for conversion?" And I said, "I don't know. I'm in rabbinical school, I don't know how to do this, this has never been done. Let's wait a little bit."

So, I learned more with them, and then on a trip to Colombia I went and visited them, and we spent a week together with these people, and I saw how they lived, and I fell in love with them, and I said, "You guys are awesome." They'd been doing Jewish on their own for six, seven years before I got to them. So I said, "I really want to guide you in this process."

We started studying for conversion with this pilot community in Santa Marta, and after two and a half years of learning every week for two, three, four, five hours sometimes, I thought "you are ready." Why did it take so long? Because this is do-it-yourself Judaism. These people don't have an established synagogue where there's printed siddurim. Nobody knows how to lead the prayers. We have really to take it from zero and give these people the tools to be autonomous. Even though they have my guidance, my guidance is always remote. So, they need a level of autonomy that most Jewish communities—brick and mortar communities—don't have.

And this really set the pattern for the work I do. I only work with four small havurot, and I really can't do more than that because it takes a lot of time and a lot of effort.

Lex Rofeberg: You've spoken about linguistic barriers, communal barriers, and geographic barriers . . . what other barriers might there be in your work? Have there been folks resistant to the kinds of conversions that you help perform? Is there resistance to working online?

Juan Mejia: Quite so. Long distance training for conversion is a hot topic. The rabbinic establishment across the movements is not really comfortable with it. It has taken me about a decade to convince colleagues that this work can be done. It is ripe with blessing. It's also very tricky. The borders, the periphery, the frontier is always dangerous. Right?

In the Wild West, for every Lone Ranger that was doing good, you had 20 mustachioed bad guys. In the periphery things get fuzzy, and since we're doing things that are new, we don't have the benefit of experience. So, there's been resistance. I think that resistance is eroding.

Once the internet becomes more pervasive and the leadership of the Jewish mainstream are Gen Xers and Millennials and people for whom the internet is not a secret and it's a neutral tool—it's actually more than a tool, it's kind of like our natural environment—it becomes easier to persuade people that you can have deep spiritual connections online.

There are limitations, but, look, I've visited people in the hospital through WhatsApp. WhatsApp is what they use in Latin America. Here in America, it's FaceTime. While people are dying, I've said *viddui* [the Jewish confession prayer before death] with people who are dying in the hospital through FaceTime. There's not a rabbi within 1,000 miles—I'm their rabbi, they're dying. I'm FaceTiming, and I'm saying viddui with you, and I'm holding your hand through the web, and I'm crying and they're crying, and it's not less of a spiritual relationship.

Another barrier has been, really, the definition of what a Jewish community is. And the best example I have is very recent: At the beginning of this year, I was helping one of my communities in Venezuela—wonderful people, I've been working with them since 2011. They converted in 2014. Soon after that, they managed to gain access to one of the established communities in Venezuela. They did not have to do their own living room havurah anymore, although that was their natural option. They got an opportunity to go to one of the regular synagogues and said, "This is what we're going to do, we're going to do Jewish together." And then things in Venezuela got really, really bad, and they decided, "You know what, I'm sick of my kid only eating one meal a day—I want to make *aliyah* [move to Israel]."

And the Ministry of Interior [of Israel] said, "No, you can't make aliyah." The Ministry of Interior said, "You did not convert in an established community." So, there's no problem with the rabbi, because rabbis, in the Diaspora—all the denominations can do conversions and have their converts make aliyah. It was not that the process was wrong.

The Ministry of Interior said, "You're Jewish. But your framework was wrong. The framework is that you should convert in a place that was already Jewish."

But that is a framework that is very quickly becoming obsolete. People outside of the analog web of relationships of the established Jewish communities are going to find our message compelling.

We have the most beautiful example—the community in Uganda. With my *rebbe* [rabbinic master] and one of my colleagues, Rabbi Gershom Sizomu, the entire community converted in 2000. They have a yeshiva, six synagogues, a hospital. Through their actions, they have reduced the deaths of malaria in that area from 2,000 to zero—*kiddush hashem*, sanctifying God's name, sanctifying the name of the Jewish people. Beautiful community.

And the Israeli government gave full confirmation that they are a recognized Jewish community only at the beginning of this year. So, the issues of recognition and who has the authority to declare that this community belongs to the Jewish people is something that is still in flux. But it is a conversation that we need to have, and Judaism is resonating in places that we don't imagine, and in places that we can't control.

And the third barrier, which is the most fascinating part of the work, is the barrier of ethnicity. And this is what fueled a great shift in my work. In the beginning, I was really focused on *anusim*, on the descendants of people who were forced to convert in Spain. And while I was doing some fieldwork and getting to meet the people, I realized that most of the people that I was working with were just taking this as a kind of an identity marker, something to give their Jewish narrative a hint of authenticity, to justify it to themselves. And on the other hand, it was also bringing in a lot of baggage, because the story of the *anusim*—the story of the Spanish Inquisition, of the exile from Spain—is a very painful one. I was seeing that people were getting stuck in the pain, and I sat down and I considered, "Do I really care if these people are descended from Jews from Spain? If I could just turn back the clock to 1491, am I doing these people a favor? They're not living in Spain anymore; they're living in Latin America. Should their Judaism just be focused on the past, or should it be reaching out towards the future?"

And what came out of that inner conversation was that I really didn't care if people were descended or not from Jews, that the ethnic component—and there's many cases in which, indeed, people are descended from *anusim*—is so distant that it's not affecting people's lives, and that I don't want them to be carrying this pain. What I want to do in Latin America is create a Judaism that is post-ethnic, in the sense that it's not Ashkenazi and it's not Sephardi; it's Mexican, it's Colombian. These people are taking the tools of Torah, the tools of Judaism, and retooling it and creating a Judaism that fits them, but that is not connected to any particular ethnic model.

Lex Rofeberg: To what extent do you think your work really does come from a deeply personal place of your own history and your own life experience? And to what extent might it not?

Juan Mejia: I suffered lack of access to Judaism when I started in my quest to find a spiritual home for me. And I was blessed that, although I found limitations, I also had the tools—i.e., I could read English, I had the academic credentials that allowed me to get into Israel through, like, an academic gate. My story of being unable to access Judaism motivates me to create a Judaism that is accessible, and, ideally, also create communities that are accessible.

But I don't think my story is the only source of empathy. There are other rabbis doing this work, and they are Ashkenazi American rabbis. There are also Sephardic rabbis in Israel who are doing this work. And their empathy is fueled by something else than personal narrative.

This work is beautiful—when you are there in a community of people who love Judaism so much, it's an incredible spiritual high—but the only thing that I would want to caution is that in other places, in the past 20 years, there's been cases of what I would call spiritual colonialism. People are coming in with no knowledge of the culture, no knowledge of the inner workings of society, and they've offered a Judaism that is foreign. And sometimes it works and sometimes it doesn't.

So, when I speak of my work with emergent communities and with peripheral Jewish communities with rabbinic colleagues I always warn them, "This is great. Support this work, open your congregation's or your organization's minds to the possibility of a Judaism that transmits itself not through—using a biological metaphor—not by sexual reproduction, but by spores.

Judaism is now reproducing, yes, in the traditional way, but we also have this new disruptive element of the internet, which is creating spherical Judaism, which is you have these bits of Torah flying around, and they fall on the ground, and people will flock to them and retool them and adopt them. If you're getting involved in this, make sure that you're doing it from a place of openness.

Dan Libenson: A lot of people take pride in the idea that Judaism doesn't proselytize. But, in a way, what you're describing is an accidental proselytization, right? I mean, just by putting the material out there, people get interested in it. And once they come to you and they express interest, it's not proselytizing anymore. How do you think about that, and how do you talk about that with people who are more used to thinking in traditional terms about Judaism as an ethnicity, or as a family?

Juan Mejia: I think the best metaphor for addressing the proselytization accusation—which gets leveled against me quite often—is the movie "Contact" with Jodie Foster and Matthew McConaughey. The premise of the movie is that we throw messages into space, right? We've been broadcasting, from Arecibo and the large array, this message to aliens. Guess what? Somebody listened, and now they want to be in contact with us.

These rabbis that are posting blogs are doing it for their flock, and they're doing it for what they see as the extent of the Jewish people, and it's either a spore, or we've been broadcasting. It's been completely a kind of unintentional side effect of Jews taking to the web.

One of the great things about working for Be'chol Lashon is that I've been able to connect with the other "Juans"—the African people who are doing this work in Kenya, in Uganda. The people who are doing this in Asia, in the Philippines. The motto of Be'chol Lashon is "we are a global people," which we tend to forget.

Why do we tend to forget? Because right now we are in a process of de-diasporization, if that is a word. We are a global people because Jews went everywhere, created Judaism that is extremely diverse and rich, but now we're seeing kind of a centripetal force that is bringing everything back to the two big centers—America and Israel—and everything else gets thrown by the wayside.

What I envision is that we truly are a global people, but that with the tools we have right now, we can transcend that and become a global religion. Which is a very different thing. Being a global people means that we have Jews from one core that have expanded and are now everywhere. But being a global religion is having the same values and stories and rituals being replicated throughout the world in slight variations, without this necessary connection to ethnicity.

I still think that the ideal is that all the members of the Jewish religion are members of the Jewish people—that is the definition that we have of Judaism. I don't want to disrupt that.

Dan Libenson: What if I was an Orthodox rabbi, and I found out that there are 100 million non-Jews out there who are desperate to convert to Judaism and would all be Orthodox? I think there's something deeply embedded in their understanding of what it means to be an Orthodox Jew, something fundamentally ingrained, that would say, even if this would solve our demographic problem forever, we wouldn't jump at it.

And I think that should be puzzled out, because the traditional Jewish movements or traditional Jewish practices that are struggling with the Jews sort of bleeding away and looking for something different, nevertheless are not actively seeking converts, and maybe they ought to. I mean maybe that's a disruptive innovation within traditional Judaism that could actually be very effective. Maybe that's a sustaining innovation, but of incredible power.

And I think that that is adjacent to another question that I wanted to ask you, which is the sense that it might be better to risk not growing as much as we might just to make sure that it's somehow safer and more predictable. Like you said, we don't know what's going to happen with all of the global Jews, right? They might be Orthodox, but they might invent some completely different form of Judaism.

I'm wondering how you think, particularly as a Conservative rabbi, about how much to embrace the unintended consequences of the global, internet-enabled Judaisms. It seems that we have to contend with the fact that as we are actively putting stuff out there, even if we believe that we're doing it in an extremely responsible way that's extremely patient and slow, it's probably opening up a chain of events that leads to people jumping in and taking it further than I feel personally comfortable with. And I'm wondering how you think about that.

Juan Mejia: I have a group of friends—we have our secret little space—and we're all converts who became rabbis, which is a growing demographic, by the way, and it's a demographic that I think is going to be really important in America in the coming decades.

Between female ordination and LGBT ordination, the curve started to go up for converts going into the rabbinate. And it was not as publicized or as controversial, but I think it does have a great power of change. Imagine that a third of the entering class at JTS [the Jewish Theological Seminary—the rabbinical school of Conservative Judaism] in this year were converts—a third!

So, the numbers are going to pile up, and these are rabbis who might not have one single *bubbe* or *zayde* [the Yiddish words for grandmother and grandfather]. What does that mean—that they don't have a Jewish grandparent? What does that mean for their Judaism? What is their Judaism about?

So, we talk and we commiserate that all this talk in the Jewish community about demographic erosion is so frustrating because what we're seeing is the wave. People are crying over spilled milk on the beach with their backs to the tsunami.

And the tsunami is not intentional—it's inevitable. We don't have to seek converts, we don't have to knock on doors. What we have to do is to institutionally be ready to deal with a massive spike in Jewish interest. And part of what that means is being willing to admit a level of discomfort with Jews who are not like us—ethnically, politically, racially.

We are here in Oklahoma. This is a slightly right-of-center state, to put it mildly, and we have a very robust number of converts in our congregations. When my wife invites rabbis from other places in the country to sit with her in *batei din* [rabbinic panels] for a conversion, sometimes it's uncomfortable. These new converts in Oklahoma don't vote like Jews, they don't follow what the rabbis recognize as political and social patterns of integration. But they believe in Torah, they believe in Jewish history, they see themselves connected as it, and once they go through conversion, they're halachically [according to Jewish law] members of the Jewish people.

One of the things that I see as the greatest boon that American Judaism has provided is that most American Jews have a non-Jewish grandparent—at least—and have non-Jewish friends and family and coworkers and spouses. And this is also now going to apply to rabbis as well—I know tons of rabbis who have a Catholic grandmother, an Irish grandfather, who have Native American, African-American narratives also. This prepares us to transcend this adversarial relationship with the gentile that we have had over 2,000 years of tragic Diaspora history.

Let's rethink the *goy* [Hebrew word for non-Jew], because the gentile is no longer the Cossack coming to burn down my village—might be, there are some anti-Semites in the world—but the goy is also my grandfather, my mother, my father, the people from whom I learned Torah.

People are really surprised when I tell my conversion story and say, "How did your family take it?" And I say, "Look, my family—it was hard for them, but at the end of the day when I sat with them, I said, 'The religious values you gave me brought me here. I am living out your ethics and your love and your passion for God in a different way, but you're still my *rabbeim* [my religious teachers].'"

One of my rebbes, in a deeply spiritual way, is the headmaster of my Benedictine school in Colombia. This guy taught me everything I know about devotion and hard work. So, I can bring part of my Benedictine upbringing to my Judaism. That doesn't make me Christian. That enriches my Judaism.

Lex Rofeberg: Are there any final thoughts that you'd like to share or new topics that you think are important for listeners to hear?

Juan Mejia: One of the areas of my work that doesn't usually come to the fore is, people almost always think that I am doing Judaism in Spanish south of the border. But there are an incredible number of Spanish-speaking Jews here in America. It's one of the things that we're starting to realize. The immense number of Latino Jews—by choice and by birth and by immigration—that are currently part of the American Jewish world is something that gets ignored. And it's a demographic that relates very differently to institutions, to Torah, to community.

In many cases, they have been innovators. Where are the rabbis from B'nai Jeshurun in New York from? They are from Argentina. They brought the kind of Judaism that Marshall Meyer, of blessed memory, created in Buenos Aires that was very musical and very spiritual. And, being incredibly talented guys, they brought it to New York, where it flourished.

I would just emphasize the great opportunities that we find in cross-pollination.

QUESTIONS FOR REFLECTION

- What surprised or intrigued you most about Mejia's life story?
- Mejia offers a new metaphor for how Judaism is growing as he calls for broader recognition that internationally, Judaism has shifted from a "sexual reproduction" model connected to genetic lineages to a "spores" model in which Jewish communities can grow up from seeds that find their way to far-flung places. How does this spore metaphor challenge or enhance how you've been used to thinking about the expansion and continued vibrancy of Judaism?
- Mejia says, *People are crying over spilled milk on the beach with their backs to the tsunami.* What do you think he means by that? What might change in your thinking or practice if you opened to the possibility that this "tsunami" is already building?
- Mejia shares his vision for Judaism as a "global religion" that is not necessarily connected to a shared ethnicity. What elements of his vision do you share? Are there aspects of this vision that you find personally challenging?

PART THREE
Reinventing Jewish Practice

Early Incarnations of Third Era Judaisms

After the Exodus comes Sinai, the beginning of the transition from what is left behind to what is yet to come. Many of us have been taught to think of the Revelation at Sinai as the moment God gifted to Moses and the Israelites a fully complete, new system. But when we read the Torah, we can clearly see that the Israelites remained an unruly bunch long after Sinai. The Revelation at Sinai is better read as a story of the early development of a mishmash of new ideas that only became systematized much later. Sinai is a beginning, not an end.

The early Rabbis seemed to understand this clearly, and they re-imagined the Sinai moment accordingly. In one version, they dreamed up a scene in which Moses is transported forward in time to the classroom of Rabbi Akiva in the second century and doesn't recognize the Judaism Rabbi Akiva is teaching. Moses becomes depressed. How could it be that Judaism has become unrecognizable to the very person who received the revelation at Sinai. And yet Moses is relieved when Rabbi Akiva explains to his students that this new version of Judaism was also given to Moses at Sinai, which God confirms, explaining that new Jewish practices are encoded even in the decorative flourishes atop the Hebrew letters in the Torah.

Innovation is not all about what we create; it's also about what we leave behind. As we think of the Sinai moment and its aftermath reenacted in our own time, we do well to invoke the wisdom of Japanese tidying expert and best-selling author Marie Kondo. During our trek through a new post-Sinai wilderness, intrepid wanderers and creators of new Jewish practices are implicitly using Kondo's method to examine the texts, history, and raw materials of Judaism and to decide what we need to keep and what we can no longer carry. When tidying our homes, Kondo suggests asking whether any given object "sparks joy"; when tidying Judaism, we might ask whether a practice helps us find meaning in life or helps us live the lives we yearn to live. Kondo insists that we thank every item we are not keeping, expressing gratitude for its service on our journey up to this point but explaining that we cannot bring it with us any farther. This is what the Rabbis did with Biblical-era Judaism, and it's what we see today's bold Jewish innovators doing with elements of Rabbinic-era Judaism. The process of "Marie Kondo-ing" the tradition is a critical part of the tradition of reinventing Judaism, and the willingness to do so is a hallmark of the innovation we need.

In Part 3, we introduce you to 18 practitioners and their projects. These innovators are making choices about what pieces of Judaism they want to reclaim and how they think their experiments will resonate. Some are reimagining Jewish institutions, while others are focused on artistic expression. Still others are creating new Jewish residential communities or empowering others to learn about and practice Judaism in a new way.

They are all inventors trying new things, and, by nature, some ideas may take off and some will have a short lifespan. We are as interested in how these practitioners think as we are in what they have done. In the years since we conducted these interviews, quite a few of the projects we talked about no longer exist. We do not see this as a failure, but rather as the natural way that a new approach to Judaism emerges through trial and error—we shouldn't be expecting a new system of Judaism yet, but rather a large number of new ideas emerging, some of which will "make it" and some of which won't.

For an organization to become stable, it needs to have more than a powerful animating idea; it needs to find an audience, get funding, and successfully organize itself. The stars don't always align. But even if an organization ends, its impact continues to be felt as its founders or its participants go on to new projects. Think of it as more akin to a relay race than to a sprint or a marathon; as long as the baton keeps moving forward, you're still in the race.

In our first few episodes, we proposed an idea we called the "Chutzpah vs. Knowledge Curve." It was a U-shaped curve that suggested that sometimes more Jewish learning results in less creativity as people absorb an idea (often taught within mainstream institutions) that Judaism has to be a certain way to be "authentic." That's the left side of the U shape—the decline of creative chutzpah as knowledge increased. But if they keep learning, people evetually learn so much that they realize changing the tradition *is* the tradition, when change is needed in order to accomplish the purposes of the tradition, and they get more creative again. That's the right side of the U. In these pages, you will meet some practitioners with only a little Jewish knowledge, and some who have a lot. What they have in common is a lot of chutzpah in the best way—"I am authorized," they let themselves say, "to bring my artist's eye and my Marie Kondo eye to the tradition." As we meet these innovators, we imagine their innovations ripening into entirely new ways of being Jewish that would be unrecognizable to both Moses and Rabbi Akiva and yet also validly tracing their origins to Moses at Sinai.

As you read this section, we invite you to imagine a primordial soup where the "molecules" (new Jewish ideas and experiments) come into contact with one another, recombine, and evolve. Part 3 is meant to give you a taste of the primordial soup. Let these ideas recombine in your head. It's not the parts, not even the sum of parts, but this soup of parts that will bring us to the next Jewish future.

Miriam Terlinchamp

> "...it's our job to imagine this moment—not what's going to happen 50 years from now, but just what's happening right now, and what can we do about it."

Embrace the Weird

Miriam Terlinchamp is the current Executive Director of *Judaism Unbound*! At the time of this interview, Terlinchamp was serving as Senior Rabbi of Temple Sholom in Cincinnati, Ohio, where she worked for 13 years. We were excited to talk to her about her innovative work as a congregational rabbi where she took a small synagogue, divested from the land, sold the building, dispensed with the dues model, reorganized the board, produced over 50 videos on Jewish vision and values with millions of views and grew the congregation by 70% in 7 years.

Miriam Terlinchamp also founded JustLove, a multi-faith movement for activists. She teaches classes in *Judaism Unbound*'s UnYeshiva and at HUC-JIR. She is active on several boards and committees within the Cincinnati community, including serving as the current President of the Board of Rabbis, Artistic Advisor Committee for the Jewish Bicentennial Mural project, and she sits on the National Clergy Advisory Council for Faith in Action and HIAS.

Terlinchamp received rabbinic ordination in 2010 from HUC-JIR, Los Angeles, and received her BA in Philosophy of Religion and Studio Art from Scripps College.

Dan Libenson: Please walk us through the story of Temple Sholom and how you are reimagining what a synagogue is all about. What have you learned about the business of being a synagogue and how to make some really challenging decisions?

Miriam Terlinchamp: When I first saw Temple Sholom, it was dying by every traditional standard. We were half the size that we had been ten years before, or five years before. We were running out of money, and our building, which was 30,000 square feet on six acres, was suffering.

I took the job, and I thought, "All right, I'll be here for a couple years, and we'll see how it goes." We started changing things immediately, and nothing happened—it didn't grow, it didn't do anything. After about three years, I wasn't feeling like we were moving at the pace we needed to move.

Then, I saw a video that my cousin, a filmmaker in Los Angeles, had made for my mother. I said, "I wish we could do that for my synagogue," and he said, "Oh, Miriam, I'll come out there and do it for you." So he came and he tried to research and talk to people and see what our message was. Then he came back to me and said, "Miriam, there's nothing original about you guys."

I told my congregation, "You guys, we have nothing to offer—there's nothing unique about us, except that, basically, we're the nerds on the street. Not the cool nerds. The ones that no one wants to have lunch with." I was like, "We're never going to be the cool ones—but we could be Portlandia. We could change and embrace the weird and be bold with that, and then figure out how to run with that."

My cousin and I ended up making this movie, our first movie, and it was about vision. If you don't have a cheeky sense of humor, you would think it's the lamest thing ever. We cast people who weren't so excited about what was happening in synagogue. We cast them complaining about things. We turned it into this movie, and then we showed it to the congregation at the annual meeting. They had no idea it was coming.

And the end of the movie, the building speaks and says, "I'm your inheritance—sell me." That's how we began the conversation about the possibility of taking the capital from our building and using it to invest in the future.

At that point, 80% of our budget was being spent on infrastructure—and we wanted to flip the percentage within five years. We wanted to grow as a community, in terms of numbers, but also in terms of differences—embrace Portlandia and expand our arms really broadly, not just by putting stickers on the window, but by actively searching out to build a Portlandia in Cincinnati.

Now we're in this place where we've grown 10% every year. We've completely changed our financial model, and our percentages of younger and marginalized members are through the roof.

Dan Libenson: Am I right that the community ultimately decided to sell the building and the land to completely monetize the value of the building?

Miriam Terlinchamp: I was totally uninterested in selling the building and land just to go and buy more building and land. So we sold the building and the land, and we took half the proceeds and put them into an account we couldn't touch, so that it could grow as fast as it could. We put all these protections in place, so if we accessed it before five years, we had some kind of penalty, and at seven years it freed up again.

The other part of the agreement was that we got to spend the other half all the way down in five years. We planned that we were going to take that whole half of the proceeds and invest into the vision. It's pretty high risk.

We built in a failsafe checkpoint at two-and-a-half years so that if we weren't hitting specific measured goals, and it looked like we were bleeding money or something, they could stop the plan, pull the money out, spend it on a building, fire me—all of it. It was a pretty big jump for a congregation to do.

Dan Libenson: Where do the activities of your synagogue take place now?

Miriam Terlinchamp: We are currently in an office park in a suburban area of Cincinnati. The most amazing part of our story, I would say, is that when we moved we lost only 2% of our population. Most stayed with us. I think it's because, once we made the decision, we continued to check in with each other. Our listening campaigns went on cyclically—we were constantly saying, "We're still here, right? We're still here, right?" We're in the middle of the seas, and we're looking for promised land. But it was hard.

I think that we're in this amazing moment in our Jewish world right now where we don't know what's going to happen in the next generation, but we've got the next 20 years where we're moving from this cusp to the next cusp, and it's our job to imagine this moment—not what's going to happen 50 years from now, but just what's happening right now, and what can we do about it.

I find myself saying that over and over again—we're just going to do this. Not for the next generation, either, just for us. Just for the Jews who are here right now—let's just figure out for us, in this moment, and then we'll figure out what's on the other side.

That conversation just seemed to work.

Lex Rofeberg: When you say that you're looking to Portlandia, and to becoming a Portland in Cincinnati, what do you mean by that, and how were you able to start taking steps towards becoming that?

Miriam Terlinchamp: The biggest issue that my congregation faced when I assumed the role as their spiritual leader was that they weren't proud of themselves—they had bad morale about who they were, and so they weren't recruiting anyone, because they didn't like themselves.

Our first marketing effort was internal—why are you here, why are you still here, why do you want others to be here? That survey found that a lot of the people who came to our congregation were people from other parts of our country and world—which is a little unusual in Cincinnati. It turned out that Temple Sholom was a place where, if you weren't from here, you could still belong here, and that our particular niche was belonging . . . being a new tribe, really, for those who had no tribe.

When I say we're like Portlandia, I meant to fully embrace the weird, to celebrate it, and to welcome fellow travelers who are like you. When you come to a service here, there are tattoos, there's piercings, there's a lot of queer folk, different races, economic statuses.

And, we have continued making movies. There was one called "The Way We've Always Done It Demon." If you see the cover of it, it's this guy covered in green—it's super freaky. I was like, "This is Temple Sholom in a nutshell—we just put weird Golom freaky movies out there about change, and it works for us."

It turned out that that was the first one that had 400,000 viewers. I was like, "Man, there's a whole Jewish community of weird people wanting to listen to weird and celebrate that. We're not alone in this—we have a really wide community that wants to hear this message."

Dan Libenson: What you're describing is a new way of organizing Jewish life. I can even imagine that people join your synagogue who are not Reform because they gravitate towards the sense of what this community is about, or they like the vibe—and it's not about Jewish denominational ideology at all. I wonder whether you're on the cusp of discovering through experimentation some new organizing principle for Jewish community?

Miriam Terlinchamp: I'm thankful to my colleagues who are keeping the status quo in a really positive way. Because of them keeping synagogues stable, I am able to experiment in a safe way. If I fail, it's just me—and my community can still go and join other congregations afterwards, they'll still have a Jewish home. But if other synagogues failed, I don't think I'd have the foundation to do it.

That being said, I do think we're working towards something really different. I don't like organized religion, and I don't think that many people my age like it either—the idea of affiliating with an institution. I felt like I had two choices—one is leave institutional Judaism and go fly this flag someplace else, or try to change it from the inside. So that's what we did.

Lex Rofeberg: I want to ask you more about this lack of self-confidence that you found in your community. What would you say to folks who think of their congregations as something they're not proud of? How did you help people identify what is special in your congregation?

Miriam Terlinchamp: I wasn't very nice about it. I said to my community, "No one wants to join us, because no one wants to go on a date with the guy who doesn't have any self-confidence. If you don't think you're cool, then why should I go out with you? You got to go after the greatest looking one over there—you have to believe that you can get that date."

We talked a little bit about that, and I just named it. It's really not fun to be with people who don't think that they're interesting—it's not fun to be with people who don't believe that they're loved, especially when they're sitting in the land of plenty—there's so much going on that should be loved.

I think the confidence thing is not just in our congregations—I think it's a systemic Jewish issue. I run into it with converts a lot. I feel like many Jews are surprised when someone chooses Judaism—they're like, "Why? Why did you want to convert? We have so many freaking holidays, and weird restrictions—why would you want to be part of us?"

So, while most synagogues spend 1% or less of their budget on marketing, we spend closer to 8 to 11%, depending on exactly what we're doing that year, which is more in line with most small businesses.

The first year we focused entirely on internal marketing—trying to raise awareness and being able to sell our vision to ourselves. From there, we started to realize that our message was more universal. At first it was self-serving—we have an online community, and we wanted higher awareness, and we wanted to get some income from the online community. We put out something at High Holidays that was fun, and that year all of our High Holiday needs were paid for by our online community. That was the first time we got a taste of what it could be.

We continue to create somewhere between four and six high-end videos a year, and then lots of small ones internally, because we never let go of the internal stuff—that's always the number one.

We only cast members of our community. Now, people who started out barely able to speak on camera know how to mic up, they understand the takes, they understand lighting. We've upped the ante in terms of being able to articulate ourselves, and deliver messages, and Jewish messages at that. When our members go into other places and speak about us, they understand our mission very clearly, because they've had to do it eight thousand times for the camera.

Dan Libenson: Can you tell us a little bit about where you are now, five years into this process? What it is that you're now doing differently as a synagogue?

Miriam Terlinchamp: The biggest change is that we didn't grow in terms of numbers of people, but the types of people changed. It was like a blood transfusion that happened. Our average age went from upper sixties to closer to the forties.

Financially, we've raised 10% more this year than we did last year and we've doubled our endowment. We had, I think, 10 legacy gifts—maybe a little less than that—and now, this year, I think we have 33.

The first thing that we started to do was change our welcoming. We now do something we call "Shul and Fuel." This would only really work in a liberal environment, but I think it's the most successful thing that we do. Every day after services, we say "Where is the restaurant?" and they pick a local restaurant that's affordable. It's just shul, and then they go to fuel. About 75% of the people who come on Friday nights will go out to dinner together. It's built in engagement, it's built in something that you can do, it's affordable. We did nothing to make it happen, and it's a fun part of the services that people look forward to.

We also changed our entire board structure. The youngest person on our board was 50, and he was the youngest by 10 or so years. So, we moved our board meetings to quarterly, and they're only vision-driven. We got rid of almost all of our committees, and we moved to teams. Now when you ask someone to do something, you create a two- or three-person team and give yourselves one-year assignments. They are all very small, mission-based things that are accomplishable. In the two years since we started that, we flipped the ratio of age and demographics on our board.

Cincinnati is an incredibly great place to be if you're Jewish, and you're a Jewish institution, because we have the Jewish Foundation of Cincinnati here, who has offered seed money to those who are looking to do innovation. A lot of what I have done, almost all of it is because of them.

Lex Rofeberg: I'd love to hear—what does the justice programming that you do look like? What does it look like, for a congregation like yours, to really step up its justice game?

Miriam Terlinchamp: When the uprising started happening in

Ferguson, I was really affected. St. Louis is not that far from Cincinnati. I was obsessed with it, and I couldn't stop watching the news. I was so upset.

I think the call of justice, for the rabbinate, is pretty awful. I wish the call to the rabbinate was improving camp songs or Sunday school, or something within my reach than racial and economic justice for our world. I just wish it was something I could do.

Then the election happened in November. The day after the election, two-thirds of my community reached out to me. I wrote this email to the community, and I was like, "We can't tolerate this. There's so much grief in the world. Everybody show up at the mosque in an hour, and we're going to overflow that place with love." And 60 of my people showed up, and they were there . . . and seven people left my congregation that day. It just continued from there, that there was a group of people who started to join, and a group of people who started to leave.

It took me a while to find a voice of passion, rather than a voice of fire. The next step happened where we declared ourselves a solidarity congregation in the Sanctuary Coalition. A woman named Maribel Diaz was going to be deported—she's a mother of four children and was here illegally. Forty-eight hours after we got the call that she was going to be deported we had 500 people showing up. We had a meeting with our senators, we got our governor to agree—it was incredible. I thought we were going to do it . . . we were on the Rachel Maddow show, we were in the *New York Times*. I was like, "Our voices matter." And then she was deported anyways. I don't think I ever cried as hard as I did in that moment.

I sent another email, but this one was very different than the one I sent in November, and I said, "Okay, let's come together again. All of us who are activists, we need something, too." People showed up from all different faiths. That's when JustLove was born.

Our name is JustLove: A New Way to Belong. Whether you're searching for faith, or God, or religious activism—whatever you're looking for, it probably boils down to finding meaning, relationships, and belonging. We say that we're trying to empower human beings with the knowledge, inspiration, and spiritual support to form meaningful connections for the purpose of furthering justice in our world.

What JustLove does is create a liturgy for social justice—that's what I call it. Someone once told me that it's spiritual sustenance for the resistance—which I like. We create original music, and we have these spiritual gatherings once a month that are led by all different clergy. Then we have small activist groups that are working for systemic change. We've built this body of people who show up regularly—much larger than the group who show up at my Shabbat services—who are from all walks of life, and we're building justice in our community right now.

I think that it's great to do social action project... we're part of a soup kitchen, we work in a shelter—all of those things are incredibly important. But knowing that you can move the dial on systemic change—and to do that from a faith-based perceptive, with a broad range of allies—I think it fuels the spirit.

The team for JustLove is myself, as founder, and then there are three pastors. We do this joke—one is an African American pastor, one is a gay pastor, and one is a white pastor who works in a Hispanic church, and then we also have a friend who is an imam. Together, we sort of are all the clichés put together. Through our little group of friends we've been able to transform one another's perspective and opened our minds, and our language, and our assumptions about what people get in this world, and then translate it back to our own communities.

We found ourselves taking leadership roles in ways that our synagogues and churches couldn't. We serve as arbiters in a lot of places when different justice organizations need help and need support.

Dan Libenson: Lex and I have talked a lot, over the years, about this aspirational belief that if more congregational rabbis were willing to stand up for justice, it would create a great interest in joining the Jewish community. Of course, it would also alienate some people.

The fear of alienating those people and risking that they would leave the congregation prevents many rabbis from doing what, in their hearts, they really would like to do and what would actually attract large numbers of people who now feel that Jewish institutions don't stand for what they stand for.

How have you resolved that fear? You say that you've paid the price. How did you do it?

Miriam Terlinchamp: I talk a lot about my why—not what we're doing, but *why* I'm doing it, why we, as a synagogue, exist in the first place. If it's not for justice, then what is the point—if it's not for shared humanity, then what is the point?

I think that as Jews we've been trained to intellectualize and to think through things and to question . . . but we haven't done a lot of feeling—at least not post-Holocaust—about connecting to God and God's path, and also walking our walk. We're really good at *thinking* our walk and *saying* our walk—but walking our walk is really hard.

I have found that, in my rabbinate, I only want people who want to be here. I want every Jew to have a home, and to feel like they belong—and that might not be with me. I'm a really unique taste, and that's not everyone's taste—so let me help you find a home that works for you.

I think being really honest about the price is important—not just in fewer people or less security, or that you'll get increased hate mail. But also that, once you start doing justice work, everything else starts to feel meaningless unless it's there.

I found for myself that, in order to be present in a moment, I have to be authentic. That sounds so obvious—but it's really hard to walk through the world without that armor of my learning, my books, this is the way I'm supposed to be, but instead to focus on human-to-human connection, asking "what do we need to build, what do we need to risk?"

Shira Stutman

> "At Sixth & I, we try to bring in anyone who wants to make Judaism of use to them."

Spreading the Good (Jewish) News

When we recorded our conversation, Shira Stutman was the senior rabbi at the Sixth... Historic Synagogue in Washington, DC. Sixth... is housed within a building that was once fully a synagogue as we understand it, but that is now a center for arts, entertainment, and ideas, as well as a synagogue that reimagines how religion and community can enhance people's everyday lives.

At the time of publication, as founder of Mixed Multitudes, an organization that exposes diverse groups of Jews and fellow travelers to the beauty and power of Jewish life, tradition, and conversation, Shira Stutman currently works on a variety of projects including co-hosting the "Chutzpod!" podcast in which she provides Jewish answers to life's contemporary questions and helps listeners build lives of meaning. She also serves as interim rabbi at the Aspen Jewish Congregation. Stutman was named one of "America's Most Inspiring Rabbis" by *The Forward* and a T'ruah Rabbinic Human Rights Hero. She graduated from Columbia University and received rabbinic ordination from the Reconstructionist Rabbinical College, where she was a Wexner Graduate Fellow.

Dan Libenson: Please tell us a little bit about what Sixth... Historic Synagogue is all about, and what it means to be the senior rabbi there.

Shira Stutman: Sixth... is a unique place in American Jewish life. I know the word "unique" is quite overused nowadays, but I'm using it on purpose. We are, in part, a secular arts and culture center, meaning that we have book talks and concerts and podcast recordings and comedy shows. Some of the performers are Jewish artists, but our secular programming is all open to the general community. The second part of what we do is, in a way, the more experimental part: We are a spiritual community for people in their twenties and thirties without kids.

What we are trying to do is create community for people at a certain stage of life, with the understanding that they won't be able to stay at Sixth... forever. We don't have kids programming, by and large, we don't have a Hebrew school, we don't do bar or bat mitzvahs. We are really trying to engage the millennials, or people in their early adulthood stage of life, in understanding what it means to live a full and vibrant and substantive Jewish life—with the hope that one day they will take what they have learned and bring it to the wider Jewish community.

Dan Libenson: Can you tell us a little bit about the history of Sixth and I? How did this unique combination happen?

Shira Stutman: The building was constructed in 1902 as the second home for Adas Israel, which is the largest Conservative synagogue in DC today. When Adas Israel moved to upper northwest DC, the building was sold to Turner Memorial AME Church. Then, after about fifty-five years, the church parishioners started to move out to the 'burbs, so Turner Memorial wanted to sell the building, but they couldn't find anyone to purchase it.

Finally, in 2002 or 2003, the building went under contract with nightclub owners. It was going to become a nightclub. Then, three Jewish philanthropists in DC found out about this deal, and they decided that this building that was once a synagogue, and then a church, could not become a nightclub—however sacred a night of dancing at a nightclub could be. They decided to buy it with literally no idea what they were going to do with it.

They pulled together some young Washingtonians in a focus group, and they said, "What should we do with this building?" Out of that conversation—and a few other conversations—came this idea of creating a space where young professionals could go to meet other Jewish young professionals.

Now, this was 15 years ago—there was no Birthright Israel NEXT, there was no Moishe House, there was no OneTable. All of these things that now are part of the everyday life of a young professional in Jewish America weren't even around. Sixth... was one of the first organizations in DC specifically to really want to engage Jewish young professionals, help them be together, help them get to know each other and get to know themselves and their own heritage and history and people.

I would like to tell you, for the purposes of this podcast and posterity, that we were incredibly strategic about Sixth... and how we grew it. But honestly for those first years, we really spent a lot of time figuring out what type of programming to do by actually doing it. Sixth & I—especially the original staff—had a tremendously high tolerance for failure. Instead of spending hours and days and weeks and years planning out a certain program, we would just try it. If it didn't work, we wouldn't do it again—or we would cancel it before it even happened. By doing that, we were able to really develop a track record of experimentation. We didn't have as many misses as we could have, and we had a lot of really successful programming.

There were two different reasons that the secular programming started. One, if I'm being totally honest, was the desire to—as one of our founding donors would say—"get butts in seats." He's a real estate guy, so he would think how much of a week, in a given synagogue, the whole synagogue sits empty. If you think about a sanctuary in your average 20th century huge synagogue, how often is that sanctuary filled? Yom Kippur and Rosh Hashanah is basically it. His real estate brain couldn't wrap his head around it. He just wanted to get butts in seats as often as possible. I would say it in a more spiritual way than he ever would, but the idea is that the more people you have, the more energy you have; the more energy you have, the more people it will bring in.

The second reason for the secular programming is that we bring in people for Jewish programming because they came for the secular programming. Someone who is partnered with a Jew or is Jewish themselves or has Jewish heritage might come for the first time and say, "Oh, well, if Melinda Gates was here for her book talk, or Karamo Brown from Queer Eye for the Straight Guy was here, then this is a safe place for me. Maybe I'll come back to check out Jewish life." That's really how Sixth... was born and how it continued to grow.

Dan Libenson: Do you think this could be a model for many other cities? What might the obstacles and barriers be that could prevent something like this from happening in every city?

Shira Stutman: First of all, there is something unusual about Washington. You have so many young people, so many of whom are Jewish or Jewishly connected. DC is also more compact than New York or Los Angeles. I don't think that an organization just for young professionals would work the same way, necessarily, in Peoria. Also, the economic engine of DC, for better or for worse, is not going anywhere—people are going to be cycling in, working in NGOs or on the Hill, and then cycling out.

Another one of the answers is that Sixth... had to break a lot of eggs to get to where it is today. The original team that Esther Safran-Foer—one of our founding executive directors—brought together just weren't interested in playing by the Jewish communal rules. They didn't even know them. So, part of the reason Sixth... was able to grow so quickly was because it happened outside of the established Jewish framework. Sixth... was able to build and grow really quickly, because they didn't take Federation money.

I don't think the model of having all young professionals is a necessary model in every single city, but I do think that it is critically important for people in their twenties and early thirties to have community with other people who are in a similar stage of life. If you are in a city where there are five or six synagogues, each of which has 15 or 20 or 30 people or even 50 or 75 people in their different young professional groups at each of these different synagogues, that strikes me as problematic. It would be more beneficial to the young professionals themselves to get them all together in one space, even if it was to the detriment of the individual synagogues.

One of the critiques of Sixth... when it first started was that we were taking the 10 people from synagogue A and the 12 people from synagogue B and bringing them together with another 300 people that wouldn't have gone to synagogue in the first place. The synagogues felt that we were taking their people and their next generation. I understand where the synagogues were coming from, but I still think when we're talking about what's good for the Jews writ large, it's better to have young people be with other young people.

We say, when kids go off to college at the age of 18, that they're now adults. But that's often factually inaccurate. A lot of young people only really start living as adults when they graduate college and enter the working world, and the challenges of that life stage can be quite significant. Everything from tremendous loneliness to a moment of trying to figure out who they really want to be, as separate from being part of some sort of educational institution or their family of origin. Being able to be around other people who are in their same age and stage—not just two of them, but 200 of them—can really help young people figure out who they want to be as adults in this world.

Lex Rofeberg: When I was a summer intern in DC, I went to Sixth... three different Fridays and I found a thoroughly different service each time. One of them was a Reform-style service, one was more Conservative, one was a renewal-fusion situation. There were three totally different things.

I'm curious about the basic presumption that a synagogue can do that—be a different thing each week and draw super-different crowds for each. What's the rhythm like at Sixth & I?

Shira Stutman: What you're talking about is part of the magic and the challenge that is Sixth & I. At base of the religious programming part of our work we are a *kiruv* organization—we are an outreach organization. Our goal is to bring people closer to Jewish practice, because we believe that Judaism is a meaning-making technology that can actually help people lead more meaningful lives. What we don't presume is that we know for every single person what will help bring them closer to Jewish living and Jewish life. It's not up to me to decide what kind of davening or service is right for you. What's up to me is to help try to connect you to God, to people, to yourself, and then to offer a bunch of different inroads for doing it.

With that in mind—every single week at Sixth & I, we will have one or two different Shabbat services going on, and they're radically different. The first Friday night of the month, we have an Orthodox service. The second Friday night of the month is the service that I lead. It's actually a Reconstructionist service, but because, unfortunately, the majority of American Jews don't know what Reconstructionism is, we call it the Jewish summer camp-style service. The third Friday night, we have a Conservative service, in that we do all the Friday night prayers—but it's very soulful, with the instruments and a lot of a lot of singing. The fourth Friday night we have an old-school Conservative service with no instruments—with a guitar, but fewer instruments. The fifth Friday night, when we have one, we have a Jewish Renewal service. So, depending on which Friday night you attend, it can have a very different taste and a very different feel.

A downside of our multiple different services is that you can sometimes lose the ongoing feeling of home—the sense that you can show up to your synagogue any time you want and you know exactly the comfort food you're going to be served. We don't have that at Sixth & I. But what we do have is the ability to really see the diversity of American Jewish life all in one space.

In a perfect world, one day you'll get to come to Sixth… and instead of having a different service every Friday night, we'll have three or four services going on simultaneously so that you could choose. We're just not big enough yet.

Lex Rofeberg: Sixth… as a building is obviously really important to your identity—your location is even your name. What does having a building do for your organization? What does it allow you to achieve and what are some of the challenges of it?

Shira Stutman: We are a very building-centric organization. Part of the reason for that is because so many of the young professionals we're working with are living far away from what they would call "home."

Their home is in DC, but they are from somewhere else. The synagogue serves as this wonderful third space for them that is a home away from home. There is something about always knowing where services are, always knowing where classes are, always knowing where they can go that they will be anchored and feel like they are at home.

There's also something about the feeling that we are evangelizers. One of the things that Shelton Zuckerman, our board chair, says a lot is "We can't get them here the second time unless we get them here the first time." The first time they come for something secular—and then, God-willing, they'll come back again. And, if you come to Sixth... for the first time to hear a comedian, or hear Jill Biden talk about her book, you've already sat there and laughed—you've already sat there and heard. So you're coming back into a space where you already feel comfortable.

One of the things we always say about our target group for the religious programming at Sixth & I, is that if you know what the phrase *kehillah kedoshah* means, Sixth... is not your place. *Kehillah kedoshah* means a holy community, and if *kehillah kedoshah* is something you are reflexively searching for when you move to DC, we'd love to have you, but you are not our target demographic. Our target demographic are people who never have stepped foot in a synagogue since they were bar mitzvahed, or they have one Jewish grandparent, or they are partnered with a Jew.

Dan Libenson: I'd love to explore the distinction that you're making between secular events and religious events. Are there ways of understanding what we often call secular as also deeply Jewish in some fashion? Is this possibly an artificial distinction? And, in this time of transition and reimagination of Judaism, how is the process of connecting people to Judaism as a meaning-making technology intertwined with this process of figuring out what Judaism even is, or what it ought to be?

Shira Stutman: First of all—one of the things we know in the 21st century is that binaries are outdated. Even if we go back to the Talmud, the rabbis also would say, "Something is kosher or it's not kosher—except sometimes...." "Someone is a man or a woman—except sometimes...." This idea of binaries—forget it.

So yes, this idea that the secular part of Sixth... is entirely separated from the religious part is somewhat facile, it's not true. There was this great *This American Life* episode in which Ira Glass was talking to one of his parents' friends from Baltimore. The friend was trying to convince Ira that *This American Life* was an intensely Jewish podcast. Ira Glass was like, "No. There's nothing Jewish about it." The guy was like, "You're an idiot. The whole thing is about people telling stories—this is so Jewish."

I do feel that about a lot of our what I will call, in quotes again, "secular programming." It's incredibly Jewish in that we have ideas being thrown around the room almost every single night of the week. We have boundaries being pushed—more often than I, as the rabbi, would like here at Sixth & I. We have justice-seeking people talking about their work. What can be more Jewish than that? To a great extent, whether the person on the bimah identifies as Jewish or not, what we do at Sixth... is incredibly Jewish.

And, there are these exquisite moments, like when Idina Menzel—the singer—got up to do a concert at Sixth & I, and started by singing her haftarah from her bat mitzvah. Or Karamo Brown from Queer Eye. He spent, I would say, 20% of the evening talking about how meaningful it was for him, as someone who grew up in a religious environment where he couldn't be out and gay, to be in another religious environment being able to be out and proud. That's not entirely secular, or Jewish, that's everything all at once. That is really when the magic of Sixth... hits.

And this "everything all at once" idea leads to the second part of what you were saying, this idea of Judaism being a meaning-making technology. All you have to do is open any code of Jewish law to know that Judaism was never meant to be lived just in the home, or just in the synagogue—it was meant to be lived with every single breath you take.

If you take the sparks of holiness from most faith traditions—I happen to know Judaism, it happens to be my technology—it can help elevate in holiness all of your daily acts, from the way that you commute in the morning and how you treat the people that you see when you're waiting at the bus stop to whether or not you compost or recycle or the ways that you eat, to the way that you behave in the office or in your business practices.

It's not only Jews who get to use this technology. In the 21st century, especially at Sixth & I—and many other synagogues as well—I assume that a full third of people who call themselves our congregants are not even Jewish. Shabbat is open to everyone. Eating ethically is open to everyone. Tzedakah is open to everyone. Again, with the bifurcation into Jew and non-Jew, a lot of what we do as Jews is something that really is open to anyone. At Sixth & I, we try to bring in anyone who wants to make it of use to them. Then, of course, God willing, it will ripple out to the world.

Lex Rofeberg: Let's talk a little more about evangelizing. You've talked about *kiruv*, often translated as outreach, but which also means bringing people near to something. What are you bringing people near to?

Shira Stutman: I think the question of what we are [working to bring people closer to] is the critical question. Is my goal that everyone ends up with two sets of dishes? When I say we are doing kiruv work, I understand the implication in the broader Jewish world of about kiruv and what evangelizing means. I'm using it both seriously and a little bit flippantly as well.

We see our primary goal as welcoming people in, no matter who you are—whether or not you're a Zionist, whether or not you're going to circumcise your child, whether or not you eat pork on Yom Kippur and call it Shabbos. Whoever you are, we want to welcome you in. We want to help bring you closer, in a way that we all need, to holiness in this world. That's what I want for myself, too. I'm a rabbi—I have a tremendous amount of work to do to be being brought closer to holiness in this world.

The research on conversion in America right now is quite astounding. Depending on who you read and how you read it, between 24 and 43% of all Americans will convert to another religion in their lifetime. Sometimes they're talking about going from Methodist to Presbyterian, which is obviously a little bit different than going from Methodist to Jewish. But the idea that you can take on a new religious identity and religious tradition over the course of a lifetime is not something that is foreign to a surprisingly high number of Americans.

With that in mind, when we talk about evangelizing, or doing outreach to people, our goal is to work with people who are Jewish or have Jewish heritage, or are not Jewish at all.

Thank God, we don't have to stand out on street corners. Thank God I don't believe that non-Jews are going to hell. There's not that extra pressure on us. But I do believe that Judaism has something to teach and to add to the world. I do believe that this world could be a more beautiful place if more people adhered to the traditions.

With that in mind, at Sixth… we actually do a lot of conversion work. We can only fit around 45 people a year into our conversion class, but at this point we already have a waiting list of well over 300 people for our conversion class that starts in September—and that was as of March of this past year. That's without ever advertising our class. People are searching for religious sustenance, and many of them think they might be able to find it in Judaism. Our job is to take those people and welcome them in if this is right for them.

Dan Libenson: Strategically, I wonder what it would look like to have a network of organizations that was collectively able to create a path for people. Each organization could specialize in a particular age, or a particular area of interest. Organizations who are successful because they're doing an amazing job of working with one particular niche, whether that's an age demographic, or people who love the outdoors, or whatever it might be could be spared the pressure they now get from funders to grow or to scale or to change their mission. What would it look like to have some larger-scale, networked view of the possibilities?

Shira Stutman: We've been thinking about this a lot. We are very lucky in Washington in that we have a number of really extraordinary synagogues in the city. That's helpful to us at Sixth & I, because even when we are transitioning or trying to help people transition, we're transitioning them to some of the best synagogues in the country—and they just happen to be in the city itself.

We are playing with dozens of dozens of different ideas, because, as I said, this really is a unique experiment of bringing people in, teaching them about *kehillah kedoshah,* and then sending the people out. Other synagogues can't believe that we consider our greatest goal when we get an email from someone that they're joining Temple Sinai, or they're joining Temple Micah. But we have the next group of young adults who are coming in for the summer internship and then coming back, and we have to be ready for them.

Lex Rofeberg: I love the idea that Sixth & I's success would be measured by whether the people who cross your path end up interacting with meaningful Jewishness in the future. Could you say more about the metrics you are using?

Shira Stutman: I'll begin with some of the challenges. One of the challenges is that it's much easier to measure Sixth & I's success by saying how many people come a year, how many people come more than once, how many people become donors. It's more of a challenge to measure how someone behaves a few years out. Remember, our substantive religious programming is only about 10 years old. A lot of our families are only starting to get to the place where we would want to see where they are, and what Jewish life looks like for them.

I guess part of our gamble is that we are only one part of a much larger ecosystem. Our job is to really help carry and love and educate and stand with young professionals in a certain stage of life—and then it will be someone else's job, God-willing, to take them for the next stage of their life.

Think about the average experience of the average 30-year-old who steps into the average synagogue, even very successful ones, on a Shabbat morning or a Friday night. Whenever we have people who are trying out the next place—and especially when we were first experimenting with this—at first they would come back to Sixth & I, and I would say, "How was it to go to Shir Tikvah?" I said, "Did anyone talk to you?" To a person, what the young people would say is the same thing—they'd say, "Oh, yeah, everyone talked to me. Every single person there came up to me and said, 'Hello. We're so excited to have a young person here. Who are you? Where are you from? Do I know your aunt? Do I know your uncle?'" They'd play Jewish geography. First we thought no one would talk to them—but instead, every synagogue is desperate for these young people.

I do think that if more synagogues focused on their core groups, whether it's young families... or, God forbid, if a few of them would just focus on baby boomers, which is an extraordinarily large contingent of Jews who also, turns out, still need their own spiritual sustenance—then we really could have a vibrant community.

Lex Rofeberg: Does Sixth... have a membership model?

Shira Stutman: Sixth... really capitalized on the idea of changing the business model of what it means to be part of a synagogue. Yes, we rely on donors, like a lot of synagogues do, and we rely heavily on donors, like a lot of Hillels do. But we also rely on earned income. There is no membership at Sixth & I—you can't become a member. You can become a monthly donor, and we would love your money—don't get me wrong—but you can't become a member.

We make money off of our book talks. We make a little money off of our concerts. We don't lose as much money as some places do off of our religious programming. If you want to come to services, services tend to be free—not always, but usually. But if you want to come to dinner after, or kiddush after, you have to pay. If you want to come to a class, you have to pay.

We are trying to change a little bit of the conversation of what does it mean to pay into a system. It's a little bit more American than I would like—I do feel like the Jewish model is more about paying into the system, not just to the things you're actually partaking of yourself—but it does help us keep Sixth... alive and afloat and nimble. We are able to make changes if we see that we are doing things that are not relevant to the community.

Lex Rofeberg: What would you say to listeners who hear about an organization like Sixth & I, and the main takeaway will be, "Ugh, I don't have that where I'm listening—I wish I had that. Bummer." What would you suggest to them?

Shira Stutman: We get this question at Sixth... all the time. "Oh, if we had Sixth... in my city, I'd go to synagogue." I'm like, "Yeah, okay."

Here are the things that anyone could have. Anyone could create an authentically welcoming environment. Any synagogue—from Jackson, Mississippi, to Washington—could be a synagogue where there are some people who are "Israel, right and wrong," and some people who don't believe that Israel needs to be a state for the Jews. We might choose not to do that—but anyone could do that.

Any synagogue can be a space where you feel welcomed in whether or not you're Jewish, whether you're partnered with a Jew or not. Any synagogue can be that sort of space. Anyone could have a synagogue where they have couples like one of the Sixth... couples that had a bristism for their child (that's a combination of a bris and a baptism). Maybe they wouldn't hold the bristism on the bimah during Shabbos services—but that the couple could still feel that their synagogue is their home. Any synagogue, any community in America could do that. Some might choose not to for really good reasons, again, but it's possible. Any synagogue could have workshops for interfaith couples, like we do. Any synagogue could have a vibrant conversion class.

Any synagogue could have services that make people cry and laugh and dance and actually feel something. When we are planning our services at Sixth & I, we think about every single minute of the service. Any synagogue could do that if the clergy and the congregants cared to.

Any synagogue can be a place where you can have secular conversations in addition to the Jewish ones.

When people bemoan the lack of a Sixth... in their city, saying, "Oh, I wish someone else would create this. I wish someone else would do this." I say, it's not someone else—it's you. You're the one. You'll do it.

Dan Libenson: I have a two-part question for you. One is, what do we need to do in order to get Judaism to a place where it believes so strongly that it is good and worthy that it is open to sharing Judaism with everyone? And the second is, what do you think are the unmet needs of young adults in DC that seem to be driving them to take an interest in Judaism? What is it that they're finding in Judaism that they're needing? I think maybe in the connection between those two questions we'll find an agenda for some of the work that we need to be doing in Judaism.

Shira Stutman: I haven't talked at all about my deep and abiding and ongoing love for non-Jewish partners. I understand the challenges of intermarriage—I really do. I've read every single piece of research, and I know that it's complicated. There are six kids in my family system, and I'm the only one married to someone Jewish. So, it's personal for me, but it's also in my professional life. I think non-Jewish partners are one of the greatest blessings to liberal American Jews, because they're the ones who remind us that Judaism is that good.

A lot of Jews don't realize the beauty that is part of our tradition. Some of it is our own internalized antisemitism and our own sense of trauma. Some of it is that the average Jew in the pew shows up, at best, only for Rosh Hashanah and Yom Kippur—so they get one type of theology, and it's not the most welcoming in of all the Jewish theologies that we have out there. Their experience of good Judaism is almost entirely nostalgia-based.

They don't have any experience of what a lived Jewish life can be until they start dating this non-Jew, and they say to the non-Jew, "Look, I want to have Jewish kids." And the non-Jew might say, "If there's no beauty in Judaism, then I'm going to raise my kid nominally whatever. Why should we raise our kids Jewish?" And then the conversation can really begin about what does make Judaism beautiful—where are the pieces that can be additive to anyone's life?

Our converts who are single tell amazing stories about their first dates with Jews. The born Jew is like, "Why would you want to be Jewish? Why did you convert? That's so ridiculous. How could you want to be Jewish?" The convert has to then spend their whole time defending this choice. It's so crazy—and totally unsurprising to me. The average American Jew doesn't understand that Judaism is not just about oppression and Holocaust—it's also about beauty and joy and vulnerability. One of the things converts and non-Jewish partners do is force the question in a really important way.

Which brings me to the second question you were asking—what is it that young professionals specifically need and want from Judaism? There is a tremendous amount of loneliness in DC. People in Washington are very busy from the second they wake up. They take a run, they walk the dog, they do their yoga, they go to work, they work twelve hours, they go to a networking event. They don't get home until 11:30 at night. But in between, there's no place that they ever went deep. There's no place that they ever sat with someone and just stared into their eyes.

What we're able to do at Sixth... is we're able to provide a space for Jewish practice that our people can lean against, like a tree, and be quiet for just a second and know that they will be loved no matter what. The 20s and 30s, for many people—not for everyone—is a time when they are looking for and then finding a life partner. There's a tremendous amount of identity formation and growth that happens during this time period. When people imagine what their life partner is going to be, they imagine someone basically exactly like them. Then you actually find the person, and you realize there's always a lot of work to be done. There are a lot of questions about what is our life going to look like together. One of the things we help do is help couples figure out what it means to choose to be together.

I'll say one last thing about the needs of young professionals. Some people, of course, have family systems that are functional and that they can lean against when they need it. But sometimes, in DC, either those family systems are very far away, or they really aren't as functional or functional in the way that you want them to be. One of the things we're able to do at Sixth... is create an extended family for a lot of people who can be siblings and cousins and advisors to each other, and help each other along.

Lex Rofeberg: Do you have regular gatherings or spaces that are majority not Jews, or draw large numbers of folks who are not Jewish and not partners of Jews? How do you work with people who are adjacent to Judaism in some other way?

Shira Stutman: Anytime I lead a service, I assume that a number of people are not Jewish. Not only people who are partnered with Jews, but people who came in off the street or who are interested in Judaism or who are interested in spirituality. I hear, "Well, I work a few blocks away so I thought I'd..." and we have a number of people who grew up Catholic and are looking for another faith tradition. And, of course, sometimes we have people who are practicing multiple faiths at the same time, which is a whole other ball of wax.

Judaism has something to offer to this world, and we are living in such a 21st century syncretic open-minded time, in which Jews are the most-liked religion in America right now according to the Pew Forum. Now, that's a little bit complicated, but in general, the Jews are the most-liked religion in America. I'll just take that statistic. People are interested in Judaism—even people who are not Jewish themselves.

Dan Libenson: Could you reflect a bit on how you work with finding a balance between knowing that we have to be extremely adventurous, and yet also knowing that it is so valuable to emphasize our connection to the past?

Shira Stutman: Throughout all of Jewish history, what the Jews have done in every place we've lived is we've taken from the cultures that we are part of, and we bring what we learn to Judaism, to Torah, and to the thread of Jewish teaching and learning that goes all the way back to Sinai.

We have a bunch of one-liners that we use at Sixth & I, and one of them is, "The Torah can take it." What we mean by that is that moment when you take the Torah out of the ark and you're holding it, and everyone's like, "Don't drop it, don't drop it." We're much more careful with our Torahs than we are with our infants, in this way that is at once beautiful, but also kind of problematic.

The Torah—and by this I mean Torah with a capital T and a lower-case-t—has endured for thousands of years, because Jewish tradition and teaching has, at its core, teachings about justice, about holiness, about compassion, about community that are True, with a capital-T, at their core. The Judaism that we are teaching is the same Judaism that has always existed, with some American touches added on. They're really additive—they don't take away.

I'll give you a story about what we did last year the evening of Yom Kippur. One of the things that happens on the opening of Yom Kippur is we say this prayer called Kol Nidre, and we repeat it three times—which is very good, because I had this idea. What happens is you take the Torahs out of the ark, and someone is holding them on the bimah, on the pulpit, while we're saying this Kol Nidre prayer.

I was thinking to myself, Okay, so we have this line at Sixth... that's called "the Torah can take it." What does it mean that the Torah can take it? What does it mean physically? We are an embodied people. We go into the mikveh to convert, we eat matzah, we sit in the sukkah, we do ... everything we do, we try to do with our spirits, we do with our bodies. I think, How can we embody this idea that the Torah is so strong and enduring that we can bring to it all of the beauty and challenges of the messy, chaotic American Jewish community, and it can only be additive?

I decided at that moment that, after we finished the Kol Nidre prayer, instead of putting the Torah back in the ark, we were just going to pass it around the room. We were going to pass it from person to person to person for the rest of the night. What's the worst thing that happens? The worst thing that happens is someone drops it. Then we figure that out—we figure it out next. Over the course of the rest of the evening, it just got passed around the room, and people held it, and some cried, and some couldn't get rid of it fast enough, and some people were uncomfortable, and some people it was the first time they had ever held the Torah, and some people were Jewish, and some people were not, and some people ran out to get a tallis, and some didn't.

It was such a perfect encapsulation of what we're trying to do at Sixth & I—and God willing, in 21st century Judaism—which is give Torah to the people. Trust the people that they can take the teachings and the learning of Torah and use it to build meaning in their lives. And that, when the time is right, they'll also give Torah back to us. The Torah can take it—and so can we.

Denise Handlarski

> *"I think a lot of folks are going to get something from their in-person communities and are going to get a lot from digital communities, and there's no reason why we should have to choose or feel like one is a threat to the other."*

Secularsynagogue.com

Denise Handlarksi is the founder of SecularSynagogue.com, an online community for those looking for meaningful cultural Jewish learning and experiences. When we spoke on the podcast, she was also the rabbi of Oraynu, a Secular Humanistic congregation in Toronto, Ontario, Canada. She also serves as a Jewish doula, helping to bring Jewish spirituality into pregnancy and birth.

In addition to her work in the Jewish community, Handlarski is also a Professor at Trent University's School of Education. Denise Handlarski received rabbinic ordination from the International Institute for Secular Humanistic Judaism and holds a Ph.D. in English Literature from York University.

Dan Libenson: Tell us a little bit about what SecularSynagogue.com is, when it came about, and what you're trying to achieve there.

Denise Handlarski: The vision for SecularSynagogue.com is to merge what goes on in Secular or Humanistic Jewish communities and to do it online. There are Jews everywhere who are not finding spaces that meet their needs—they're in smaller communities, they're in places where Jewish life tends to run a little more conservative, or just places where they haven't found a community that's a fit for them. I thought, why not bring the great things about communal life, learning, practice, ritual, community, all of that good stuff, into the digital sphere to connect those Jews who aren't being served.

There is, I think, a deep desire to connect to the Jewish world, and in a lot of the organized Jewish world, the way you connect is through synagogues. If you're someone like me, who is a secular Jew and a very involved Jew—I practice Judaism daily—I felt always excluded from a synagogue space, because the main thing that goes on there is a prayer service.

Dan Libenson: When you say, "I practice Judaism daily," can you give us a little bit of a flavor of what that practice is, what Jewish things that you do that you think of as a practice? And, how are you building communal organization around those things in your local congregation and on SecularSynagogue.com?

Denise Handlarski: There's an interesting dynamic that informs a lot of my work, where what has been termed Jewish practice has very often been defined through a religious lens or a religious experience. Lots of us have been told if we're not keeping kosher, or if we're not doing daily prayer, then we're not practicing Judaism the right way.

That drives me bananas, frankly. I think there are lots and lots of ways to practice Judaism. Often the secular cultural Jews have internalized that narrative, so we ourselves don't think we're practicing Judaism when we may be. In my daily life, some of the things I do are I read Jewish media, I talk about topics of interest to Jewish communities. This morning, I was part of a meeting on combatting antisemitism and white supremacist movements more broadly. I see that as Jewish practice. I read Jewish children's books to my kids. We sing Jewish songs. I personally have a weekly Shabbat practice—not everybody does. I see Judaism as informing a lot of my daily life, and it doesn't have to be prayer for it to be serious, meaningful Judaism.

The community I serve in Toronto is called the Oraynu Congregation for Humanistic Judaism which is an affiliate of the Humanistic Jewish movement. We get together for services that don't look like traditional prayer services. We have creative liturgy that is earth-centered and human centered, beautiful, moving, meaningful poetry, music, readings, meditations. We do that together around Shabbat or around holidays. We have all kinds of other programming going on—speakers, social events, cultural programming like plays. All of that I see as Jewish practice that we can do together.

In the digital space, we have the opportunity to get together more often. In my community in Toronto, when we get together in person, the logistics of the busy-ness of life and space and all that kind of stuff, we tend to have a program about every two weeks. I'm interacting with congregants one-on-one sometimes, but truthfully, there will be moments where weeks go by before I will interact with a congregant, and sometimes longer.

What I notice about SecularSynagogue.com is that we're not getting together in person, but we're hanging out every day—there's conversation going every single day. The intimacy that you get in an in-person interaction might be different than the intimacy you get in digital interactions, but they're both special and meaningful in their own way.

Dan Libenson: Can you describe a little bit about how SecularSynagogue.com works? I join it, and what happens to me?

Denise Handlarski: When you join, a few things happen. You get access to a part of the SecularSynagogue.com website which is for members, and on there there's stuff like "Run a DIY Shabbat." In that file there's information about some secular blessings that a lot of people have never had the opportunity to learn. There are suggestions for readings and practices and things you can do. There are parenting resources. There's fun stuff like have a scavenger hunt where you live to discover the Jewish history of the place. A bunch of different resources.

The main platform of the group is a closed Facebook group. I am not sure it will always be Facebook, but for now, that seems to be the platform that works best for folks, in terms of where we are anyway and where we're used to having some of these conversations.

Sometimes people have said to me, "Why would I pay for access to a Facebook group when there's so many Facebook groups to access for free?" To answer that question, I would say what you're paying for is access to a community. Unlike Facebook groups that are not membership-based, where people drop in and out, this feels to me more like a community. We know each other. We share more personal stuff than, perhaps, goes on in other kinds of Facebook groups which have a more public face. We offer each other real support—sometimes people put out there, "I'm struggling with mental health," or, "This is an issue that's going on in my marriage." We're offering each other real, meaningful communal support in addition to doing Jewish learning and Torah study and mitzvah Mondays and all different kinds of stuff together.

Lex Rofeberg: What have you noticed about the differences between the in-person synagogue and the digital synagogue experience?

Denise Handlarski: When I started SecularSynagogue.com, I launched it to coincide with the Rosh Hashana-Yom Kippur period. It was amazing to see the beautiful, meaningful, and intimate connections that formed in a pretty short time. I would argue that takes longer, sometimes, in the in-person communities where people are getting together less often.

The fact that we're seeing each other every day adds something that you don't necessarily get in many congregations. I know there will be some people who say, "I go to my Orthodox synagogue every day," but I serve secular folks who usually don't go to their spaces every single day. I think that the immediacy where digital Judaism can reach you is very positive.

Also, sometimes when you are in a traditional synagogue and you don't know or understand something, you might be inclined to feel like an outsider or pressured to have to pretend I know something you don't. In SecularSynagogue.com, I can see all the conversations that go on and I wouldn't let somebody feel that they didn't know something. Every time somebody says a term in Hebrew or mentions something, a Jewish idea—even if it's something that I assume many people know, like "tzedakah," I'll always gloss it. I'll always explain what it is just so that people don't feel like they have to do that work on their own.

I never want people to feel left out of conversations. As the leader in a digital space, I can better ensure that everybody feels like they have the opportunity to come along with whatever conversation is going on.

What I found with SecularSynagogue.com is a bunch of people who joined it are also members of in-person communities—and so am I. I don't think it has to be an either/or situation at all. I think a lot of folks are going to get something from their in-person communities, and are going to get a lot from digital communities, and there's no reason why we should have to choose or feel like one is a threat to the other. Ideally, they complement each other.

Dan Libenson: Can you help us understand what folks in the world of Secular Humanistic Judaism mean when they say "humanistic"?

Denise Handlarski: Historically, Secular Judaism, as a movement, really came from the secular Yiddishists that we think of as being foundational in creating North American Jewry, from Ashkenaz, in the early 20th century. They were very anti-religion, very anti-hierarchy. They were rejecting anything that seemed like religious Judaism, or structural Judaism. They had no use for anything that would be called synagogue or rabbi. If you suggested they do some Torah study, they'd be like, "Why would we possibly want to do something like that?" And yet, they were deeply Jewish. They started *The Forward*. They educated their kids Jewishly. There were things that were very important for them to retain in terms of Jewish identity, culture, and language.

Humanistic Judaism was started by Rabbi Sherwin Wine about fifty years ago. It came from a more religious viewpoint—not that the philosophy of Humanistic Judaism is religious, but the structures are more familiar to those who come from a religious space. Sherwin Wine was ordained in the Reform Movement. He was used to a synagogue space, he was used to something called services, he was used to celebrating all of the Jewish holidays, even if we were celebrating them in a different way. The Humanistic Jewish movement is more like that—it has rabbis, might do text study, might look, in some ways, more traditional. But the content of what we do tends to be rather untraditional—we create our own liturgy.

What I would say now is that the differences between these two strands matter much less than our commonalities. I think what we're trying to do, in any of those communities, is create meaningful, beautiful Judaism for folks who are secular and cultural Jews. Whether you like to use the word humanistic or you don't, what you're doing is probably pretty similar.

And, what counts now is what are we actually doing in our spaces together. If what we're doing is serving us, making our lives better and making us better forces for good in the world, then that counts much more than what we call our movement or what the history of our movement might be.

Dan Libenson: When you say, "I practice Judaism every day," it feels to me like the quest is to find a Judaism that can be practiced every day by people who don't believe in some of the premises that they've been taught and who might have felt excluded because of that. I'm curious whether you feel like doing SecularSynagogue.com is giving you a new insight on some of that?

Denise Handlarski: When a lot of us folks would go to spaces—whether they were synagogues, or whether they were JCCs or youth groups or camp, or whatever—and say things like, "I'm Jewish, but I don't believe in God," we were told, "You're not a real Jew—secular Judaism isn't real." When you're dismissed like that, you do tend to disengage. It shouldn't be surprising that a lot of secular folks were like, "There's no place in Judaism for someone like me."

The movement of Humanistic Judaism and the secular Jewish groups that are around have been very good for creating spaces for those folks who felt excluded elsewhere. But I don't want Judaism, moving forward, to be a reaction to exclusion. Frankly, I'm over it. If you don't think I'm a real Jew, I don't care. I think a lot of people are with me, that we're done with the judgement.

I pitched SecularSynagogue.com—and I really believe this in my heart—as a co-created community. That's, I think, what people like about it. When people say, "We should have a digital seder," I'm like, "Amazing idea." I would have never thought that we should have a digital seder—but of course we should. We'll work together on a

Haggadah, we'll each make our own little seder plate, and at home, we'll dip the parsley together. That's so beautiful and enriching, and something that came out of the community—not from me.

Although I see myself as a rabbi affiliated with the Humanistic Jewish movement, SecularSynagogue.com is independent. I want it to feel really free and open as a space where people can bring their ideas, bring their energy, and create it. It is completely secular—we don't do any prayer, although, as I mentioned, I will sometimes share traditional prayers for the sake of learning, or we'll look at Tanach, which is Jewish Bible texts, together. But we're not reading those words with reverence. We're not praying. It doesn't mean it has to look the way any previous community has done it. We get to figure it out together.

One of my taglines, when I created the community, was, "Meaningful Jewish community from the comfort of your couch." What I said to folks was, "What if it was possible to have a meaningful Jewish life in five to ten minutes a day?" What if we let go of the narrative that if you don't speak Hebrew, if you don't keep kosher, if you don't attend services, if you're not part of a synagogue that meets in person, then you're not a real Jew. What if we say, actually, I'm doing more Jewish now in five minutes a day than I ever have before, and it's enriching my life and making me see the world in new ways, making me want to do good in the world, because I understand Jewish imperatives around ethical behavior better. That is a huge success story to me, if that's what we're able to achieve.

Dan Libenson: I'm wondering if you could reflect a little bit about what the word synagogue means to you in the context of what SecularSynagogue.com is?

Denise Handlarski: SecularSynagogue.com is definitely not what most people think of as a synagogue. That's what I like about it. What is a synagogue space? It is meant to be a place of gathering, a house of study. We can do that online, we can do that together, we can do that as people who are culturally Jewish, or secular Jews, or however you term yourself. I saw it as a take-back-the-synagogue phrasing.

One of the challenges, when folks try to start stuff that's new, is that we want to get so specific in what we call it that nobody knows what we're talking about. If I called it a digital space for cultural Jews who are getting together and doing Jewish stuff together ... people would say "What are you talking about?" But if I say synagogue, people kind of have a sense of what I'm talking about. If you say secular synagogue, then they're like, "Huh, different from what I might expect." If you say SecularSynagogue.com, my hope is people will be like, "Okay, so I'm a cultural Jew who wants to do Jewish stuff online—this might be something interesting for me."

We're excited by the possibility of what can a synagogue be. It doesn't have to be what we grew up thinking it was.

Dan Horwitz

> "The original thought behind The Well was, what would Chabad look like if it were liberal and actually inclusive?"

The Well

Dan Horwitz is committed to fostering a joyful Judaism that is inclusive, inspiring and relevant. A lifelong learner, in addition to rabbinic ordination, he holds 3 masters degrees and a law degree. Now serving as the CEO of the Jewish Federation of Greater Nashville, Dan has been a pulpit rabbi at a 900 family synagogue, the CEO of a large JCC, the organizational rabbi for Moishe House globally, and was the founding director of The Well, a young adult outreach and engagement initiative which under his leadership transformed young adult Jewish engagement in Metro Detroit and beyond. He is the author of the recently published book "Just Jewish: How to Engage Millennials and Build a Vibrant Jewish Future" (Ben Yehuda Press, 2023). Designated by *The Forward* as one of "America's Most Inspiring Rabbis," Dan is a lover of hummus, Jewish music jam sessions and shooting hoops, and is grateful to be building a life and home with his spouse Miriam and their three rambunctious children.

Dan Libenson: Tell us a little bit about your organization, The Well.

Dan Horwitz: Let me start with a bit of backstory. I was staffing a couple Birthright Israel trips back in 2009, 2010 and late in the trip we got all of the participants to the Wailing Wall to hopefully have this meaningful spiritual experience at the heart of Jerusalem. Before we actually get up to the wall, we're met by a Chabad rabbi who has a permanent tefillin cart installation and this rabbi is asking of all of these young men that I'm leading, right outside where the Temple used to stand, "Is your mother Jewish?"

If the answer was yes, he would invite them over to wrap the tefillin around their arm and put it on their forehead. If the answer was no, he ignored them, as if they were subhuman. Right before what would have been this uplifting moment, you had this moment of separation, of judginess, of feeling not included in Judaism.

My feeling at that moment was, "Holy crap—where is liberal Judaism's tefillin cart equivalent? Where is the warm, wrapping embrace to have people feel excited and welcomed into the community—to still have it be rooted deeply in tradition with meaningful content and all of those pieces, but in a way that is going to be inclusive of everybody who's identifying as a Jewish person?" We know that nowadays something like 50% of young Jewish millennials have parents who are interfaith. So that was a huge wakeup moment.

I looked at my hometown of Metro Detroit, and I saw multiple Orthodox outreach organizations who were doing *kiruv*—or ingathering—kind of work. But there was really nobody outside of the physical synagogue structures and Federation—which does awesome work in Metro Detroit. There was a need and a void in that space for a truly inclusive Jewish voice to go and connect and build relationships with folks in their 20s and 30s who, as we know, are overwhelmingly not finding their homes within physical synagogue structures.

The original thought was, what would Chabad look like if it were liberal and inclusive?

Dan Libenson: When you were starting to conceive of this liberal and inclusive Chabad, what did you think such a thing would look like?

Dan Horwitz: For me, it was a home-based Judaism. That first year, we were hosting Shabbat dinner out of our house multiple times a month. Sukkot, we had eight straight days of programming out of a super-cool sukkah made out of recycled doors from city of Detroit teardowns and decorated in tribute to something called the Heidelberg Project—which is a well-known art installation in the city of Detroit that's just completely out there. It was rewarding, and it was exhausting—my wife is a saint, because she did not sign up for that.

Then, when we had our second child a little over a year into having started The Well, we knew we needed a little bit more peace and quiet around the house and that was the impetus to really evaluate what we were doing. What I saw was that we were building a Jewish community that was not empowered—it was rabbi-centric. For you to have a meaningful Jewish experience, you come to my house, I'll create that experience for you, and then you'll walk away hopefully feeling great—but you're certainly not in a position to do anything that we just did on your own in your home.

That was when there was a significant shift in our organizational approach. We moved away from striving to mimic Chabad to say: We're going to strive to be empowerment-centric co-creators. We are going to help you host Shabbat in your home for the first time, and coach you through that process, and help you with the guest list, and, yes, help underwrite if necessary. We're going raise some money to buy seven sukkahs that we're going to lend out specifically to young adults who have never had a sukkah before in their own backyard—with the caveat that they have to invest in the roof and the decorations, and host at least one larger-scale gathering of ten or more people for a meal during the course of the holiday.

Dan Libenson: How many people are participating now in The Well? What are some of your key program areas?

Dan Horwitz: In our first two years we grew significantly when we moved away from the Chabad "everything has to be at my house" model, and really rededicated ourselves to the empowerment-centric co-creation model. In year one, we had 65 young adults help plan and host a gathering for the Jewish community. In year two, that number jumped to 170.

Our shared interest groups have grown to the point, now, where I think we're at about 17 of them that meet every month. We had over 160 gatherings in year two alone, after having 81 in year one. We had multiple thousand unique attendees at our programs, and well over 5,000 in total attendance. The Metro Detroit Jewish community really only has about five to six thousand young Jewish and Jewish-adjacent adults—so to have had a couple thousand unique participants in our gatherings feels really good.

We have a text-based learning series called CSI—Coffee, Study, Interpret—where we are investigating the role of text and issues in our lives. We are very intentional about framing the topics for discussion around secular issues that people are really interested and passionate about. Then we use the time together to see what Jewish tradition and other traditions have to say about the topic, so that folks will walk out having a sense of appreciation for what the Jewish wisdom tradition might have to say about something—and how that fits into a broader universalistic world outlook that respects the different experiences and traditions of others as well.

We do a CSI at least once a month, and our speakers have included everyone from two Syrian Muslim refugees whom we welcomed to come and share their stories, to Judge Bernie Friedman, who wrote the DeBoer v. Snyder opinion that ultimately got looped into the Obergefell gay marriage decision, to the CEO of the Detroit Zoo who came to talk about Harambe the gorilla. We've talked about everything from mass incarceration to what makes food Jewish.

At least once a month we partner with other local organizations and do an out-of-the-box spiritual experience, whether it's kabbalah yoga, or Jewish mindfulness meditation, or an alternative service or worship experience, to help people connect in those ways.

Shabbat dinner is another huge piece of what we're doing—often, if it's not at my house we're out at other people's houses in order to help them create and facilitate, every month, a Shabbat dinner experience.

But our best stuff is the stuff that people bring to us. It's when people in the community come and say, "Hey—we're really interested in making X happen—can we try this? What would that look like?" The response, overwhelmingly, is, "Yeah, of course—we would love to help you make that happen. How can we be of most help to you?" I would say we're doing something community-generated every month.

Many people view what we are doing as a significant value add above and beyond their synagogue membership, because we're doing the kinds of programming and community building that speak to them, that most synagogues are not equipped to do for the 20 and 30s demographic.

Lex Rofeberg: Tell us about why you called your organization "The Well?"

Dan Horwitz: We knew we wanted the name to be in English so that it would be as inclusive as possible. My wife, whose name happens to be Miriam, suggested that we call it "The Well." There's midrash—the creative narrative part of our tradition—that talks about Miriam, Moses's sister, as the one who was responsible for the water—or the well—that was with the Children of Israel as they wandered in the desert for 40 years. When we dove into exploring what that meant, we were excited—both because of traditional symbolism of water being a source of sustenance, and Torah being likened to water. Plus, if you look at everything that happened in the Bible, if it was cool, it happened at the well—it was the singles bar, it was the office water cooler, it was the hangout spot.

We really liked that Biblical groundedness and rootedness and intentionality behind bringing tradition forward, while, at the same time, being as inclusive as possible to the broader Jewish community and beyond.

Dan Libenson: Given your emphasis on inclusion, how have you wrestled with sustaining a connection to tradition and history and authenticity alongside your emphasis on innovation and co-creation?

Dan Horwitz: For me, I keep the traditional Hebrew whenever we're offering blessings at anything that we're doing. Some of my own formative Jewish memories were watching my father and grandfather saying kiddush over a cup of wine. Now that I have children of my own, having that opportunity to do that and share that and pass that down feels good, feels authentic. I love singing in Hebrew and praying in

Hebrew, because I can get lost in it—because I don't have to think about every single word as I'm saying it, because it has that rhythm, because it's the music that actually moves me. My dream prayer service probably actually has no words, and is all just *niggunim*—which are the wordless melodies, "Lai lai lai, nai nai nai, dai dai dai," and that, to me, is going to move me spiritually just as much as actually offering words would.

I always provide transliteration for anyone who might not read Hebrew. My translations are overwhelmingly what I would call inspired by the original text, but they are written in order to be as broadly inclusive as possible. So the standard blessing of, "Baruch atah Adonai, eloheinu melech haolam, asher kideshanu b'mitzvotav v'tzivanu ..." I translate as, "We acknowledge the unity of all, and express gratitude for the opportunity to connect by ...."

What I love about the concept of acknowledging the unity of all is that if you are a traditional believer, you can fit into a traditional Jewish construct with that. And if you're not a believer, the unity of all is still is a concept that resonates very much with 20- and 30-somethings who are universalistic in their outlook.

Lex Rofeberg: What roles and experiences do Jewish-adjacent people have at The Well?

Dan Horwitz: I think that we have inherited a beautiful wisdom tradition that can help people self-actualize as they go on their lives' paths and journeys. I don't think limiting that exclusively to Jews is a smart decision; I don't think that it's a practical or realistic decision. I'm not advocating for formal proselytizing, in terms of trying to get people to convert, because that's not a priority of mine—but in terms of making them feel welcome within the communities that we're building, absolutely.

If young Jewish adults are hanging out on a Saturday night, they're inviting their friends who are not Jewish to come with them. If we, in some way, say, "You're not invited because you don't happen to be Jewish," we're also going to lose all of the people who happen to be Jewish who want to hang out with their friends. Creating spaces where everybody can feel welcome and included is essential to making the community approachable for those who happen to not be Jewish—but it also really helps attract Jewish people to want to come to these things, because they know that they can show up with their whole selves, and with their whole friend group, and not feel like it's going to be awkward for the others.

Dan Libenson: How is The Well different from other existing Jewish organizations? Is The Well charting a course that could eventually consolidate into being some kind of new type of synagogue? Or is The Well fundamentally making something new in the world?

Dan Horwitz: I don't see us becoming our own independent synagogue. I don't see us offering Hebrew schools, or bar or bat mitzvahs, or things of that nature. There are lots of folks who are doing that kind of work very well in Metro Detroit already, and the donor class in Metro Detroit is affiliated with traditional institutions and want to see them succeed. And our revenue model is based on the investment of the same donors who are also supporting these other institutions.

Also I really don't want to be a pulpit rabbi—and if I did, I would go to a synagogue and work for a synagogue in a pulpit capacity.

I also don't necessarily think synagogue is the only way or the right way to live what people perceive as authentically Jewish lives. We're all about embracing the Ron Wolfson relational Judaism philosophy. I personally had 300 one-on-one coffees last year—and now that we're a full-time team of three, my team is actively out there having multiple coffee dates on a weekly basis. That's the beginning of how we cultivate relationships and bring people into what we're doing, without question. It takes the most time—and it's the most rewarding thing that we do, as far as I'm concerned.

As we grow, and as we get closer to when it might be time to think about creating pathways for The Well participants into more traditional institutions, my hope is that I'm going to be able to start spending some time with synagogues in town, as well as other Jewish communal organizations, to figure out how they can maybe start to look a little more like us, and how we can start to look a little more like them, in order to see if that makes sense.

Part of my role, as I perceive it, is to have one foot in the institutional world and the other foot in the non-institutional world and to see how we can bridge those two together in meaningful ways.

QUESTIONS FOR REFLECTION

- In the conversation featuring Miriam Terlinchamp, she mentions her synagogue's choice to sell its historic building, and how it helped plant the seeds for the community's growth moving forward. How do you relate to having a particular Jewish "home base"—where your Jewish life is grounded? What fears arise, and what excitements arise, when you envision (or experience) a Jewish life that does not have a particular building or institution as home base?
- Sixth & I Synagogue, the community that Shira Stutman once led, has anchored itself to a historic synagogue space (at the intersection of 6th & I in Washington DC—it's even in the name!). That said, they deploy the space in a variety of creative ways. What can we learn by comparing the approaches of Terlinchamp's community in Cincinnati and Stutman's in Washington DC?
- Denise Handlarski and Dan Horwitz both express desire to move beyond some of the more common models of Jewish place. Handlarski mentions that she wants SecularSynagogue.com to "push what a synagogue can be." Horwitz tells his story of moving The Well past "Chabad's model of everything has to be at my house." Where would your dream Jewish community "live?" In one place? In multiple spaces? Online? A mixture of the above?

New Communal Structures

August Kahn and Tal Frieden

> *"I think there's an intellectually ravenous Jewish community on college campuses that is champing at the bit to explore Jewishness on a whole new level that they can't find in their Jewish institutions."*

Judaism on Our Own Terms

As we discuss in the episode, JOOOT is a national movement of independent college campus Jewish organizations committed to promoting student self-governance and radical inclusivity. Its goal is to shape the future of American Jewish discourse and community, grounded in the belief that the independent Jewish communities of today will foster the independent Jewish leaders of tomorrow.

When we spoke to them, August Kahn and Tal Frieden were college students leading independent Jewish groups on their respective campuses. August Kahn was a rising senior at Pitzer College in Claremont, California, studying religious studies and gender and women's studies, and one of the co-founders of Nishmat at the Claremont Colleges. Tal Frieden was a student at Brown University and a founding member of Friday Night Jews, a radically inclusive non-hierarchical and non-denominational Jewish community.

Kahn and Frieden are now living and working in New York City. Kahn works in public programs and education at the YIVO Institute for Jewish Research, and Frieden is the Raise Up NY campaign coordinator for ALIGN NY, organizing a coalition of labor unions and grassroots community groups to raise the minimum wage in New York State.

Dan Libenson: Let's start by finding out a little bit about what Judaism On Our Own Terms is all about.

Tal Frieden: Judaism On Our Own Terms is a new group of college Jewish communities. We're built around the principle that independent Jewish communities are an important part of the college experience. Specifically, we're interested in building Jewish communities that are not bound to the political views of donors and are able to build their own vibrant Jewish life on campus.

The communities that Judaism On Our Own Terms is hoping to foster are built around the principle of open and honest dialogue around the hardest issues facing the Jewish community today, without litmus tests or without forcing anyone to leave their opinions at the door.

August Kahn: One of the greatest premises of our organization is that the people who should have the most say in building Jewish life on campus are those who are practicing it themselves—namely, the students.

Lex Rofeberg: To what extent is each of the different Judaism On Our Own Terms groups independent from the others, and does each have its own set of values and identities?

August Kahn: What we're practicing is very much a college Judaism. It's one that reflects the ideas and identity of a campus. I think, for everyone, a good college education is rooted in taking everything apart and being willing to reevaluate everything. Our groups are the same way. We are willing to totally take apart everything and put it back together if that means maintaining the integrity of our group.

We're really trying to explore the very boundaries of what Jewish identity can be, knowing that it will be real and sacred for us. That means that what we do is very much rooted [in] the needs and ideas of different student groups. What that could mean for us could be very different from someone from Brown, or what that could mean for Wooster could be very different than for Stanford.

Tal Frieden: I want to underline that I think the real commitment in Judaism On Our Own Terms is to taking apart the things that we take for granted in college Jewish communities.

If you look at our guidebook, there are parts devoted to talking about Ashkenormativity and how the emphasis on Ashkenazi experience is something that we need to question and tease out of what we think it means to be Jewish. We're interested in assessing the landscape of what college Jewish experiences traditionally look like, teasing out the parts we want to examine more closely, and then putting back together what we think creates a really authentic, whole, and beautiful college Jewish experience.

Dan Libenson: I think it's clear that there's an issue on college campuses about where people stand on issues relating to Israel, and there's concern among many students that campus organizations aren't allowing a robust discussion of those issues. Are there other areas where campus organizations are somehow limiting the robustness of the experience—intentionally or not?

August Kahn: Even without policies regarding Israel/Palestine, there still is a deep need for an organization like Judaism On Our Own Terms. One of the things that we try to do is really hone in on the values and needs of individual Jews. We're trying to examine anything that is at the forefront of Jewish exploration today.

The way that Jewish institutions talk about the future of Jewish continuity already rests on preconceived notions of what a Jew is, or where can we find Jews. Judaism On Our Own Terms is trying to push back against that and say that some of the best minds for the Jewish community may not be found in traditional Jewish spaces, but instead are looking to bring something else to the table from somewhere else.

In many ways, we're training future Jewish leaders who will be able to explore their own Jewishness through this individual lens for the first time.

Tal Frieden: On our campus here at Brown, there has been super-robust conversation in the beautiful independent Jewish community that we've built here called Friday Night Jews ... FN Jews, get it? We've been able to host important conversations about things ranging from the divestment campaign that was going on on our campus to BDS writ large to anti-Zionism as a Jewish practice or Jewish ideology. Those conversations just weren't possible elsewhere on campus because of the constraints placed on institutionalized Jewish college spaces.

A big part of what makes these communities different, aside from Israel/Palestine, is the commitment—at least in my community—to non-hierarchical organizing spaces. There are no elections and boards and executive boards and trustees we have to communicate with in order to make decisions. Decisions are made collectively as a group of students on an ad-hoc basis. Leadership changes every week, basically. That organizing principle and structure radically changes the way Judaism operates on campus.

The flexibility of a non-hierarchical structure allows us to change to address the needs of each week. It also means that we miss things. Sometimes we'll sort of flop and won't have a huge Hanukkah party, but maybe we'll do Hanukkah at the next Shabbat and fold it in that way. The tagline of every email we send, is that things happen if we make them happen, not because they're supposed to happen.

We see a really large number of Jews from interfaith families at our events. We also see unaffiliated Jews, or Jews who came from families that were unaffiliated with a synagogue, or Jews who didn't grow up with a ton of traditional practice at our Shabbat dinners and other programming. That doesn't mean that we don't also attract summer camp Jews, or Jews who grew up with rich exposure to Jewish practice.

We're committed to making our spaces not just welcoming to but inclusive of and sharing ownership with Jews of Color on campus. Jews of Color have been involved with my campus community of Friday Night Jews since its inception, but we're always working to make sure that it's a more comfortable and inclusive and shared space.

We also offer something important to folks who have grown up in Orthodox families and who don't identify as Orthodox anymore. I know a lot of folks who have a strong, deep connection to Judaism but may feel like if they enter a normative Jewish space, they're going back into what they received. They—like all Jewish students—are asking how do I reflect what I've received, and how do I enfold that into what I'm currently feeling today.

Lex Rofeberg: Can you say more about what you are pushing against in terms of how other campus organizations operate or where they focus?

August Kahn: All good activist groups—and I'd say most student clubs—started from some form of discomfort. I would say even maybe most Jewish movements or Jewish innovations started from some feeling of discomfort with what was currently existing. We're in a long, long legacy of Jewish innovations that have been started because of something new that was not being picked up by the organizations or ideas around them.

That's always changing, and so too should our organizations keep changing. Especially on college campuses, where people keep graduating and new people keep coming in, we have to keep reevaluating what our organizations are doing. Continuity is important, but I think we should only have discussions about continuity in dialogue with how we meet the needs of this ever-changing body of people who are benefiting from these organizations. The only way to do that is to be unafraid to fail, and to constantly reevaluate and to constantly deconstruct.

I believe that the future of Judaism and the past of our Judaism is really a Judaism on our own terms. Whether it's our synagogues or our camps or our day schools—all of them can reflect this idea, too. If not, we will be in denial of who's actually in the group, which will create this total dissonance with what Jewish communities are offering and who's actually practicing in them. I think it could lead to the demise of Jewish institutions if they're not willing to listen to who is actually in those spaces.

Dan Libenson: What do you think the future is, and ought to be, in terms of donors—whether that has to do with existing organizations or your organizations?

Tal Frieden: Part of the answer is asking the question, what do we need to have a vibrant Jewish community? Do we need our own building, or is it okay to have Shabbat dinners in someone's living room every other week? How much staff support do we need? How much do we need to spend on catering, and things like that? All of the costs that are associated with Jewish college life are taken for granted at this point.

I once spoke at a conference of Jewish donors in Boston where the central questions were, "How do we get young Jews excited about Israel?" And "How do we get young Jews excited on college campuses?" It was right after the election in 2016. It was absurd to me because to me those were entirely the wrong questions. Jewish students were excited; Jewish students were talking about Israel and Palestine; Jewish students were talking to each other about Jewish things all the time. But if you start with the question, "How do we get them excited about the thing that we're excited about *in the way that we're excited about it*," that's not a conversation, and that's not an open dialogue between equal partners.

August Kahn: I welcome donors who are interested in continuing Jewish practice and discussion and the conversation on a very robust level. That's a goal that I share with them. However, I think that the best way that we can continue this is to say if you care truly about putting your money in the name of Jewish continuity, then do it knowing that it's going to be a Judaism that may not look like yours, but it may look like ours.

It has to be premised on the understanding that there's a new group of folks who are having conversations that you may not be having. They may not sound like Jewish conversations to you, but for the folks involved, they are distinctly Jewish conversations. If you're interested in the future of Judaism, and open to the idea that Judaism will be practiced enthusiastically and wholly by a new generation, then you have to say, "Where I put my money, it may look different than what I expected—but at least some of the core values I have will still continue."

Lex Rofeberg: I think what you're creating is also an incredible resource for smaller campuses. Your guidebook was designed so thoroughly and so thoughtfully around how people can start up their own small Jewish groups.

What advice would you give people who already have a very small organization and who are trying to make their organizations sustainable? What would you say to folks who are trying to create Jewish life without many resources?

Tal Frieden: Friday Night Jews here started as a group of friends who were like, "Let's make Shabbat dinner every other Friday night, and let's do it in each other's apartments, and let's rotate." It was maybe 12 or 15 people at the beginning. From there, it's grown to consistently 50 people every other week. Our listserv has over 100 people.

So, I would say that it's totally possible to start an independent Jewish community from a couple of friends who just want to have Shabbat dinner, or whatever the practice that you end up choosing may be. My advice would be to center it around a practice that brings people together—whether it be Shabbat dinner or havdalah [prayer marking the end of Shabbat] or some other practice that you find special. On a campus with a small number of Jewish students, the intimacy that a ritual like that can provide is really grounding. I would say that the key, perhaps, to making an independent community work is rooting it in shared ownership and a practice that brings people together.

Dan Libenson: It strikes me that some of the funding of college Jewish organizations is premised on an assumption that campuses are a kind of war zone, a place where students are at risk and need protection. I'm wondering if you could share your sense of what it's like on college campuses these days?

August Kahn: What I see in people and institutions outside of the campus is this deep anxiety and fear of the intellectual power of a college campus. Historically, campuses have been a hotbed for intellectual innovation and for rebuilding new ideas and for trying them out and seeing what works and what doesn't. Our Jewish students who are products of these organizations, of this kind of learning, are going to take it to every place that they want to take it.

It was very interesting in Claremont to see that there were many folks who were in Jewish Studies departments, taking Religious Studies classes on Judaism and Jewish thought, who were not going to current Jewish institutions for Friday night. It wasn't because they weren't interested in Judaism—or because they were just taking the classes for the grade. It was because they felt that they were being treated in the classroom with a dignity and respect for their own ideas and their own thoughts that they couldn't find at Shabbat dinner.

If you're not willing to take Jewish students seriously, there's going to be a deeper bed of students who are going to go elsewhere and create new spaces. I think there's an intellectually ravenous Jewish community on college campuses that are champing at the bit to explore Jewishness on a whole new level that they can't find in their Jewish institutions.

Lex Rofeberg: Can you tell us more about the activities and rhythms of your groups?

August Kahn: The group of friends who started Nishmat got together in the library and said, we're looking for a Jewish community and we can't find it here. We wrote down a list of adjectives of what we wanted Jewish community to be, like mindful or *heimish* or homey, inclusive, all this different stuff. We said, "Okay. We're going to have a Shabbat event with dinner on this date, and we're going to see what happens."

We threw out the word and got all these folks. It turned out that we were very singing-heavy. We did a lot of singing *niggunim*—wordless melodies that come from the Hasidic movement. I think is so notable that they don't have words, they're trying to evoke something that's beyond words, which also means that a lot of folks can participate in them without having to know the words.

After Pittsburgh, I think, was a really notable time for our Jewish community. We were able to host a long antisemitism workshop for the entire campus that Nishmat students helped organize and lead.

I think that we're interested in routine, but we're not super-dedicated to routine. We're really, really excited to pick up the pieces as they go. We're creating a space that's not only bringing what we've learned from our own different backgrounds together, but also learning our own Jewish ethos together as a community.

Lex Rofeberg: Tal, can you tell us a little bit more about the origins of Friday Night Jews and how it looks today?

Tal Frieden: Friday Night Jews really started as a bunch of friends who wanted to have Shabbat dinners in each other's apartments potluck-style. I would also say it started pretty directly in response to non-Zionist and anti-Zionist Jews feeling left out of institutional spaces on campus and wanting to find community elsewhere.

Since then, we pretty routinely have Friday night dinner every other week. Our Friday night ritual usually looks like people arriving and schmoozing, chatting for a little while. We also this year started doing niggunim—wordless melodies—at the beginning as part of our ritual section. That ritual changes if the person leading that week wants to do something else. We've also had someone read poems, we've had someone teach a prayer or a melody to a prayer. Our ritual section varies continually.

Then we go into the dinner section of the evening. We always have a facilitator and a conversation topic. That has ranged from Jewish role models to responding to Pittsburgh and what community safety looks like to us. Some really important conversations that we've had have been about how to institute restorative justice practices into our group.

Dan Libenson: I'd love to know how you reflect on where this is all going, or where you hope it might go. Is your vision that there should be lots of Jewish organizations on campus that are student-created, and they might wax and wane, and they might come and go, and that's totally fine, and nobody should worry too much about making sure that every Jewish student is connected? Or is it your view that you're hoping that these organizations are going to grow over time with the hope that more and more Jewish students find a place to connect?

Do you have a concern that what are now these tiny new organizations that you're building could turn into institutions that then start to feel like they need money, and then they need to find donors and then they have to get stuck with these donors' agendas?

August Kahn: We're not the first organization that has recognized that Hillel is not the center for Jewish life on campus. Chabad has already done that. Chabad has already exposed, in a really interesting way, that while many needs are Jewish you can't find it in the same place at the same time. We're not, I think, blazing the trail of saying that a vibrant Jewish community is a diverse Jewish community, and that Hillel's mission of being the center for Jewish life on campus has revealed a lot of deeper problems.

At the same time, I think Hillel is doing some great work in having a strong presence on many different campuses all around the country, and I think all around the world, and being for many people the first opportunity to really be enfolded into the Jewish community. I think that's really important.

I would say I hope for the future of Judaism On Our Own Terms is that we can keep being an organization that does the same work, and does it in our own way—just like other Jewish organizations before us have done. This is something that someone said to me at Nishmat—that I go to Hillel and I get what I want. I know exactly what I'm going to get. I have my dinner, I sing songs, I feel like I'm back at home. I have this beautiful experience that's very, very nostalgic and very, very warm of going to my Reform temple. Then I go to Nishmat too, the next week, and I have this other completely different experience. I have to reevaluate what is my entire place in the Jewish community, and what is my voice.

Those are two Jewish ideas, but they're very, very different. We're meeting a need that may not be met by other Jewish organizations. They're doing the same for us, too. What I'm looking for in the future is that we're going to be part of a conversation alongside different organizations that will ultimately lead to a more robust dialogue on the future of Jewishness itself.

Tal Frieden: At Friday Night Jews we had an interesting moment this year when there were first-years coming to our Shabbats and saying, "I got to Brown and realized I could choose between Chabad, Hillel, and Friday Night Jews." That was a really interesting moment of being like, Okay, if we're part of this ecosystem, what is it that we're going to do that allows us to keep doing what we're doing in the way that we're doing it, and not become institutionalized? I think a huge part of that has been our leadership structure and the fact that the facilitator changes every week—the ritual coordinator changes every week. You won't see the same person standing in the front of the room all the time. That allows every experience to be different.

Lex Rofeberg: I think this isn't just about campuses. I think that you're actually a model for something I would like to see among all age cohorts. I don't know of other networks with multiple independent entities from coast to coast who are in regular touch through conferences, making guidebooks, and all these things. I don't know of networks for independent-minded groups that are ultimately just people coming together and creating their own Jewish life.

What would you say to a person, any person, who wants to create their own local Jewish community of some sort, or has started an independent Jewish community and is looking to connect with others like them around the country?

August Kahn: I would say that our Judaism has gone through thousands of years of challenges, of frustrations, of anxieties, of deep unimaginable fear. In those places of deep tension and deep frustration, there has been so much beauty. We have to recognize that our Jewishness is a product of circumstance. That our Jewish inheritance is one that has always been in dialogue with what is going on around the community and around the world—both within the community and outside.

Those who have been able to understand and acknowledge that history of circumstance have been able to build deeply successful, deeply robust, innovative Jewish communities that all of us, I think, benefit from today. If you're looking to be part of this kind of Jewish organizing—one that is experimental, one that is really trying to reach as far as we can ... that's the essence of our Jewish tradition. You're not alone in being part of a long, long chain of discussions. We are a drop of water in this long river of understanding about what is the future of Judaism and what is the future of Jewish identity and what does that mean for those who are practicing it today.

David Cygielman

> *"What I think we're tapping into is creating Jewish life, Jewish learning, and Jewish community in a setting that is already naturally happening for the population we're trying to serve."*

Moishe House

David Cygielman is the founder and CEO of Moishe House, which is one of the most successful and admired Jewish innovations to have come about in the last decade or so. David has been much lauded in the Jewish world.

Dan Libenson: Tell us a little bit about what Moishe House is and what it's all about.

David Cygielman: Moishe House started 10 years ago to engage young adults who were finished with college but hadn't yet settled down. 22- to 30-year-olds are our core demographic. And the idea is simple: We have 3-5 young adults who live in a home together, and in addition to their full-time jobs or graduate school, they turn their home into, essentially, a community center for their peers and friends of friends. Their houses turn into a place to go for Shabbat dinners, films, discussions, and all sorts of activities one to two times a week.

It started off with one Moishe House in the East Bay—in California—and then a second in San Francisco, and today there are 85 Moishe Houses spanning 20 countries. So that's Moishe House at its core.

And over these 10 years, we have also built out several other programs that have to do with Jewish education and content, learning retreats, and alumni programming through Moishe House Without Walls.

Dan Libenson: How did Moishe House get started?

David Cygielman: Moishe House got started through a funder who gave me an opportunity to meet with him once a week while I was still in college and share ideas of things we could be doing in the Jewish community. Moishe House was one of those ideas.

I had gone on a trip to Israel when I was in high school, and after college, four of the people from that trip were renting a house together in Oakland, and we figured we could use that space for a potluck Shabbat dinner. With some text messaging and emailing, 72 people showed up for Shabbat dinner—and that's really how it began.

That original funder allowed us to operate the program out of his foundation for the first two-and-a-half years, fully funded. But as a result of an economic downturn, that foundation closed down and in a two-week period, Moishe House went from fully funded to having zero funding. At that time, there were around 20 houses. We had four full-time people and a real operation going.

Dan Libenson: This story touches on the precariousness of the funding of innovation in general, and I think also in the Jewish community. So, what did you do at that point?

David Cygielman: Our hypothesis was that it was going to close down. We were about a million dollar a year budget at that point, with around 20 houses and staff, and we didn't even have a bank account, let alone a business entity. Initially, the goal was to be able to let the folks in Moishe House get out of their leases. A lot of people in Moishe House are living in homes that they can't afford without our share of the rent.

Then we started to figure out what it would mean to become our own organization. I asked some of the folks who had been encouraging if they would join the board. I let them know that it would probably be the shortest board term that they had ever experienced, but that we needed their names and their buy-in. And we had a few friends and supporters put in enough funds that we could last six weeks, but that was it.

And then an amazing thing happened. Lynn Schusterman of the Charles and Lynn Schusterman Family Foundation had known about Moishe House and heard about what was happening. She came to us gave us funding for six months, saying, "Either this will give you an opportunity to close down more gracefully, or in a perfect world you'd be able to find another six months of funding and continue to go." Once we had that, we tried to see if we could find more—and piece by piece, we were able to, and eventually we got some larger grants from folks like the Jim Joseph Foundation and Righteous Persons and Leichtag, and others.

Dan Libenson: So tell us a little bit more about Moishe House's basic model. How do you work with your residents in terms of rent subsidies, and how do you support their programming?

David Cygielman: There are four types of programs that every house has to be doing, which are social gatherings, Jewish culture and holidays, Jewish learning, and repair the world. The young adults not only put on the programs, but also invite their friends, and friends of friends, and create the atmosphere out of their homes that then engage tens of thousands of people.

The rent subsidy and the program budget are proportional to the number of programs they're doing in a month—so for houses in larger cities with more residents, you're looking at a 75% rent subsidy. In addition to a rent subsidy of 75%, they also have a $500 a month program budget—and they're doing seven or more programs a month.

Dan Libenson: And tell me a little bit about what these programs tend to be like—do they tend to be traditional, non-traditional, a mixture?

David Cygielman: The best part about the programs is that they take on the identity of the residents. So, when you have young traditional folks living in the house, you see some traditional programming. When you don't, you don't. Even Shabbat dinner—which is happening in all of the houses—can look incredibly different. You can go to a Moishe House where they have Friday night services and a kosher kitchen, and you can go to another house where they do the basic blessings, and everyone's going out afterwards together. It really takes on the identity of the three to five people living in the house.

Lex Rofeberg: I know you have houses in large cities, but how have you also been able to be successful in smaller and mid-sized communities?

David Cygielman: We have houses in London and Moscow and Paris, but there's also Moishe Houses in Prague and Khabarovsk—cities throughout the world that aren't typically thought of today as the central hubs of Jewish life.

Because of our model, the largest line item in our budget is the rent subsidy, so mid-size cities provide a huge opportunity for us because the rents are so much less than in San Francisco and New York and DC or LA. We are focused on serving the needs of young adults in Raleigh-Durham as much as we are in Washington, DC. Any mid-size city is going to have enough young Jewish adults that creating community and building Jewish life is an opportunity. It's been amazing to see the turnout in those places.

And Moishe House Without Walls does play into that. One of the key findings of our first large-scale evaluation in 2011 was that Moishe House residents were facing a fairly steep cliff when they moved on from their house. They went from having hundreds of people in their home, running programs a couple times a week, to maybe moving somewhere by themselves or with a significant other, or maybe with one friend. Even with all these skills and networks, but it was a slamming on of the brakes, to some extent.

What they were asking for was basically a format and support to run some programs. So, we created Moishe House Without Walls for former residents. They could lead up to two programs a month that were continuing to build Jewish community and Jewish life. Over time we started allowing alumni of other programs to also become eligible for Moishe House Without Walls, including learning retreats that we or partner organizations put on. That's what we've seen, really, spikes Jewish life in places like Jackson. In fact, the leaders of our Moishe Houses in Las Vegas and Raleigh-Durham both started as Moishe House Without Walls hosts who got enough of a following that they opened Moishe Houses. So they have led into each other nicely.

Dan Libenson: Why do you think it is that people are wanting to live in Moishe Houses? Essentially, they're signing on to be quasi-professional Jewish programmers, and they're not necessarily people who feel so confident about Jewish programming.

David Cygielman: Our data shows that the rent subsidy is not one of the top factors, though obviously that is a draw. What I think we're tapping into is creating Jewish life, Jewish learning, and Jewish community in a setting that is already naturally happening for the population we're trying to serve. 22 to 30-year-olds are already wanting to live together—they're already wanting to create homes that are conducive to having people over and engaging in larger community and participating in these kind[s] of social and spiritual activities.

The issue is that they're not usually given the opportunity to lead them. And our study and evaluation has shown that of the folks who we might look at as strong, young Jewish leaders, less than 25% see themselves as leaders in the Jewish community. Moishe House says to them, "Listen—you guys are the leaders of the Jewish community. And we're not telling you that to pat you on your back—we're actually telling you that because you are in charge."

Dan Libenson: What is your sense of what comes next for Moishe House residents? Are you working to connect them into our organizational infrastructure, or is there some other way that they're Jewishly connecting in their lives that doesn't go through the institutional infrastructure?

David Cygielman: The big measure for success for us is, are people who come to Moishe House getting involved in Jewish life outside of Moishe House? Two-thirds of the people coming to Moishe House have gotten actively involved in other Jewish organizations and activities that they learned about or discovered through Moishe House. So that's super important. We do 20% of our programs and partnerships with other organizations because we know that if they just do Moishe House, that is only a short-term answer.

Dan Libenson: A number of new organizations are focusing on homes as an important site of Jewish learning. Organizations like Moishe House, Kevah, OneTable, and Hello Mazel, to name a few. I'm just wondering if that's something that you think represents a broader shift in American Judaism from building-based institutions to communal spaces?

David Cygielman: I think that the buildings we've built were coming from a really good place. But, for the institutions that have invested so heavily in buildings, the challenge is the cost of maintaining those spaces. Half a million dollars a year may be going just for the upkeep of a space. And that becomes a challenge when you're trying to innovate.

And it's a very big challenge to go to another generation and say, "Hey, you didn't build this, but our expectation is you're going to maintain it," which is the less fun part, and less interesting part. And so what you're seeing is a lot of people saying, "Rather than doing that, we actually don't need that infrastructure of space—we can just do this in our own homes and living rooms. And when we need a larger space once in a while, we can just rent it out." I think it's really coming out of just the simplicity of it.

Dan Libenson: I remember being at a meeting with you years ago with a bunch of highly experienced Jewish leaders of various kinds, and we were going around the table, talking about our organizations. And I think you casually mentioned that at Moishe House, you had all kinds of Jewish education going on for your staff. There was a staff communal learning once a week, and you said you had a rabbi on staff who spent an hour one-on-one with each staff member working on an individualized Jewish learning program for that person over the course of the time that they would be working at Moishe House. And I remember the mouths dropped open of everybody around the room. I think that somebody asked you—maybe it was me—"How did you come to this idea of having this investment in learning for the whole staff?" And you just said, "We were just thinking that here we were running a Jewish organization, and we didn't necessarily know that much about Judaism—and so we ought to be learning."

David Cygielman: Absolutely. I think the same is true around Jewish education as it is around service work. We work to have monthly volunteer service projects during our staff time to go and get involved. I think both the Jewish education and the service opens your eyes. We're never coming in saying, "We know everything about what there is to do here," so we're constantly trying to improve ourselves. And improving ourselves both as a group, and also individually.

Now that we're doing learning retreats, we encourage and support and pay for Moishe House staff to go to at least one learning retreat every year. In addition to that, when we do our all-staff training, we build in Jewish education. It's not enough to say we value it—it's important to show how we're doing it.

Dan Libenson: What is it about you that allowed you to create this organization, and what do you see in others that are doing similar work?

David Cygielman: I think it's a couple things. One is that I think you have to care. Where that level of care comes from is going to be different for everyone. For me, it was spending every Sunday at the home of my grandparents who came to America after the Holocaust and having that experience of people who had to really fight and lose everything for their Judaism. And it was the experience I had in college when my dad got sick, and I applied for a Hebrew Free Loan and the committee—an anonymous group of people—came back and said, "Rather than giving you a loan, we're going to actually give you a grant for your tuition for the last two years of school, as long as you commit to continue volunteering and working in the Jewish community."

So one is you have to care, and two is that you have to be solving a problem for yourself. To just sit around and talk about what young Jews should be doing or shouldn't be doing—I'm not sure it gets us very far. But when you have a group of young Jews saying, "Wow, I'm too old for college stuff, I'm too young for young adult stuff—what's there for me?" and solving a problem for ourselves—that's a really important way of thinking about it. I think that matters a lot.

Dan Libenson: One of the things that I've always been really interested and impressed by is your process—you seem to be able to accomplish big things with a scrappy start up approach. Can you talk about how you set priorities and get things done?

David Cygielman: One example would be when we were building our internal computer system, the "Mintranet." From the start we knew that if we sat down with a whiteboard to map out all the things that we might want, we'd end up with Yahoo—but we were clear that we were trying to create only what we need, and that's it. We viewed bells and whistles as a negative—we just wanted to get you from point A to point B. Are there certain days when things could be a little easier if we had this or that function? Yes. But I don't think that's come close to outweighing the fact that it's just quick and dirty and done.

And the other piece around our process is—when you are trying to solve problems, are you thinking about things in a meeting in your office—or are you thinking about them out loud in an open space? We've worked really hard to be transparent and authentic. We raise a lot of money—tens of thousands of dollars—a year from the residents and the participants, in addition to the rent subsidy and all of those things. That's close to $2 million a year coming in from the residents' rent portion plus about $60,000 in donations. So, when we have the residents all together once a year, we sit down, and go line by line in the budget. Because it's totally unfair to ask someone to give and participate in something if they have no idea where their money is going, or what it's needed for.

I think one of the big lessons that we can all learn together is that if we're trying to engage this population and this generation, we're going to have to be overly transparent and overly authentic. People don't want to get involved in a situation where budgets are only for the executive committee of the board and we're keeping all these things hidden and private. This generation can't really feel a sense of ownership and commitment to something that they don't know about or have the ability to impact.

Sara Levy Linden and Shira Rutman

> *"The opportunity for our group to evolve with us is something really special about the group being small, about it being organic and having some structure but not too much."*

San Francisco Urban Kibbutz

At the time we recorded this episode, Sara Levy Linden and Shira Rutman were leaders of the San Francisco Urban Kibbutz, which sought to enable Jewish and multifaith families to build Jewish life together to help their families thrive and find meaning in San Francisco. The Urban Kibbutz, a non-institutional initiative uniquely led by both those working professionally in the Jewish community and by those with professional careers in other fields, was seeded as part of Hakhel, a Jewish intentional community incubator run by the Jewish environmental organization Hazon. In the wake of the COVID-19 pandemic, many families moved to other places, and the SF Urban Kibbutz is no longer active.

Formerly a biomedical engineer for medical device companies and start-ups, Sara Levy Linden has spent the past ten years organizing Jewish community programs and anything related to American Mah

Jongg. She created Mahj Club, teaching mah jongg as a method of community building. As a Jewish professional, she served as a program manager at the San Francisco JCC and as an administrator at the Jewish community high school in San Francisco. She and her family subsequently moved to Long Beach, in Southern California, where she continues to teach Mah Jongg.

Shira Rutman lives in San Francisco with her family and works as a public health researcher at UCSF, focused on partnering with communities to understand and address health inequities.

Dan Libenson: I'd love it if you could start by telling us the origin story of this urban kibbutz that you've created.

Sara Levy Linden: The headline in *Jweekly*, the weekly paper here, was, "Families squeezed out of San Francisco, leaving, leaving." It resonated with me and my family, but at the same time, we were like, "We're going to be one of those families that stay."

I thought, what could we do? What could we do positively to work around the cost of living?

We had already been practicing sharing many things among our friends who happened to be Jewish. Several of us lived on the same street, many of us had young kids, and we just started sharing stuff. We had a small apartment, and our friend across the street had a house, so they offered to house our parents when they came in. They happened to have two cars and we had one car, so once in a while if we need an extra car we would share. Our kids were about six months apart, so we were constantly passing things back and forth. It felt good. On top of that, we were surrounded by this caring community through our friends in preschool. People were bringing us meals constantly as we were having our kids.

We were really inspired by that and started wondering how we might even add to it, how we might make taking care of each other our Jewish practice, including reducing our environmental footprint by sharing things.

We were doing that as of 2013. Then during my maternity leave, I wrote an editorial in the *Jweekly* explaining what we were doing and how we were thinking. That really sparked conversations amongst our friends and some new ideas.

Dan Libenson: Shira, can you give us some examples of what you actually are doing now? It's now about six years since the initial op-ed. What does it look like today? Are people actually living together?

Shira Rutman: We're not living together, although there are a good number of us who are in the north part of San Francisco, not too far away from each other. It's nice to run into Sara on her walk to work and run into other members of our group who go to school across the street from our house. Even though San Francisco's a small city, for me it's a big advantage to have people walking distance, because we prefer to live that way. It's one of the reasons we like to be in San Francisco.

We did talk a lot about the idea of cohousing and I think many of us felt like it was just not realistic in this city. We considered it but decided there are ways of being in community without living together. So we're doing that.

Since I've been a part of the group—and our family has been engaged with this group for about two years now—we have started to form some structure within the group.

We have a babysitting co-op where we support each other in that way. We have a social justice committee. That group, so far, has done a couple different things, including volunteering in the community together—as community building. The other committees include Jewish learning.

We created calendars—using the Jewish calendar to guide our activities. Some of the things we've done are make Shabbat, make *havdalah*. We've had a Tu BiShvat [Jewish holiday centered on ecological awareness] seder in the park, we wandered through Golden Gate Park and stopped for different pieces of our seder at different points in the park together. We had a Passover, Pesach, in the park as well where we had activities for the kids that were related to the themes of the holiday. Those are some examples.

Lex Rofeberg: What drew you specifically to do this through the lens of Judaism when you could have just done it with people who were similarly looking for cost-sharing and community support opportunities?

Shira Rutman: For our family, Jewish practice is a critical component of being part of this group. The opportunity to be creative and flexible in our practice is also important. As my family has grown, each of us is needing something different in our Jewish practice at different stages of our life. My kids are six years old and ten years old, and even at this point it's different from a few years ago, the way that they connect to Judaism and the way that my husband and I do as adults. As my kids have gotten older, I have more space to bring in intellectual learning. I have more space to bring in more personal energy, to bring in spiritual seeking and practice.

The opportunity for our group to evolve with us is something really special about the group being small, about it being organic and having some structure but not too much. That's really different from what we might experience in a larger institution that just can't necessarily grow with our children and our personal desires.

And each of us brings something different. For me, the way that we do Jewish is really an important piece. Somebody else brings community organizing. I'm not a Jewish professional, but there are a number of them in our group. They bring a different connection to Judaism than I would.

Lex Rofeberg: You've mentioned that there's not a ton of structure to your group, but what's the rhythm of this urban kibbutz? If somebody were to shadow you for a month or two, what would they see? What do you gather around, where do you gather, how frequently?

Shira Rutman: Our core group has a monthly meeting. One of the nice things is that one of our core households works at the Jewish Community Center, and so can help us with a space—which is a trick in San Francisco, finding a space to gather. Through those meetings, we've been forming more of the structure.

We created these subcommittees, one of them being the calendar. That calendar I see as really forming the structure of our day-to-day. We've started to move towards this idea of having a monthly Shabbat, or a monthly havdalah. At each of the Jewish holidays, we try to have some getting together that's really, for some people, the only way that they're going to observe whatever the Jewish holiday is that's happening. They may not be going to a synagogue or another place to practice or observe that.

But I would say that the consistency and the rhythm of the group is still forming.

Sara Levy Linden: I actually want to expand on the origin story. Part one, was our organic nature, being a village, and how we want to live our lifestyle as a family. But part two is that I received a small seed grant from Hazon and the Israeli Ministry of Diaspora called Hakhel. Hakhel is the Jewish intentional community incubator.

There are about 30 to 40 communities that are picked each year to be part of this incubator cohort for three years. This happened to us in 2015. So the stage we are in now is maybe proof of concept, thanks to this Hakhel grant, which we've been able to use to expand our community building skills and networking.

I've been very inspired by hearing other people's stories, because intentional communities can look many different ways. They don't have to involve cohousing—they can be around music, around food. I think ours centers around raising kids and trying to be flourishing human beings ourselves. Hopefully that will lead to our kids learning and growing as flourishing human beings as well.

The Hakhel grant also came with the opportunity to attend the Jewish intentional community conference once a year, and a trip to Israel which I went on last November. It really was Community Building 401, or the master class of community building. There was no sightseeing—it was all going to kibbutz and moshav [cooperative communities] every day, seeing mission-driven communities. That really inspired me.

It was an amazing experience to be in a group of 20 people representing different communities. It got me, and I hope us, to this place of really being able to focus around the work to be done and the many small successes we can have without focusing on housing. I feel like we're really rocking it with taking care of each other and just being.

What that translates to is . . . we are slow about things. We try to get together once a month for our steering committee, but we don't always. We try to get together Shabbat. It doesn't always happen—or maybe just two of us do it, and that's enough because that would work. For us, especially at this time in our lives when things are constantly changing with young kids and cost of living and everything else, we really just appreciate each other and try to be there for each other and do the best we can.

Lex Rofeberg: Why did you choose to call your project a kibbutz and not some other form of community? What meanings of kibbutz are you playing with?

Sara Levy Linden: When this first idea started, and we were searching for language to talk about it, we'd say, "It's kind of like a moshav." A moshav is like a village in which people have their individual ownership but also come together in community. In the United States, it might look like a condo association, if you will, where you have your own private spaces but you contribute to the community.

When I would explain that, people in the know would say, "Oh, moshav." But those who weren't in the know, would say "Like a kibbutz?" That's kind of how we settled on the name. It was familiar to more people. Recently a friend said, "You're kind of like kibbutz without walls."

My vision of what I think kibbutz did well, and what I'd like to see continue, is optimizing talents and sharing resources. Shira has this rich background in seeking spirituality that she brings to the table. I have a community organizing background that I bring to the table. How can we bring that to the table and then resource share—so that we all get to benefit from it.

Dan Libenson: What kind of resources do or don't exist currently that could sustain the kind of work that you're trying to do? I can imagine a future in which people's Jewish life is based on these ephemeral comings-together of five or 10 families in these time-limited condo-association-like intentional communities. What would it look like if the institutional world of Judaism were built to support that structure?

Shira Rutman: Some of the events that we've had in our homes have had 40 people at them. We have these small San Francisco apartments, and it's a lot with the kids running around. It's wonderful—it's really amazing to just have a pot of chili and the people going and gathering for blessings and then scattering. On the other hand, sometimes we really do need space.

I have thought that partnering with larger institutions that have space could really be valuable. Particularly if those institutions had some flexibility in how they used their space, I think they could better support these organic communities like ours.

Another thing that I think about is our rituals. For years my family has really made our own—we just make it up. I go online, I pull from different places. I like Ritualwell a lot. I want to pull this piece that has meaning for me, and this prayer that has meaning for me. My husband is in early child education, and he thinks about, how do we make it meaningful and practical for the kids in our group, and how do we keep their attention?

Something that could help people navigate how to create those rituals might be really helpful. I don't think it is about creating a manual, but something that helps people design rituals themselves. Something with a lot of flexibility, and the opportunity to pull together elements that have real meaning for us, and that practically works for our families. A set of options so we could gauge things that are short or longer, things we can do walking in the park, things we can do in different seasons.

Lex Rofeberg: Could each of you name a moment where the full glory of the kibbutz shone through, where it encapsulates the magic of your community? And what do you think would change about the world or the universe if everybody—or at least many more people—did what you're doing?

Sara Levy Linden: A shining moment was when we had a small book club meet at someone's house before Rosh Hashanah and the High Holidays. We met and talked about Alan Lew's book, *This Is Real and You Are Completely Unprepared*. I had read this book the year before, was so inspired by it. I now had the platform that I could send out 40 emails and say, this is the night we're meeting, and we're going to talk about this book. Five other people showed up and we had this great conversation.

A more macro moment was walking into Golden Gate Park for our Tu BiShvat seder. Shira and her husband Adam led a seder that highlighted their skillset and joy of being outdoors and doing Judaism their way. It included a little bit of noshing, a little bit of singing, a little bit of pausing and reflecting on the environment we're in and doing that stage by stage. About 30 people came and it felt like a quintessential San Francisco Jewish experience.

Shira Rutman: The reason that seder was also a highlight for me is that it touched on so many different pieces. We've had Tu BiShvat seders in different ways before, even some outdoors. But being in the redwood grove in Golden Gate Park, we also decided to incorporate a social justice piece, in a way that was doable for this group and for our children. We talked about how Tu BiShvat is an opportunity to think about the ways that, historically, we have, as Jews, thought about contributing to our environment. We did a trash pickup and we talked about that.

It wasn't just a Tu BiShvat seder, but it was also a way of really being in an environment that had meaning to us, thinking about how we're a part of that, historically, as a people, and also how we're doing it with our kids—we're just picking up trash in the park. We're also singing. We're praying. Even something as simple as that, bringing together all of these elements of meaning for us brings it to another level.

For us, going to a synagogue and sitting in a room and reading a book with other people is just not suiting all of those parts of our humanity in the same way. Our children aren't going to sit there, so they're over in childcare, maybe, or maybe we even have to get a babysitter because they don't have childcare. It's not really suiting our full family and our full humanity.

What spirituality looks like, what religious practice looks like, is so different to different families and individuals. This, I think, is a way to seek out what does it look like for you, what are the bits and pieces to pull together for you. And how to do that in community, and how are the other people in your group supporting you in that process. That's something that we all need in life in general, and maybe as Jews in this time in particular.

Lex Rofeberg: What would you say to people who are thinking, "Hmm, I could give that a go"? Do you have any practical words of advice?

Shira Rutman: When I was growing up, my family was in a *havurah* as a part of our synagogue. That is a group that's put together, often by the synagogue, of families that might have something in common, and they come together for Shabbats or other opportunities. To me, our group is kind of like a havurah-plus—we've added in all of these pieces.

But start out with just making Shabbat. Or, we've actually leaned more on havdalah because Friday nights are really rough for us to try to gather or host. But Saturday evening—we can do that. We can come together and make a ritual and then wind our way into a Saturday night together.

Start out with one consistent activity that you're doing that's centered around the Jewish cycles of the year or of the week, and then add onto that. Think about what has meaning for you—what are the needs of your group? Is it related to supporting your children and families together? Is it related to sharing resources? Is it about political or community and social action? You can just start adding on. Do we want to do Jewish rituals or Jewish prayer or spirituality? Do we want to be at a playground and just try it out?

Sara Levy Linden: It's just as important to have the small as it is to have the big. I would encourage people to find one other household that you really feel all-in on, and just try to be with each other and try to help each other, try to listen. Enjoy the great times, and then give each other a break when things are tough or life is happening.

From there, let it expand out. When you talk to a friend who says, "Hey, that sounds kind of cool—I want to try that too," you say "Great—join us for this dinner, or join us for this thing." Again, continue to be with each other and not always have an agenda. Thinking as family and what you would do for the other person, or how you would be.

When we were in Israel, my mind was blown that in the kibbutzes there, a hundred individuals [could be] sharing one bank account. But that didn't happen overnight—it started in the youth movements.

Be patient with it—it's not a condo. I walked out of the Israel trip saying, I am not going into cohousing because that is a contractual agreement. It's going to take longer, but I want to invest the time to find the people that I really see eye-to-eye with and understand. I think in the long game that's going to be better for my family, myself, and the greater community and the world.

Beth Finger

> "It's an amazing time to be Jewish, because there's so much freedom now to be creating new things that are really relevant to people, and that are interesting."

Jewish Without Walls (JWOW)

When we interviewed her, Beth Finger was running Jewish Without Walls (JWOW), a grassroots organization that she founded, headquartered in Suffolk County, Long Island, New York. JWOW functioned as a volunteer-run, low-budget organization that provided Jewish experiences, life, and connection to people across denominational and affiliational boundaries.

In the years since JWOW ceased operations (2018), Finger has established a presence in environmental and sustainability activism and education. She was the project manager for Huntington Mobilization for Sustainability, or HUMuS, which is a project of Kehillath Shalom Synagogue, a Reconstructionist synagogue based in the Huntington, Long Island, area. She is a naturalist and teaches in the Outdoor and Environmental Education department for Long Island public schools.

Dan Libenson: Beth, thank you so much for joining us today on *Judaism Unbound*. Tell us a little bit about your work and your organization, Jewish Without Walls.

Beth Finger: Jewish Without Walls is a grassroots, independent venture that builds vibrant Jewish communities across denominations and affiliations. There's no membership, it's inclusive, and everybody is welcome. We have over 50 programs a year and they're all run by volunteers in our community.

Right now we're located primarily in Suffolk County, New York, on Long Island. In this area of Long Island, the Jewish community is perhaps not the way a lot of people envision Long Island Jewish communities. According to the 2011 New York Jewish population survey, Suffolk County had the highest rate of intermarriage and also of non-affiliation—so this area really needed some injection of vibrant Jewish life.

Dan Libenson: Tell us some more about what kind of programs you do, and what kind of people you serve—and why it needed JWOW to come along to do those things . . . why didn't those kind of things seem to be coming about from existing Jewish organizations?

Beth Finger: In every part of our lives, we have so many options and choices—but when it comes to finding a Jewish community in the suburbs, we really only have one or two choices. One is joining a synagogue; and if you have a Jewish Community Center nearby, perhaps you can join the Jewish Community Center to find other Jewish families.

But we know that many families will never join a synagogue, and others won't join a synagogue, perhaps, until their children are ready to start Hebrew school. So, what about the period of time between when your children are born and when they are seven, eight, nine years old and ready to start Hebrew school? There's really—amazingly—nothing for them. There's no way for them to find other Jewish families. And I just can't believe that no one thought of this before me—because it's such an obvious need.

JWOW does primarily serve families with children ages 10 and under—but we do have programs all through elementary school, and also programs just for adults so that we can get together and learn to cook Jewish foods, or read Jewish books together, or do other fun things. But we are primarily geared towards young families.

When newcomers come out to Long Island, they don't know where to turn to find other Jewish families. There had to be a way for families to find other Jewish kids for their children to make friends, and also for them to make Jewish friends. I know you've said on previous podcasts that Jews are everywhere, and admitted everywhere, and welcomed everywhere. But I have found that despite that, Jewish people still have some invisible connection to other Jewish people—and especially when they have young children, they want their children to have other Jewish friends.

Dan Libenson: So you're serving a group of people who are looking for Jewish friends for themselves and for their children, are interested in Jewishness and Judaism in certain ways—and yet are not thinking "Let's join a synagogue"?

Beth Finger: JWOW actually has several goals. One of them is to provide a way for people who are not synagogue members to find Jewish community. Another one of our goals is to provide a way for people who *are* synagogue members to be able to meet people from other synagogues so that we have one Jewish community.

We did a comprehensive survey last year that found that we're about evenly split—JWOW participants are about 50% synagogue members and 50% non-members—and we love that combination. It shows that we are really pursuing both of these goals to break down some of the walls among existing institutions, and also to provide ways for people who are not currently part of the established Jewish community to find a way to make Jewish friends and explore their Jewish identities.

Dan Libenson: Why do you think it is that those synagogue non-members are interested in Jewish things and yet they're not joining synagogues?

Beth Finger: When it comes to synagogues, you have to look at the return on the investment. Synagogue membership around here is about $3,000 a year for a family—and that doesn't include Hebrew school. So it's quite a significant financial investment that people no longer feel obligated to make.

Once it's really a choice, the question is what am I getting out of my membership? Am I going three times a year? That's a thousand dollars a day. What else is my synagogue offering me that really excites me and interests me and makes me want to join? And I think people are finding that the answer is not much—and so they're not joining.

Lex Rofeberg: What is it about the "without walls" factor of your organization that is particularly helpful, beneficial, or appealing to the people that work with you?

Beth Finger: Without walls means a few different things. First, it literally means we have no walls—so I'm sitting here talking to you from my kitchen, not from an office in a building someplace. And what that forces us to do is to be really innovative in where we have our programs, and sometimes programs that might start out as "blah" turn into "ah!" because we have to find some really cool place to have them.

But no walls also literally means we don't have the albatross around our neck of needing to raise enormous amounts of money to support those walls—to fix the roof and the parking lot and everything that comes along with it. So that is a huge relief—something that I don't envy the synagogues who have to deal with that kind of pressure and stress all the time to maintain those walls. No walls allows us to do a lot with the money that we do have—because we can spend it all, really, on our programs, which is what people want.

And then figuratively, we have no walls—which means that everybody is welcome at our programs. We have a really flat structure in terms of the way that we're organized. Everyone is welcome, everyone is equal—there are no insiders and outsiders, there's no membership, and there never will be membership. If you participate in a JWOW program, you're part of JWOW—you're a JWOWer, and that's it.

Dan Libenson: It sounds like what you're building is something that cuts across the lines that used to functionally divide us, and, in a sense, you are revealing an interest in being one people that was almost invisible under the old structure.

Beth Finger: Yes. I think people today don't care about those lines—they're not theologians; they can't tell you the difference between Conservative theology and Reform theology. What we're talking about—in suburbia, at least—is secular Jews who still feel very proud to be Jewish, who want to be able to pass along Jewish traditions to their children, who want their children to be able to celebrate holidays with other Jewish children. And there are old walls that were put up by insiders, some of whom might still feel very strongly about those walls, but regular people in the street don't even understand what these walls are about.

Lex Rofeberg: Who are the kinds of organizations out there—maybe geographically close to you, maybe not—that you see as your peers, that are similar to you?

Beth Finger: Even since we started JWOW there are many more organizations that have been created to support Jewish startups, which is nice. People see the writing on the wall, that we need to be in a lab right now testing out all kinds of new inventions on how to engage Jews. You have everything from Slingshot to UpStart, Natan, Joshua Venture, ROI . . . you really do have all of these incubators and organizations that are trying to help startups.

But JWOW is unique—there is nothing else like it. There are some really cool startup volunteer-driven *minyanim*, which are synagogue-based startups that are doing awesome things—but at the end of the day, they're a synagogue. So what makes JWOW unique is that we are not a religious organization; we focus on Jewish culture and Jewish friendship and experiential Jewish education.

Big Tent Judaism is an organization that has taught me a lot in terms of public space programming, and how to be very sensitive in the way we advertise our programs so that we take down all the walls and make it so that everybody feels included and part of us. Just as an example—when the community was planning to do a community event for Lag BaOmer, they wanted to call it a Lag BaOmer picnic. And I said, "No one's going to know what Lag BaOmer is—even Jews don't know what Lag BaOmer is, let alone any kind of interfaith family—and as soon as they see that, they are going to shut it out. They're going to think this isn't for me." So what we have to do is say "Family picnic" in really big letters, and then in small letters you can write, "To celebrate the Jewish holiday of Lag BaOmer." So we're not immediately putting up a wall that turns people away.

We also go out into the community to connect with unaffiliated people. We are in the supermarket during Passover in the matzah aisle and we are at local street fairs over the summer with our table and arts and crafts. Our biggest program each year is Hands-On Hanukkah—which is a Big Tent Judaism registered program—and we do it in two local shopping centers. About 1,000 people come to these programs. The shopping mall is decked out for Christmas—green and red everywhere with a big Santa in the middle of the mall—and then suddenly there's this oasis of blue and white for three hours and we have Hanukkah music playing and all kinds of activities for kids and adults, and live entertainment—and people love it. And they are so proud to be Jewish—they love for their kids to come and see all these other Jewish kids, to show them that they're not the only Jewish kid, even though they might be the only Jewish child in their class. And they are so thankful to JWOW—I get emails of thanks all the time after that program for providing something so special and Jewish in a public space.

Dan Libenson: Was it your immediate idea that, "I should found this as a startup," or did you try for a while to get some larger Jewish organization interested in what you were doing?

Beth Finger: I had been involved in my local synagogue and found it very frustrating. And when I came up with this idea, I knew I had to do it as an independent venture—because one of my goals really was to bring the whole Jewish community together; it wasn't just to revitalize my synagogue. I had bigger, broader plans, and I knew I couldn't do that in one institution. Honestly, I didn't really know what I was getting involved in—I just had this idea and I just started it.

Lex Rofeberg: Has Jewish Without Walls done any thinking about what it might look like to take that "without walls" to another level and experiment with some online manifestations of some of your programming?

Beth Finger: Well, before I talk about the programming—JWOW would not exist if it weren't for social media, that's for sure. I remember when I used to work in the olden days at a JCC and you'd have to take out ads in the paper. But with Facebook, it caught on so fast—because everyone sees everything, and what their friends are doing. And that's basically how we grew. If it weren't for Facebook, we literally would not exist.

JWOW does have a group on Facebook and the wall is open, which means that anyone can post. And I leave it like that on purpose, so that the JWOW wall has become the central address for all things Jewish in Suffolk County. On the wall today there was someone who was asking how much is the going rate for a mohel; someone else was posting about a movie about Italy during the Holocaust. So it's just a great resource—anyone who has any kind of crowdsourcing question will go to the JWOW wall.

I also encourage all of the synagogues and local Jewish organizations to post their programs on the JWOW Facebook wall—because we have over 1,000 local members on that wall. We know that people have gone to programs because they saw it posted on the JWOW wall—including myself. I've gone to programs that I didn't know were happening because I saw it on the JWOW wall.

I spend a lot of time curating that wall—I take it very seriously. And we found from a survey that we did that people feel a sense of Jewish community, even if they've never physically been to a JWOW program, because of that wall. I also pepper the wall, sometimes, with questions—and I ask, I write, "Discuss," and I'll put some kind of a question. And people reveal really personal Jewish experiences, Jewish feelings, Jewish identity issues on the wall, and people respond to them. I spend a lot of time working to make sure that our social media is really encouraging people to explore their Jewish identities.

On Yom Kippur this year for 25 hours I turned our Facebook wall into a *yarzheit* [anniversary of death] wall, and I asked people to post pictures of friends and family who had passed away, and to write a memory about that person. We had so many people posting pictures of friends and family who passed away, and writing memories—and it was a beautiful, really ... I'm getting goose bumps remembering it, of people talking, sharing these people with the community.

Dan Libenson: So what I think is interesting about what you're doing is that it's not just saying, "Hey, come to our programs," but it's saying, "We really honor the idea that you can create your own Jewish experience for your own family and the people closest to you—and essentially we want to offer you a set of resources that hopefully will make that more powerful."

Can you speak about the dynamic of how people's homes can be a new location of Jewish living in the way that we used to think of the synagogue being the place where you go for Jewish events? How does JWOW fit into that question?

Beth Finger: Home is the backbone of JWOW—because we don't want people just coming to our programs and doing something at our program and then never doing it again. We're trying to do experiential Jewish education. We are teaching parents about Jewish traditions and values, and then, after each one of our programs, we have a "JWOW to go"—which is something that they can take home with them so that they can continue it in the home.

Home is the most important place for Jewish to happen—especially when you're dealing with young families. That's where you're passing it along to your children—the smells in the kitchen when they're baking challah [braided bread]. All of the senses—creating beautiful art together, to be used during the Passover Seder or at Shabbat. You want these things to be happening in the home.

We have a series of themed Shabbat in a Box [activities] that we've been doing this year with funding from PJ Library. We have Frozen, the movie; we have superheroes; we did a great Super Bowl Shabbat in a Box. We did a Star Wars Shabbat in a Box, because Star Wars opened on Shabbat—and so we had Shabbat Awakens for one of our Shabbat in a Boxes. And the idea here is that we should make it fun—we should make it fun and relevant to young families. The idea is that if they're making it into a party, hopefully they'll invite friends and family over to celebrate Shabbat with them.

We've gotten people who are saying—who write to us afterwards saying, "We have never celebrated Shabbat before, and on Saturday morning my son was asking me if we could celebrate Shabbat again." So it's really working—when you make it something that families really relate to, and that they love, they're more likely to do it, and to do it again.

Dan Libenson: I'm wondering, based on your work with kids and young families, whether you're seeing their parents asking for a certain kind of thing or potentially more open to a certain thing than you might have expected?

Beth Finger: One thing I've seen—at least out here in the suburbs—is that the parents are really, unfortunately, Jewishly illiterate, and they know it. And so when they're coming to these programs with their young children, and we're teaching very basic Jewish ideas and traditions, they are learning right alongside their kids. And we try to have differentiated learning at our programs—something for the adults and something for the kids—but I'm telling you, the parents are just soaking it in, because they really do have a desire for their children to know these things, and they know that they are not equipped to pass it along.

I had a light bulb moment recently. People wax nostalgic for the synagogues of the 70s and the 80s, when it was bursting at the seams and there were so many Hebrew school classes that they were meeting in the hallways, and it seemed like such a vibrant time. But then I realized—those kids who were in Hebrew school at that time are today's young parents who are rejecting all of it, and who are Jewishly illiterate. That's what that produced—that's what that time period produced. So maybe we shouldn't be so nostalgic for those days.

QUESTIONS FOR REFLECTION

- August Kahn says: *All good activist groups—and I'd say most student clubs—started from some form of discomfort. I would say even maybe most Jewish movements, or Jewish innovations, started from some feeling of discomfort with what was currently existing.* When has discomfort with what-is helped you produce or co-create a new idea of what can be—in your Jewish life or beyond?
- Via Moishe House, and via the Urban Kibbutz, we can witness different models for empowering Jews in urban environments to create their own forms of meaningful Jewish practice. What do these kinds of spaces provide that might be harder to find in more traditional synagogue environments?
- Beth Finger speaks about the power of education that serves both children and adults (in her case, the parents of children—in other cases, perhaps adults generally). Are there are other forms of trans-generational programming that could serve you and your Jewish communities as well? What would it look like to take steps toward creating them?

Artistic Re-Visions

Amichai Lau-Lavie

> "I think Judaism offers the modern human being, confronted with a smorgasbord of cultural opportunities, with a magnificent menu of options for making life meaningful on an individual and collective level."

Lab/Shul

Social activist and storyteller, writer and community leader, Rabbi Amichai Lau-Lavie (He/Him) is the co-founding Spiritual Leader of the Lab/Shul community in NYC and the creator of the ritual theater company Storahtelling, Inc. Israeli born, he's been living in New York since 1998 and received his rabbinical ordination from the Jewish Theological Seminary in America in 2016, the 39th generation of rabbis in his family—the first one to be openly queer.

Rabbi Amichai is the subject of Sabbath Queen, Sandi DuBowski's documentary film, 21 years in the making, which premiered at the Tribeca Film Festival in June 2024. In 2017, Rabbi Amichai published The JOY Proposal with a radical response to the reality of intermarriage and taking on a personal position on this issue, including his resignation from the Rabbinical Assembly of the Conservative Movement.

In 2022 Rabbi Amichai began publishing Below the Bible Belt, a daily digital project extended over 42 months, critically queering and re-reading all 929 chapters of the Hebrew Bible.

Rabbi Amichai serves on the Executive Board of Rabbis for Human Rights, is a co-founding member of the Jewish Emergent Network, a founding faculty member of the Reboot Network, and serves on the Advisory Board of the Sulha Peace Project for Israeli and Palestinian peacemakers, the Leadership Council of the New York Jewish Agenda, the Advisory Council for the Institute for Jewish Spirituality and as an advisor to Jerusalem Open House for Pride and Tolerance.

Amichai is Abba to Alice, Ezra and Cai-Hallel.

Dan Libenson: What is Lab/Shul and why did it come about?

Amichai Lau-Lavie: Lab/Shul is a contemporary congregation based in New York City. We are revamping an old favorite—the Jewish congregation. And by "revamping," I'm trying to think of who our modern audiences are and what are the sensibilities and needs of modern Jews in an urban center such as New York. And we're a lab—meaning we're trying things out, really anything and everything. And we're a shul—because we're liking the homey, cozy concept of what a congregational arena is about.

Lab/Shul is now four years old . . . we emerged out of an earlier model of a theater company, the Storahtelling theater company, that is now 15 years old. What happened very organically is that the practitioners, artists, and fans of the theater group here in the city spent so much time creating ritual space and communal space, that we simply morphed into this sense of a community and a congregation.

What Lab/Shul does is create opportunities for sacred environments—whether that is worship or study or social action. We support people in many life cycle moments. And we serve as a lab to integrate the arts as a pivotal way of making meaning out of our lives.

And it keeps evolving—we have a few thousand people who show up for the High Holidays. We are a pop up, so people come to us [at] different locations throughout the year for Shabbat or the holidays. We are God-optional, meaning we are user-friendly and everybody-friendly, that is Jewish and not, believers or not. The way that is depicted is the way we work on our liturgy and the type of environment that is really outside the box—inviting people to think about spirituality in a new way.

We are also experimenting with a lot of digital and virtual stuff as well. The conversation we're having right now is not one that's happening with people sitting and talking in person. We're wondering what that will mean for the future of our people, and all people, as far as the sacred experience. And we're young, we're supple—and it's fun. We get to ask a lot of questions and throw a lot of things at the wall and see what sticks.

Dan Libenson: I'm wondering what it is, exactly, that artists bring to the table? What is the perspective of artists on this Jewish stuff? Where do you want it to be? Where do you think all that can go, as part of building the Jewish future?

Amichai Lau-Lavie: Back in '98, '99, I had the passion to make Jewish literacy accessible to people so that the progressive agenda, the inclusive agenda, the queer and feminist agenda, is grounded in Jewish knowledge and not just in feel-good ideologies. I wanted to make Jewish literacy available to other people. One of the ways to get people engaged—and disarm the suspicion and the feeling of being inadequate—was through lower stakes and through amusement and through humor and through entertainment and through art.

My work was through the juxtaposition of theater, media, education, and spirituality as a way to invite people into the conversation of Jewish identity and Jewish literacy without the expectation that this is a religious obligation, that this is an educational enterprise. This is about aesthetics; this is about an emotional exploration of identity. And the flag that I waved by founding a theater company in 1999 was artists are the new rabbis. "Artists are the new rabbis" was my way of saying, "I don't want to become a rabbi—I want to be a theater practitioner. I want to be a translator of Judaism. I want to use the stagecraft as a way to get into the heart and invite people to the conversation, and we'll see where it goes from there."

The whole gestalt of Storahtelling was going into the synagogue arena as a site-specific theatrical artistic enterprise, opening up the Bible, and inviting people to rethink our relationship to sacred scripture and to the politics of it, and to our identity with it. I think what was so powerful about Storahtelling, as it evolved into Lab/Shul, was that we came from the point of view of art—and that is a different invitation into the heart and into why people would be engaged with it.

What happened along the way was art seemed—at least to me, after 10 years of doing it—not enough of a game-changer. In the Jewish community, art is important—but it's a garnish, it's a side dish. I felt like the impact I want to make on who is a Jew, what is Jewish, what is spiritual, what is universal in the 21st century, needed more of an insider's attitude.

My own direction went from saying that artists are the new rabbis, to saying that rabbis are the new artists—and I want to become a rabbi who uses art. Whether it's the theatrical arts, the aesthetic graphic arts, music, just architecture—the notion of how the art enhances our experience—I wanted to do that as a rabbi, and be a smarter, more strategic change agent from within. I moved my community to think of ourselves not just as artists, but as a congregation that is artist-driven. This is a subtle but a dramatic shift.

Dan Libenson: One of the things we're trying to encourage with this podcast is an attitude that Jews—whether they're professionals or laypeople—should treat Judaism itself as a material to be reshaped in an artistic way, and not as something simply to be preserved or locked up in a vault. I guess I'm wondering from you whether that accords with what you're talking about?

Amichai Lau-Lavie: For me, it comes down to the bottom line—why do Jewish, why create Jewish? Whether it's to write a play or join a synagogue or have a . . . mitzvah or open a Jewish book or listen to this podcast. My answer—and my risk, quite frankly—is that the bottom line of why interact with Jewish life is that it makes my life richer as a human being. Man, woman, gay, straight, white, black, Israeli, American, et cetera, of all ages . . . at the end of the day we want a rich life, a full life, from sunrise to sunset, from crib to coffin and in between, that is imbued with meaning, that makes my own experience of the world meaningful and makes me part of a larger eco system in a helpful way.

I think Judaism offers the modern human being, confronted with a smorgasbord of cultural opportunities, with a real magnificent menu of options for making life meaningful on an individual and collective level.

The bottom line for me is not that I, at the end of the day, am a good Jew. It's that I am a happy and helpful human being utilizing—for whatever reason, biology or choice—the Jewish system to make my life rich and full. As an artist, or someone who appreciates art—and that is all of us—what does the Jewish story and Jewish art have to offer my life, my family, my community? Is it beautifying my home? What does the mezuzah look like, and what does it mean that my threshold is marked with a prop, with a ritual signifier of coming and going? Whether it's the colors that I choose or the objects that I choose to decorate my walls. Whether it's what I wear, and how I wear it. Whether it's how I mark moments in my day and throughout my life. I think if we are reframing the why and the what as, "These are tools to make your life meaningful," then so many people who are turned away, turned off from a parochial, insular, Judaism, will actually become interested.

Dan Libenson: The Judaism we've inherited evolved in conditions where "Why be Jewish?" was not the driving question. Now the question is, how does it adjust to a reality where "Why be Jewish?" has to be the central question?

I have this intuition that artists are a big piece of the solution. The task of artists is, in part, to be able to help negotiate that kind of transition, because artists are exploring those kinds of questions.

Amichai Lau-Lavie: Human experience is the bottom line. Judaism serves that, and it's the same for art. Art is not the bottom line—it's not art for art's sake—it's art for the sake of human experience or change. Artists will tell you, "What are you talking about? I'm making art because I'm making art, because art is beautiful." People will tell you, "I'm doing Jewish because Jewish is important."

I think that that dance between doing something for its own sake or for its bigger context is an interesting place where art and religion are interacting right now. And the fact that we have more choices to not just be one thing, but many things, is a new phenomenon in the human experience and in the communal experience.

I think you're right that where artists come in as necessary change agents is in the transmission and in the translation of abstract notions into emotionally evocative experiences that people can relate to. If it is painting or if it's music, if it's theater or architecture—it's taking complicated, abstract ideas and relating them to people in a way that resonates, not just intellectually, but emotionally. I think that is the pivotal role of the artist.

Dan Libenson: Could you give us some examples of what artists have been able to do that is bringing a new lens into Jewish life?

Amichai Lau-Lavie: The Storahtelling project at the core of Lab/Shul takes the traditional unit in which the Torah is transmitted and proclaimed and ritualized and makes it into theater. You walk into a synagogue or wherever the ritual is done, whether it's somebody's B mitzvah or a Shabbat morning or High Holidays—and alongside someone standing on a stage and chanting from a scroll in Hebrew there are actors acting out the story, and asking you, the audience member, to interact and share your voice and make commentary known as *midrash*—which is a Jewish art form of op-ed-ing. Suddenly, the arena becomes a site-specific theater, and the script is challenging scripture, and we're looking at how we're negotiating our heritage and our modern needs.

We've trained hundreds of actors and musicians and clergy and educators to think of the way we transmit Torah as an artistic storytelling form. It changes everything, because suddenly you're riveted, and suddenly it's interesting, and suddenly it's theater and not just a stale moment or religious recycling.

A second example is music. At Lab/Shul we work extensively with a lot of musicians to craft fantastic music that opens us up in a personal, private, and public way.

Third is the words themselves. We've inherited a prayer book, which is an anthology of poems—that is an art form. The words we've inherited are an accumulation of hundreds of years of other people's poetic thoughts about the spirit. Part of what we do in Lab/Shul as God-optional and artist-driven is redefine what words we use. We're working with poets to retranslate the liturgy into modern norms that speak to everybody—atheist and believer—poetically inclined.

In the 21st century, books are heavy and expensive, so we don't use books—we use screens that are designed by artists. When you walk into any of our prayer, or worship, environments, the walls themselves are art, and the words there are generated by artists. Whether you're someone who's comfortable with the Jewish experience, or new to it, you feel like you are in a sophisticated, modern, sensitive environment where the aesthetic matters a great deal.

Lex Rofeberg: How have you been able to blend the worlds of art and technology so that they're working in concert?

Amichai Lau-Lavie: My friend Stephen Wernick, who's at the head of the Conservative Movement, says that the two factors that most hinder the evolution of synagogue are books and chairs—once we started sitting, and once we started reading, we lost a lot of our spontaneous being. That could be debated. But where we sit and how we gather and how we congregate—certainly for millennials and the next generations—is an interesting challenge.

The notion of the digital, not just as a means to an end, but as its own thing—that the medium is the message—is huge. By using screens as our way of projecting liturgy, we are not just making an environmental and a financial choice, but making an aesthetic choice about delivery and about getting people on the same page using less liturgy. There's a price to pay for it, but I think it's a statement about modernity and about being where we are now.

As a community that does not have its own location—we're a pop-up, and we rely a lot on virtual and digital communication—we pay a lot of attention to how our messages are transmitted. We're paying more attention to how people interact with their spiritual lives via online and via screens. Not as a byproduct, but as an intentional delivery system.

Dan Libenson: I've always been intrigued by the way that Lab/Shul describes itself as God-optional. Can you share with us what you've learned about the Jews who are not participating in your typical Jewish organizations—what are they looking for or not looking for in terms of God?

Amichai Lau-Lavie: G-O-D is a Western construct of the divinity, which is complicated, which is layered, which—at least in the Judaic vocabulary—has, and continues to enjoy, many titles and many names and many depictions that are paradoxical and sometimes contradictory. G-O-D "God" has become a placeholder for a primarily masculine, very Christian-minded, judgmental, on the throne, up in heaven, father-thing, that for many people today just feels completely off-putting, and not how we connect to the mystery of creation and being—whatever that means to us.

What we're trying to do by being God-optional and artist driven, is saying, "Okay. Let's open this up as artists do, first of all [by] translating it differently." Lab/Shul, as of last year, took G-O-D out of our liturgy. Every time you come to a Lab/Shul event: we use the Hebrew liturgy—we would use "Adonai." You can see the Hebrew there on the screen, and you can see the English poetically translated. There is never going to be "God" there. There's maybe "Source," there's maybe "Being," there's maybe "Spirit." We're not the first to do it—but we're consistent about saying, "We don't want it there," because that word is too baggaged.

Then we take it a step further by talking about being genderless, and by inviting people to think about the spiritual, or the sacred, or the mysterious, in ways that, as a 21st century theist or non-theist, we can make sense of. We're inviting participants to think and feel along, aloud, with us, about "What's my metaphor? How would I paint this differently? How am I going to look at this piece of art called life and come up with my own interpretation?"

It's a pluralistic notion. It is a notion that really honors the human experience, and challenges us to be creative and be deeply personal, and not to be beholden to one image or one depiction of what truth is. How we rebrand God is a really fantastic challenge for the modern age—and we're not the first to do it.

How we open up the text, how we invite people to be artists and co-creators, invites us all to think of these notions in a very freeing way. We are still, in some way, around the same canvas even though our artistic expressions are going to be radically different.

I'll use one last example: Last week I saw a film about the French court of Louis XIV, where dance was formal, and everybody danced in the same way. Think about how we dance today at a wedding—whether it's a hora circle or a dance party—we're all dancing in the same place, but we're dancing differently, sometimes crazy, sometimes not. And yes, there's some music. We're not all dancing the same choreographed dance, even though we're all in the same dance floor—and I like that. We get to have our own artistic expression, even and especially when it comes to how we deal with the biggest questions of life, which is how we connect to the sacred within ourselves, with each other, and with the mystery which some people like to call God, and I no longer do.

Adina Allen and Jeff Kasowitz

> *"We have found that really good things happen when we can activate creativity in adults—we can learn new insights about our lives, we can connect to one another really deeply through creative community."*

The Jewish Studio Project

Adina Allen and Jeff Kasowitz are the co-founders of The Jewish Studio Project, which describes itself as part urban art studio, part house of Jewish learning, part spiritual community. It seeks to spark a culture of creative spiritual engagement, infuse Judaism with new voices and diverse perspectives, empower individuals with creative confidence, and address our society's increased polarization and divisiveness. The Jewish Studio Project's unique methodology, the Jewish Studio Process, combines Jewish learning and creative arts exploration to investigate relevant questions about our lives and tradition.

Adina Allen, the creative director of The Jewish Studio Project, has previously worked as an educator at Tufts University Hillel and the Brandeis Collegiate Institute, as well as serving as a chaplain at Hebrew SeniorLife. In 2024, she published a book entitled *The Place of*

All Possibility: Cultivating Creativity Through Ancient Jewish Wisdom. She has rabbinic ordination from the non-denominational Hebrew College Rabbinical School.

Jeff Kasowitz is executive director of The Jewish Studio Project. He previously served as vice president of strategy and growth for the national education reform organization City Year. Kasowitz is a musician, writer, and performer of original music inspired by Jewish texts and liturgy. In 2016, he released an album entitled "Arba'im Shanah."

Dan Libenson: What is The Jewish Studio Project?

Adina Allen: The Jewish Studio Project exists to activate the inherent creativity that's within each and every one of us. We have three goals: To make our lives more meaningful; to make Judaism more vibrant, bring new and diverse voices into Jewish tradition; and to make the world, ultimately, more just.

We exist as a local hub in Berkeley. We have a studio called Studio AM, which has local community programming. It's our research and design lab and community hub. It's what fuels the fire that takes our work nationally. We have a methodology that we teach folks that we think can enliven Judaism and bring those new and diverse voices to educators, to people across the country.

Jeff Kasowitz: We're part urban arts studio, part *beit midrash*—house of Jewish learning—and part spiritual community. I think what we're most interested in is providing people tools and resources to really explore the questions that are up for them—the things that they're celebrating.

We've found that when we combine Jewish learning—for example, *hevruta* learning, or paired learning of Jewish texts—with a creative process using paint, or Cray-Pas, or collage, or something like that, we can move from an intellectual engagement with our tradition into a more imaginative, creative exploration into ourselves, so that we can get deeper meaning into the questions that we have about our lives and our tradition.

Lex Rofeberg: How did this come to be?

Adina Allen: My mom, Pat Allen, is a leader in the field of art therapy. She and her colleagues developed a way of taking art therapy out of the clinical mode into a more community practice mode. So, I grew up in a studio, essentially. From a really young age, paintbrush and pen were given to me as tools for exploring questions I had about the world, for dealing with struggles in my life, and for connecting to the divine. That was always in me.

Then I went to rabbinical school at Hebrew College in Boston, and felt so engaged by the traditional mode of *hevruta*—paired learning in the beit midrash, in the house of study—and the intellectual engagement of text. At the same time, our teachers were telling us, "You're the next generation of commentators who are going to bring this tradition forth and make it relevant to people." I felt like the information was really residing from my forehead up, and I was only accessing a certain amount of myself that could engage with the text. I found this with my colleagues, my classmates, as well, that there were so many other ways of knowing that we weren't accessing.

So I started bringing this creative process that I'd learned as a child into the beit midrash—combining beit midrash and the studio—to do this intellectual learning of text, and then to process it through these other modes. And I saw that all kinds of new interpretations were coming up, ways that these texts hit people's lives emotionally, memories that they brought up, and all kinds of new stories and interpretations were coming forth from combining those two modes. And saw that there was really a yearning and a need for that, for those new modalities.

Dan Libenson: I have an instinct that it's really important to understand the difference between the way that art is used in your work and the way, I think, that a lot of people think of art. I think, in many ways, the difference is similar to the way that people think about Judaism—that that's something that the professionals do, and they can do it really amazingly well, and I might appreciate it, but I'm not an artist, I'm not a rabbi.

Adina Allen: We almost always shy away from using the word "art" exactly for the reason that you just outlined. There's so much baggage that comes along with that word. We usually say "creative process," which is also hard, because I think that could mean so many things.

But one of our foundational beliefs is that Jewish texts are not just for scholars, and that art—creative process—is not just for artists. We use creative process as a way of investigating relevant questions about our lives, inquiring into stuck places within ourselves to see what kind of new answers or information can come forth, processing challenges, and activating information to see what new can come.

Essentially, we take two things that have the most baggage for people—their Judaism and stuff around creativity and art—and we combine them together. We often start our programs by saying, "How many of you are harboring a memory from your second grade art teacher, telling you to put down the paintbrush, you'll never be an artist, stick to math or social studies." I think so many of us have that. That's really one narrow definition of what art can be, that our society has decided on. We're really trying to open up those possibilities of what it can be.

Jeff Kasowitz: As we get older we tend to grow more inhibited. When we say that we have a Jewish arts studio, people think, "Oh, this must be for kids, because kids know how to play, and kids aren't self-conscious about their creativity—they're less inhibited." But we're focused—at least in this initial phase—on working with adults, precisely because that's where the opportunity is to activate this creativity that may have been dormant.

We have found that really good things happen when we can activate creativity in adults—we can learn new insights about our lives, we can connect to one another really deeply through creative community. It really feels like the work is around creating a brave space for people to go into this vulnerability, chip away at these inhibitions, and develop some creative confidence that can add a lot of meaning to their lives.

Dan Libenson: When I've been in the studio with you, there's this gut level feeling, like, "Wow, there's something so deep and important here." We don't think of the Jewish experience—whether that's of prayer or of study—as being creative. But at your studio the experience of Judaism is an experience of creation, as opposed to an experience of absorption or reflection.

Adina Allen: What makes this space and process really unique and exciting for us is that we come at it with this approach of curiosity—of really being curious about what are other people going to bring and add, as opposed to, "Here is this knowledge that we have to impart that we want you to take away."

It's about being curious together as a community and eliciting those insights that are going to come from individuals that have never been said before—they've never occurred before—because that unique individual has never interacted with that text or that idea in that way.

I think this is always what rabbis, what scholars have been doing throughout Jewish history. The first time that I combined this in rabbinical school was when I was taking a class on Tanhuma—a very creative rabbinic *midrash* [creative interpretation]—with Nehemia Polen. Seeing these wild, imaginative stories that the rabbis were weaving off of just one little letter, or one turn of phrase, or one word, it was like, "Oh—they were weaving their imagination, their life experience, coming to new answers through the text." That is exactly what keeps Torah alive, living, an etz hayim—a tree of life—today. That's what we're required to do, I think—both for ourselves, so it remains relevant and interesting, but also, I think, in service to the tradition, so it can continue to thrive and live and evolve in the ways that it's meant to.

The first three words of Torah are, "*Bereshit barah elohim*—in the beginning, God created." The first act of the Divine is to create—God is, inherently, the creative source. A few verses later, we're told that humans are made *b'tzelem elohim*—in the divine image. We take that to mean the Divine is the creative force; we are made in the image of this divine creative force; accessing and activating our creativity is not only the way that we mirror the Divine, but we channel the Divine into this world, and partner with the Divine in the creative process, in the ongoing work of creating the world.

Jeff Kasowitz: And it's a reminder that, if each one of us is made in the image of the Divine, then each one of us is creative—and that there's something really important and meaningful and instructive about being creative in our lives.

Dan Libenson: It seems that Judaism in America over the last 100 years or more has been largely a spectator sport. There was an expectation that Jewish practice was something that you attended at services. Perhaps one of the reasons why there's a need for something new is that there doesn't seem to be the same willingness to accept that spectator sport Judaism anymore. I think people would be interested in Judaism if it tapped into their skills, their knowledge, made them feel, "Hey, you have something to contribute—we need you to make this great." What you're starting to surface here is seems like a way of doing that.

Adina Allen: To me, what b'tzelem elohim means is to value the uniqueness of each human being. I think it's inviting people to bring their skills and their talents and their knowledge, and I think it's also beyond that—giving people a way to explore what they don't know about themselves, about the world. At its best, that's what prayer should be—it should help us tap into what is beautiful, alive, and good within us, but it should also help us work through that which is stuck and intractable, that which is unknown. I think both of those things feel really important.

Jeff Kasowitz: Dan, what you're describing is my history with Judaism growing up in a mainstream Jewish community—in a fairly observant family—where we did Friday night dinners, and Shabbat services, and holidays and everything. I always felt like I was receiving Judaism—always felt like there wasn't really an entrée into going deeper and seeing what all of this really had to say about my life and the world. It's really through this creative engagement and being able to ask these questions about the things that are up for me, or the questions that I have in my life that Judaism has become more meaningful to me.

One example of how this plays out in the studio is something called "creative commentary." Every other Wednesday morning, from eight to nine thirty, we have a program here that's part *parasha* [weekly Torah portion] study and part creative writing. A different rabbi or scholar will frame the parasha and ask some questions that spark discussion for about 45 minutes about the Torah portion, and then we partner with creative writers and authors in the East Bay, and they give us these prompts to personalize the learnings and the questions from the *parasha*. We do free writes and then we share. It's amazing what people end up saying, how it touches their lives—there's tears almost every time. It really opens hearts, and creates a really beautiful community of, "This is Jewish, and this is touching something that's alive for me—and this is really meaningful."

Lex Rofeberg: How does music play into your work?

Jeff Kasowitz: We infuse all our programs with music, because music has the power to open us up. Music sends vibrations through our bodies. It has the power to connect us through melody and harmony every time, if we're singing a niggun or a chant or a prayer. What is coming out of our mouths as musical notes or vibrations is a gift to the other people in the room. How that all blends is a way to think about what creative community can look like.

One of the challenges of using music as a modality, versus something like colored pencils, is that anybody can draw on a piece of paper—there's no barrier to entry. With music, it takes a little time to be proficient with an instrument. However, people can typically bang on a drum, people can sing a niggun. We definitely infuse those kinds of elements into our programs.

Dan Libenson: I'm wondering, based on this, if you could spin out some of the fantasies of where this all leads . . . or what this is a part of. What would a future American Judaism look like in 20 or 50 years that's infused by some of the elements that you're talking about here? What would be different?

Adina Allen: I think one thing that's so exciting—and also that's so vulnerable and scary—about this as an idea is that we don't know, and we're not determining, what should this look like in 50 years. The whole goal of this is that we don't exactly know, and that it's about being open and alive to what emerges in the moment and following that. It's about tons of people being activated and alive—opening themselves as channels to something bigger than themselves that can come through them into this world.

I think what makes me really excited is what these new interpretations, new iterations of what spirituality and prayer can look like, new ways that we come together in community can do for Judaism . . . as well as how that relates to an individual's own life and work world.

This isn't about producing more "artists," but about how you take that aliveness, that connection, and bring it into whatever work you're doing—into your parenting, into the way you make spreadsheets, into the way you interact with your colleagues.

We also explicitly create programs that are about intractable issues—Israel/Palestine and other issues in the Jewish world that feel really stuck, and where more dialogue, more discussion, more debate isn't going to get us where we need to go. We offer processes and spaces where each of us can go into those places that are hard and stuck within us and move through that. That's one way that we try to use creative process, and we've done that in a number of different communities.

What we found, and how we use creative process, is also to let that intellectual information percolate down into those other parts of ourselves. I think so often we have that intellectual engagement, it's like, "Okay, I had a few feelings—moving on to the next thing in my day." But what if we stayed with that and let things sit and percolate—what might shift and change?

Those people who find that they can't bring their full selves, their creativity, their whatever, to organized Jewish life—they don't find a space for themselves—those people who are on the margins find a place here and feel enlivened and activated.

And we do a lot of professional development work which feels really important to me. This isn't about creating something separate, it's about bringing us all into this future together. It's hard—it's hard to not know. It's hard to let things emerge. It's hard to be vulnerable with one another, it's hard to get in touch with these deep places in ourselves, it's hard to start to untie the knots of those stuck, intractable issues. But wow, if the organized Jewish world could do that, how amazing.

Dan Libenson: Lex and I have realized over the last couple years that there can be a big disconnect between thinking different and doing different. Do you think that people who have participated in Jewish Studio Project programs have more to draw upon when translating new thoughts into action?

Adina Allen: Yeah, that disconnect between thinking different and doing different, what is that? There are deep places in our psychology that block us from actually making the changes that we think or say that we want, right? That is part of what the creative process is useful for, is for going into those places that can actually work. You're, "Okay, why is that stuck, and how can I understand that and parse that apart so that change can actually move forward?"

The other thing I would say that happens at the studio in these programs is that without really knowing each other, or ever necessarily having a conversation with another person in the program, you feel a deep love for them. I would say that you can really see b'tzelem elohim when we do visual art programs. You see that visibly on the page, with the exact same time, the exact same text we studied, the exact same materials—and there is not one piece that looks like any other piece. I think there's a deep love that isn't based on knowing everything about that person, but just about our shared humanity—if that feeling infused the Jewish world, so much could become possible.

Lex Rofeberg: I think there's this perception people have that art is refuge from the world of politics or the world of justice stuff—it's what you do to forget about those things. There's also that perception—and we've talked about this on the podcast in the past—that Judaism is that refuge, that you go to synagogue, it is a sanctuary from the outside stuff. It seems like you're pushing back on that, and that part of the explicit purpose of what you're doing is to help form a better world.

I'd love to hear what that looks like in your day-to-day.

Adina Allen: Both are, and should be, true—both about prayer and creative process. Sometimes you need it to be a refuge from what's happening, and just to center yourself and forget other things—and sometimes it should be used as a way to help move forward in those realms. I think both should be true, and can be true.

I have found that often at Jewish conferences we get put into the self-care, self-healing bin—which, yeah, it can be that, but I really see it as a much harder, almost more serious tool. I don't think that we can or should do the things that are traditionally thought of as social justice work, like activism, without having another part that's processing what is . . . what are we doing, why are we doing it, what have been the effects of doing it, what emotions are coming up for us as we do it? I think otherwise, we can get into some scary places.

Jeff Kasowitz: One of the feelings that we all have when we are working in the studio is a feeling of hope, and hope is a really important thing to feel when doing justice work. Without feeling like it's possible to get to a hopeful place, or a better place in this world—it's hard to move towards any sort of positive change. What we hear from the folks who have been doing this work with us is that they feel like their hearts have been opened, they feel connected, they feel hopeful, they feel like their dreams are possible.

Dan Libenson: I think a lot of people struggle with prayer—which is fundamentally, I think, a struggle about the words, about saying words that you don't believe.

Do you think you are tapping into a new kind of prayer with this ability to put me into a creative space where I actually feel like I'm creating something worthy, where I can feel that I'm doing something that matters?

Adina Allen: I think it is. I do like traditional prayer—there are things that I really like about it. I don't think we're explicitly trying to create something to replace that. We both feel a real love and connection to traditional prayer. But the things that I wish or would hope that prayer would provide, I find—and I think people find—that this process also provides.

Jeff Kasowitz: I think some of the folks who come here are having an experience that they might view as prayer or spiritual. I'm remembering an evaluation we got at the end of one of our programs from a person who graded us pretty harshly. She was like, "Okay, this seemed just like an ordinary art workshop that had some Jewish elements—it didn't really do much for me in the moment." We were like, "Okay, it's not going to work for everybody." Then a week later she sent us an email saying, "I have the piece at my desk in my office, and I look at it every day, and it's continuing to speak to me." She's saying, "Maybe what you're doing is deeper than I had initially thought in that experience."

To me this speaks of a similarity to prayer—it may not always feel transformative in the moment, but if there's a way to come back to it on an ongoing basis—which I think we're able to provide, because something is actually created—that kind of spiritual experience or meaning can last longer.

Lex Rofeberg: What would you say to the person who is asking themselves "How could I create some form of this in my community?"

Adina Allen: Our first immersive five-day deep dive into Jewish learning and creative process is happening soon. And there's going to be multiple ones of those, we hope, where people can come from all over the country and join us. We also love doing consulting and coaching with people around thinking about their unique community and their needs and their strengths, and how can they bring this in a way that's authentic and grounded and relevant for them. We're excited to connect with folks around the country.

On a smaller level I'd say anyone can start by asking themselves where can you take a creative risk in your life? In your cooking, in your spreadsheet making, with art supplies, in your parenting technique—think about ways you can try that creative risk taking, create a space where there's no comments happening and you can just be in freeform creating mode, and then reflect on that experience and see what it yielded.

Sarah Lefton

> "The biggest thing I've learned through the last 10 years of this work is that you have to make your own meaning not just through reading the text but through actually making something from each piece of text."

BimBam

At the time of this interview, Sarah Lefton was the founding executive director of *BimBam* (formerly known as *G-dcast*), which sought to create connections to Judaism through digital storytelling. *G-dcast* got its start creating short animated videos for each weekly Torah portion, which Lefton was inspired to develop as a corrective to her own mediocre Jewish education.

BimBam no longer produces new content, but the site and YouTube channel are alive and well, housing comprehensive videos on an array of Jewish topics, from texts to holidays to *Shaboom!*, an animated series for Jewish preschoolers.

Sarah Lefton has been named one of the 50 most influential Jews by *The Forward* newspaper and was a recipient of the Joshua Venture Group fellowship for Jewish social entrepreneurs. In 2012, she received the Pomegranate Prize for exceptional young Jewish educators from the Covenant Foundation. She is currently working as a freelance video producer and Creative Director of the Digital Storytellers Lab.

Dan Libenson: We first met at a conference called The Conversation, and I remember that you were going around showing the first video that you had ever made, which was the Torah portion about Balaam and the talking donkey. Everybody was so blown away and excited.

Sarah Lefton: That was a really big couple of days for me. I was walking around that hotel with a laptop like a waiter showing it to people, and thank God, because someone who saw it there made an introduction to my very first donor, who made the series possible. And somebody else who was also there is now on our board. It was an extremely formative experience.

Dan Libenson: Tell us about what *BimBam* is and what it does.

Sarah Lefton: We are a New Media production company based in San Francisco, and we make videos. Sometimes we make apps, sometimes we make audio pieces—but we make stuff. The stuff that we make happens to be about raising basic Jewish literacy. We're best known for making animations—on the one hand for adults who want to learn the basics of Judaism, whether that's about ritual, prayer, what Jews believe, or what's in the Torah. And then on the other side of things, for young families raising Jewish kids. We have a series called *Shaboom!* which is about Jewish values; we have how-to, kind of prayer-eoke videos, if you will; and other things for that audience, apps about baking challah and things like that.

Dan Libenson: How did you get from that first little video of a talking donkey to where you are today?

Sarah Lefton: I came out of tech and new media and advertising and things like that and was a recreational adult Jewish learner. I grew up with the very best mediocre Jewish education that a girl in South Carolina could get. It was very focused on identity and belonging and camp and community and Zionist folk songs and pride and cheers, and it was awesome—and that was it.

It wasn't until my 20s, when I was living in New York, that I ran into different kinds of Jews for the first time and felt that something was missing. I was so connected to Judaism and suddenly felt that there was no there there—that I didn't have any information. I was being invited to Shabbat dinners on the Upper West Side with Jews who grew up quite differently from me—whether they had gone through day school or had done a year in Jerusalem, or whatever it was—they knew things that I didn't know. Somebody asked me once if I wanted to share a few words of Torah at a dinner, and I was mortified—I didn't know what the [Torah portion] was, and frankly, I wouldn't have even known who any of the characters were if I had. This was deeply embarrassing to me.

In my 20s, I embarked on this solo adventure into Jewish learning, and I became the littlest learner. I was showing up to lots of Torah and Talmud and Hebrew adult education classes, largely in Manhattan, and finding myself the youngest person in the room by 30 or 40 years much of the time. This is before the great explosion in cool young adult Jewish experiences that now proliferate in Manhattan and elsewhere.

So I was on this adult Jewish learning experience, and at the same time was working in advertising during the birth and great flowering of the World Wide Web. I was building websites for corporate clients and doing quite a bit of video production and animation and this and that. It just started cooking for me—why isn't there this online for Judaism? In fact, there was very little online for Judaism at all—particularly for the beginning learner like me. And this just seemed crazy to me, as someone who made commercials for shampoo and cruise ships, why weren't there commercials for Jewish ideas online? The idea started to cook for me at that point.

Dan Libenson: Just to make sure that I'm understanding this right . . . essentially, the way that you think of yourself at that time is as somebody who had a positive feeling towards Judaism, who saw themselves as someone who was Jewishly connected. But when you moved from South Carolina to the big Jewish city of New York, you had a sense that the content of your Jewishness was insufficient to make you feel good about it in comparison to others that you were encountering? Or was there a different set of feelings involved as well?

Sarah Lefton: There were two things involved. One was this feeling that I was deeply connected on this heart and this hand level, I guess, but there was no head there—I was very connected through community and feeing, but not a lot of knowledge. And as somebody who otherwise thinks of herself as fairly intellectually oriented, this was disappointing to me—how could I be such an overachiever in all these other ways—how could I be so well-read, etc., etc.—and know so little about my own background? I took a class in university called Myth onto Film, where we hand painted film onto celluloid about myth, and I couldn't think of a story to tell and ended up illustrating a Greek myth. And to the Sarah of just a few years later, that was incredibly embarrassing—how did I not have stories from my own tradition to refer to?

I was at NYU in graduate school; I was surrounded by not just Jews, but a lot of Israelis in my graduate program, and hanging out on the Upper West Side with a Jewish community on Shabbat really for the first time in my adult life. I felt "less than," and that is not a way I like to feel.

But I was picking up all this Jewish information and I wanted to share it with my friends—the people I grew up with. If only they knew what I was learning now, they would be as happy as I am. I thought, well, I just have to package it up and make it fun for people. It would be so cool if I made a website and if I made a video, like I do for work, about all this Jewish stuff—it would be so great. How has that not happened yet? And long story short, at a certain point I said, "Well, I guess I've got to do it, because nobody else is going to."

Dan Libenson: So you're in this position where you're imagining that this has to exist, but it doesn't—so what do you do next?

Sarah Lefton: What I do next is get laid off from my job in advertising because it's the year 2000, and the economy is starting to tank, and everyone gets laid off. I spend 10 months hanging out around the Burning Man scene, traveling, partying, making art, and deciding to move to San Francisco. I get to San Francisco, and there is no work to be had in new media and technology, but I meet a guy who is on the board of a Jewish organization called Camp Tawonga, and next thing you know, I am the marketing director for Camp Tawonga.

What I got out of working at Camp Tawonga was a real understanding of the institutional Jewish world and how funding and philanthropy work. And while I was there, I did my first little experiment in Jewish entrepreneurship—which is, I made some funny Jewish T-shirts that I put for sale online through a little business I called Jewish Fashion

Conspiracy. I started building a little following online of people who thought I was funny and were interested in what I had to say. I got invited to The Conversation as a result of those t-shirts.

G-dcast as a concept had been brewing for me for years before I actually made a piece. I think I hit a point where I was just so frustrated that the thing I wanted to exist didn't exist. I went on a JDate with somebody who turned out to be an animator, and we didn't really have dating *fuego*, but I said to him, "For a really long time, I've wanted to make this animated Torah portion of the week video. I think it would be so cool, and I think people would really love it. Do you want to work on something like that together?" And he said, "Sure. I mean, you have to pay me." I paid him a few hundred dollars, and we made what you can still see on our website. It's the Torah portion called Balak from the Book of Numbers, the story of the talking donkey.

I went over to my friend Andy Shapiro Katz's house—he is a rabbi and educator—and sat on his couch, and with a super-cheap microphone just interviewed him and followed my intuition. And at the end I said, "Hey, can you make a joke about ass, because donkey and ass—that would be funny?" So made a little pun. Then I went home and edited it together and made something that was about three minutes long, and then Nick animated it. I called it *G-dcast*, because I thought that was funny, and it rhymed with podcast ... and went out and started showing it to people.

I heard about this conference that was going to happen called ROI. It is now an annual event put on by the Schusterman Foundation, but this was the first year. There was this call for innovative projects in Jewish life. Nick and I and another collaborator, Matthue Roth, thought, "Wow, we should really get this piece together and bring it to the ROI conference, and maybe we can show it to Lynn Schusterman and whoever else is going to be there, and maybe we'll get funding for it." This caused us to scramble and finish the piece up quick, and we brought it to Jerusalem. I was fortunate enough that I got to pitch *G-dcast* to the room. I got up in front of 150 people and showed my *G-dcast* episode, and got a standing ovation. People thought it was so exciting.

It was through the process of animating all of these Torah portions that I really learned them all—and that is such a deep and profound thing. I think the biggest thing I've learned through the last 10 years of this work is that you have to make your own meaning not just through reading the text but through actually making something from each piece of text. For some people, it's writing a blog; for some people, it's making a podcast; for me, it was producing these animated films with other folks.

Lex Rofeberg: As much as intuition tells us that more Jewish knowledge would equate with a better ability to craft inspiring new Jewish things, we've wondered if in certain cases, innovation might correlate more with having less Jewish knowledge and less sense of the need to stay true to something original. I'm curious whether being from South Carolina, or just coming to this with an open mind and not having that base of knowledge, played into your willingness to enter into this whole new world of Jewish text in the way that you did?

Sarah Lefton: I think it's true that the more I know, the less willing I am to get into dialogue with people. I think I'm quieter in these situations because the more I know, the more worried I am about what I *don't* know—you know what I mean? Many of us are intimidated by high-level discourse, especially between academics and rabbis, and we will drop out of the conversation. So the less I knew, the more willing I was to go out and say something creative or different or wacky.

Lex Rofeberg: What's so special about the internet, and what *BimBam* does, is that it allows people to be intimidated in the privacy of their own homes. If I'm intimidated by a conversation in an Upper West Side Shabbat lunch, it can feel obvious that I'm behind the eight ball and I know less than anybody in this room. If I can go online and watch a video, nobody sees me do that—so that, "Oh, gosh, I didn't know, how stupid must I look right now," is gone.

Sarah Lefton: One thing that's really worth bringing up is that there's two kinds of distribution factors—or models—at play here. I guess you can call them push and pull. Here's a good example: I got invited to a *shiva* [the Jewish custom of visiting the family of someone who died in the week after the death]. I am completely mortified because I have never been to one, I have no idea what to expect. The stakes could not possibly be higher for me to look like an idiot and hurt someone's feelings.

I can either stay away—which is how many people are going to choose—or I can dig in and learn something. People at a certain age don't have a rabbi they're going to call and ask for advice—they're going to go online, duh. When you search YouTube for "Jewish *shiva*," you're mostly going to get a lot of videos of men with beards telling you how things work in Yiddish accents. Then you'll find our series of four videos about Jewish death, burial, and mourning rituals and customs. It is such a great way to, in 10 minutes of your own time, figure out the basics and feel totally confident to walk into a shiva, a seder, or a synagogue for the first time knowing the basics and feeling okay being a beginner. We're there with a non-judgmental, non-agenda-driven, fairly light approach to these topics for something you are searching for.

Now, the other type of distribution is the push stuff. Different institutions choose to push out certain content of ours. So, for instance, there are chaplains in the hospice world who will send out our same mourning and grieving videos to their families. There are folks in the synagogue world that specifically send out our traditions of baby naming or *bris* [circumcision ceremony] videos when applicable. The internet allows us to work both ways.

Another important audience is interfaith families, or interfaith couples that are dating, where one person is Jewish and the other one isn't—but wants to be part of a Jewish conversation. Maybe the couple has decided to raise Jewish kids, or raise the children in two faiths, whatever—the point is, there's a non-Jewish person who wants to be a full part of their partner's life, and so they watch our stuff to see, "Wait, what is a bar mitzvah? Wait, what is a seder?" And by the same token, prospective converts are an important audience—they are checking out Jewish ideas, they are on a Jewish learning adventure.

One of my favorite stories is from this woman who is in a long process of converting, and her friends tease her and ask how she knows so much Torah since she's not Jewish, and she says, "Don't you guys know about *G-dcast*?" She said, "And that's when I realized that your videos were the foundation of my Jewish education, and that's where I got all my building blocks from, and I wanted to say thank you."

QUESTIONS FOR REFLECTION

- Many spaces are what we might call "God-driven" and "artist-optional"—but Amichai Lau-Lavie speaks about Lab/Shul as "artist-driven" and "God-optional." In what ways might this dramatically alter the nature of Judaism at Lab/Shul—and in other spaces driven by artists, without any requirement of God-belief?
- Adina Allen and Jeff Kasowitz are less enthused by the words "art" and "artist" than is Amichai Lau-Lavie—they prefer the phrase "creative process." Were you moved by their approach to "creative process," which they use largely to avoid the false presumption that art is "just for artists?"
- Sarah Lefton asks the provocative question: "as someone who made commercials for shampoo and cruise ships, why weren't there commercials for Jewish ideas online?" We could hear this cynically, as a comparison between consumer products and Judaism. What might be the deeper meaning here—and what would change about contemporary Jewish life if there were more (and better) "commercials" for Jewish ideas available online?

Empowering 'Regular Jews'

Benay Lappe

> *"It may turn out, at the end of the day, that what SVARA is really about is a way to get people to fall in love with Judaism."*

A Traditionally Radical Yeshiva

You may recall Benay Lappe from Part One, in which she spoke about her Crash Theory and the notion that people with Queer identities and perspectives are most likely to lead the way in cultural innovations.

Here, she speaks more specifically about one of the innovations she has contributed, SVARA: A Traditionally Radical Yeshiva.

Dan Libenson: You're one of the most exciting innovators in the Jewish space today, and we are eager to hear about what your organization, SVARA, is all about. Could you start by describing briefly what SVARA is as an organization?

Benay Lappe: SVARA is a "traditionally radical yeshiva." What that means is it's a learning-centered community, centered around the experience of learning Talmud. One purpose is to create "players"—people who are confident, informed, steeped in the values and the principles of the tradition, who are prepared to "play" with the tradition, and make it better, and bring their insights to it. Another reason SVARA exists is to create a distribution system for what I think is the smartest version of Judaism that we have.

One of the unexpected things that [has] happened since I started SVARA is that people are falling in love with Judaism because of what they see in the Talmud. It may turn out, at the end of the day, that what SVARA is really about is a way to get people to fall in love with Judaism.

Another unexpected thing is that when people come to SVARA, they learn and they find a community which becomes their home, and learning Talmud becomes their way of doing Jewish. And I really never set out to create a new way to do Jewish, but that's what's happened, and I'm finding it really interesting, and it's shifting how I see the future of SVARA and the future of Judaism in general.

I grew up in Skokie, where there was a *shul* [synagogue] on every corner, and part of what I see in our future is that there may just be a *beit midrash* [house of study] on every corner, and instead of going to shul, some people might go to the beit midrash. It may become a spiritual practice the way prayer caught on as a spiritual practice after the destruction [of the Second Temple].

Dan Libenson: How is studying Talmud at SVARA different from studying Talmud in more traditional yeshivas?

Benay Lappe: One of the ways that SVARA is different from a traditional yeshiva is our lens on the Rabbis and what's going on in the Talmud and the tradition. I would call it a "Queer lens." And what I mean by "Queer" at this moment is not LGBT, but queer in a much bigger sense, meaning: coming from and influenced by a profound experience of marginality or otherness, which informs how that person walks through the world and the critique that that person brings to the world.

So, a person can be "Queer" even though they may be heterosexual if they happen to have an experience of marginality that comes from, perhaps, a disability, or the color of their skin, or any number of other ways in which they are not in the mainstream.

As a Queer person myself, when I learned Talmud, it was so screamingly obvious to me that the Rabbis were Queer—not LGBT Queer,

I'm not talking about, you know, Jonathan-and-David and Ruth-and-Naomi stories. That's Queer 1.0. I'm talking about Queer 2.0 which involves inheriting a tradition or a story that you know very well doesn't work in this or that regard and being willing to bring your life experience to bear on that story to change it.

And I saw that [in] the Rabbis, who inherited a biblical story that wasn't working for them in so many ways. And because of what I think had to have been experiences of otherness for them, they upgraded the tradition and made it better, even overturning Torah.

And that's what I see in the Talmud. It's this enormous document recording example upon example, case upon case, of where the Rabbis bring that outsider insight to bear, whether it's to improve the lives of women or poor people or children or you-name-it.

Dan Libenson: My understanding is that a lot of the programs you run these days are six-week-long one-night-a-week sessions, where people come for two or three hours and study. And, you insist that people read the text in the original Hebrew and Aramaic. There are no translations allowed in your room. You give people dictionaries so they can look up words, but no book Talmud translations. And as a result, of course, it's very slow going. This is not a way of learning Talmud that's covering a lot of ground. And so, the question is, why do you insist upon that style, and why do you think it has been so successful and beloved by people, even people who come into your sessions not knowing a word of Hebrew, and certainly not a word of Aramaic?

Benay Lappe: There are many parts to the answer to this. The first is, if you want to know what the Talmud says, if you're really interested in the content, you should probably go to Barnes and Noble and get a book called *Wisdom of the Talmud*, and you can read it in a couple of hours, and you'll know a lot about what the Talmud says. And at the end of those couple of hours, you'll be no different, fundamentally, than you were before.

There's an epidemic lack of confidence among liberal Jews, and one of the things we're trying to do is to instill a sense of confidence, because you don't become a bold, courageous, risk-taking player until you feel confident and until you feel you have a sense of authenticity and authority. That's one of the reasons we learn in the original.

And another reason—and it could be that at the end of the day this is really what drives all of us to learn Talmud and why Talmud has survived as one of the core Jewish practices for 2,000 years—is that it's fun. But it's not just fun. It's joyful. It creates an experience that is deeply, deeply pleasurable. A professor named Mihaly Csikszentmihalyi wrote a book called Flow* which talks about those experiences that people find most pleasurable and rewarding, experiences that create a sense of total involvement, in which you completely forget what is going on in the world around you. The common dynamic of flow experiences is that there's a narrow window of balance between your skill and the demandingness of the task, so you are absolutely present and focused when you're doing it. People find flow while they're doing sports, or playing chess, or learning Talmud. And it's a very rewarding experience.

And in the beit midrash, add to that you're doing this with another person, your *hevruta* [literally, companion, but with the meaning of study partner in the beit midrash] which becomes a very intimate experience. And, you're doing it in a roomful of people who are doing the same thing, which becomes a very intimate experience among the group of people, and very community-building. I've had students who have described to me running into another student from the beit midrash out in the street or at the grocery store, and when they see each other, even if they didn't talk much in the beit midrash, they feel like they both climbed up Mount Sinai together.

Another goal of Talmud study is understanding the mechanisms of radical change in order to be able to utilize them when you need to. Learning as a spiritual practice shapes us into people who think differently. It teaches us how to think about complex issues. We don't learn Talmud the way it's learned in traditional yeshivas because, if the material is working for you, you want to learn the material for practice. But if it isn't working for you as you have received it, that's not when you teach for content; that's when you teach for process of change.

---

* Csikszentmihalyi, M. (1990). Flow: *The Psychology of Optimal Experience.* (New York, NY: Harper & Row.)

Lex Rofeberg: What is it about the Talmud and the achievement of learning your way through a difficult text that is particularly meaningful for people?

Benay Lappe: I believe we all walk around with half-completed discernments and insights. We walk around with the shards of our life experiences that are not yet completely processed and integrated and understood, and usable. And when you learn a text with a partner, as you're trying to figure out what the text says, you'll say something, your partner will say something else. You'll then say something, they'll say something else. And something about the text that you're trying to figure out will trigger a memory, will trigger one of these half-figured-out insights, and all of a sudden it will become whole, and there will be a light bulb, there will be a click.

That's a beautiful moment, and it's a wonderful feeling. And that's one of the ways that a text, which can be about the laws of lost and found, or about truth-telling and lie-telling. It can trigger for you something that has created now a full insight, about yourself or about the world, that may be completely unrelated to what the text was about. And that's very satisfying.

And I think at the end of the day, what SVARA is about is just that we figured out a way to take this material, this experience that's been used by not even 1%—it's probably more like a tenth of one percent of Jews—and we figured out a way to make it accessible to the other 99.9%.

Lex Rofeberg: From what you described, SVARA's work is all about taking a text, the Talmud, which happens to be native to the Jewish tradition, and bringing a Queer lens to it, and finding the elements of the Talmud that speak, in particular, to Queer people. Do you work with folks who aren't Jewish, but who are interested in connecting to this ancient text from the Jewish tradition through a Queer lens? And is it different for people to come at this from a Jewish lens in particular?

Benay Lappe: There's nothing about learning Talmud that requires you to be Jewish to do it. For Jews, there is a kind of redemption that happens that's probably absent among non-Jews who learn Talmud. It happens in that moment when you realize that your tradition is really smart, and you trust it, and it trusts you, and all of a sudden you feel better about yourself as a Jew.

But there are lots of people who are not Jewish in the beit midrash at SVARA. And if we're right that learning Talmud actually can shape who you are as a person, this is something that should be available and accessible to the whole world as a practice, and I would love that to happen. We have lots of seminarians from other traditions, and seekers who come to the beit midrash, and if they don't already have their *aleph-bet* [that is, know the Hebrew/Aramaic alphabet], we put them through a one-day aleph-bet marathon, and they're ready to go. This diversity only enriches the conversation.

I think my ultimate takeaways from my experience of learning Talmud are that the tradition is really, really smart. It's smarter than you can imagine. We should recognize that it's not perfect, and it needs to be fixed, and it needs to be made better, but it trusts us, even though we may get it wrong now and then—but it trusts us, ultimately. It believes every human being has *svara* [moral intuition].

We shouldn't be afraid to mess with the tradition. What SVARA, the yeshiva, is about is giving people not only the confidence, but the learning that it takes to mess with the tradition in a responsible way. The Rabbis never thought that you needed the title "Rabbi" to do that. You needed to have two things: You needed to be *gamirna* and *savirna*—you needed to be learning/learned, and you had to have *svara*. And everyone can have that.

Brett Lockspeiser

> "You might think of the Jewish library as a bunch of books on a shelf . . . a bunch of discrete rectangles that are somehow separate from one another. But that's not actually the shape of the tradition—that's not actually how it functions."

The Future of Torah

Brett Lockspeiser is the cofounder of Sefaria, a free living library of digital Jewish texts and their interconnections designed to create space for more people to engage with the textual treasures of Jewish tradition. When we spoke, Lockspeiser was Sefaria's Chief Technology Officer, a position he recently left to start a new venture.

Before founding Sefaria, Lockspeiser was a product manager at Google, where he led the team that created the Google News Archives. His work at Google inspired his vision for Sefaria's platform. Due to the highly convoluted and connected nature of Jewish text and discussion, Sefaria's code is incredibly complex, and designed to be a living platform rather than a preservative archive. All of the platform's code is intentionally released under an open source license so that anyone can reuse it or conduct research.

Dan Libenson: Am I right that the goal of Sefaria is to bring, essentially, every Jewish text from the past online in a free—and, ideally, in the future, translated—way?

Brett Lockspeiser: Yes—that's the big vision. If it's part of the giant Jewish conversation in text, then we want it to be freely available and interconnected to the rest of the texts in the tradition. We're currently working through the core canon—the library is now about 130 million words of texts, so it's a growing and large database. It's the largest database of English-language Torah texts anywhere, and the largest free database of Hebrew and Aramaic texts anywhere.

Dan Libenson: What's available there now? You have, obviously, the entire Torah, and the entire Talmud—what else?

Brett Lockspeiser: We currently have about every text that I've ever heard of. Better scholars on our team are taking over the prioritizing—because they're aware of texts that even I'm not as familiar with.

We have the Torah, the commentaries, the Mishnah—complete in English, a lot of Mishnah commentaries. The Talmud. One of our big pieces of news from the last year is that we were able to broker a deal with Steinsaltz and the Koren publishers to make a complete English translation of the Talmud available for free online—so you can go to Sefaria now and read the Babylonian Talmud in English.

Beyond that, we have a lot of halachic texts—these are the legal codes about how Jewish law is actually applied from the Talmud. A lot of texts in Kabbalah—Jewish mysticism. A lot of texts in Hasidut—all sorts of mystical and moral dimensions of understanding the Torah. It goes on and on—we're starting now to include some contemporary texts as well, and getting into more contemporary commentary.

Dan Libenson: And, you've networked each text to the others in this way that these brilliant rabbis, centuries ago, kept in their heads—but now you're able to follow all those trails through the way the software is designed, right?

Brett Lockspeiser: Yes, the interlinking is a core focus of the project. It's something we see as modeling a value in Torah itself—is that it's about connectedness and interconnectedness. Anytime you say something, you cite a source, or you cite an opinion that came before. In any case, you want to be connected to the other texts and the other voices that are in the tradition. It's a great example of where this ancient tradition and new technology really converge—we're building a network, we're building a graph that interconnects all of these conversations.

We often talk about how you might think of the Jewish library as a bunch of books on a shelf, because that's how you've seen it in a *beit midrash*, in a learning hall, or in a library. You might think that it's a bunch of discrete rectangles that are somehow separate from one another. But that's not actually the shape of the tradition—that's not actually how it functions. And if you're a great scholar and you've learned for years and years, you get to appreciate that—but it takes a lot of hard work to build up this visualization in your mind about how it's not just a thousand rectangles, but it's actually one conversation, one network that spreads across time and space.

We have the opportunity to make that awareness a priority in the application and in the data. You can experience that by clicking on a line of Torah and seeing all the commentaries, all the places where it's requoted, following those lines along. You click from one to another, and then that leads you somewhere else—you get to build these wonderful trails as you traverse this network. And we get to visualize it in other ways, too—we can actually take that data and make interactive graphical visualizations that show this network connectivity in ways that haven't been visualized before, except in the imagination of great scholars.

Dan Libenson: How do you think about the mission of Sefaria?

Brett Lockspeiser: Our purpose is to create the future of Torah—to do it ourselves, and to help others create the future of Torah. When we think about Torah, we think that it has at least two sides to it—Jewish tradition talks about a written Torah and an oral Torah both being given at Sinai. On the text side, we have this amazing tradition of every generation adding layers and dimensions into an interconnected text-based conversation. That's something that's fixed and that we're trying to bring online—make accessible to more people, make it free, make it reusable, make ways for people to get at it in its original and in translation.

Then we're also thinking about the oral dimension of Torah—which is about conversation, about making meaning, about having face-to-face interactions, about bringing an ancient text and making it relevant to your contemporary life. That's, in some ways, a more challenging side of the project. We're thinking about what we can do in technology to make oral Torah—the experience of meaning-making—more interesting, more relevant, and more engaging for more people.

I think many people have a preconceived notion about what religious texts are. They think it's about the Christian Bible—you're going to Bible study, you're reading the Bible. But the world of Jewish texts is so much deeper than that. Once you get beyond the Bible, and you get into the Midrash, and you get in the extra stories that are added on on top of the Bible, and you get into the Talmud—it's surprising. Some of them are raunchy and weird and racy and violent, and all sorts of things that are interesting. I want to help people get beyond the surface level of, "Oh, this is about the Bible," and realize that the world of Jewish texts is just a lot weirder than that—and you might find something that surprises you or interests you in it.

Lex Rofeberg: Where do the texts all come from?

Brett Lockspeiser: Today, most of our texts are coming from scanning and digitization work that we do ourselves, together with partner organizations in Israel and New York. We're actually taking books and physically scanning them, running through the process of turning images into actual text, and then taking that digital text and structuring it into the database. Sefaria is all about having a structured data for the text—not just images like PDFs. We're working with actual books.

For the translations, primarily we're finding publishers that have high-quality translations, and we're trying to broker deals with them. The model that we've been using—which is, I think, relatively novel in the world in general—is that we do the fundraising to pay a bounty to a publisher, and they release the text with a Creative Commons license, but they retain the copyright—we don't buy copyrights from publishers. The publishers are still free to do everything that they're doing, but in addition, the text becomes available for free online—and not just for Sefaria. These deals generate a broad license for the world at large, that everyone can use and reuse these texts in all sorts of novel ways that we have even yet to imagine.

We also have a whole platform on Sefaria where users can pick from our library and create their own source sheets. Source sheets are a practice of Jewish educators to make a mixtape from the library of Jewish canonical sources—to pick a theme and take lines, paragraphs, from a variety of sources that all help to illustrate a particular topic. It's a very Jewish practice in that it's about being polyvocal—it's really about having one piece of paper with multiple voices on it. The sources on a source sheet don't necessarily agree with one another—and maybe that's part of what you're teaching, is how they disagree with one another.

To make source sheets, people had to know 18 different websites and pieces of software, remember which one had which texts, and then they had to copy and paste the text into Microsoft Word, and they couldn't get the bilingual formatting to look right all the time. It was just a painful process, logistically, for them to get through. We were able to build an app that makes that process easier for educators to do.

The Sefaria source sheet builder lets you say the name of a text, type in a citation for a text, and it magically appears on your sheet in English and in Hebrew. The layout is flexible and dynamic, so you can move things around in their orientation without breaking everything, and hopefully it looks good all the time. As you're browsing the library or searching anything you can find, you can just click to add it to one of your source sheets. And you can add more things—you can add your own questions, your own comments, you can edit and change the translations that are in your source sheet that happen just in your copy of something.

We also let people publish them. It used to be a big problem—there wasn't a good resource for sharing or finding other people's source sheets, and educators would often send out an email to some list or to a bunch of colleagues saying, "Hey, I'm working on a source sheet on violence—what sources do you have? Do you have something for me?" Everybody had Microsoft Word documents sitting on their hard drive which were inaccessible to anyone else. It was this great big waste, that there was all this great knowledge that a lot of the educators were willing and happy to share—but it was just stuck on their computers.

To date, over 80,000 source sheets have been created on Sefaria. Most of them are private, developed by a teacher for their particular class. We've got, now, almost 9,000 public sheets—and those public sheets get tagged as well, so people can say what are the general topics that the sheet is about. That has created—totally from the wisdom of the crowd—a topical index of the all of the most important themes that Jewish educators, today, are thinking about in their teaching.

In essence, through source sheets, we've created a user-generated space on Sefaria where people are expressing themselves—where they're having opinions, they're adding contemporary questions, they're adding images and videos—not just texts. But everything they do is connected to the primary sources in the library.

Dan Libenson: How did you and your partner come to this incredibly audacious idea, which has now translated itself into an organization with 17 staff members in, what, five years? It's incredible.

Brett Lockspeiser: Josh Foer and I met on the Bronfman Youth Fellowship and had fallen mostly out of touch. He became a science journalist; I got involved in technology, started working at Google. Then, a mutual friend of ours heard that we both were dismayed at the currently bad state of these texts online and put us back in touch. We couldn't find Mishnah online; the Talmud wasn't there, which was shocking to us. It seemed like there were so many obvious and interesting things that could and should be done if somebody would just go ahead and give it a try, so we started working on it.

I had not been involved in Jewish life after college; I didn't see myself as having a career as a professional Jew at all. But when Josh and I started talking about this idea it just felt like it was a great intersection for me, personally. I had enough of a picture of what the Torah conversation looks like and a background in technology. Google had indoctrinated me with the sense that access to information is inherently empowering.

We heard about a grant opportunity, a fund that came together specifically around Jewish new media innovation projects and thought this was a perfect way to launch our idea. We shopped around the grant proposal to a number of people, and everyone was sort of like, "Yeah, right."

Dan Libenson: Were they like, "This is too unbelievable—this is too big," or something like that?

Brett Lockspeiser: Yes. Neither of us had a background in the nonprofit world, neither of us had a background in the Jewish world at all. Even though we had done other things, in this world we were outsiders—who were we? We were proposing this really big, audacious project. Everyone said, "Nobody's done it yet—why would you be able to do it?" or, "How much is that going to cost?" or, "The copyright holders are never going to want to work with you, because they're trying to make money."

We realized that the idea didn't communicate on paper, that a grant proposal was the wrong way to pitch this idea. It motivated us to say, "The way we have to do this is we have to show people—we have to demonstrate to people what this is going to feel like." We spent about two years working on a prototype—building a demo that people could get excited about. Early on the focus was Genesis chapter 1—and it was like, "How many connections can we add to Genesis chapter 1 in an interactive environment?" We started recruiting volunteers saying, "Help us fill out more and more of this database. It doesn't have to be complete—it just has to be exciting. It has to have enough paths to follow to get you excited."

It really changed things. When I brought an iPad to a meeting and showed people, "Here's the text, I click on this line, look what pops up," it stopped being, "That's too big—we can't do it," to, "Cool—we want this."

Dan Libenson: When I think about your story, I'm thinking about what a regular Jew can do that a professional Jew can't do. Your background at Google allowed you to conceive of the idea that we could organize all of the Jewish information. In the context of Google where they're trying to organize *all* of the information, the idea of trying to organize just all of the Jewish information sounds like a small project. Whereas for anybody who's in the Jewish community, it feels overwhelming and crazy and ridiculous, which maybe explains some of the early resistance to giving you a grant to do something that sounds insane.

Brett Lockspeiser: Yes, coming from Google, I was able to conceive of this project as actually small. It's a huge project—it really is—but from some perspective, I was able to sit down and think, "You know what, we're talking about the core—we're talking about 1,000 books. That's totally finite." This was part of our early pitch, too, to say, "Google is putting up billions, if not trillions at this point, of webpages in its index—we're just talking about getting 1,000 books really well structured in a database."

In fairness, it's actually a bad comparison—because what we're doing is actually a lot harder than what Google has to do in indexing a webpage or in scanning a book. We're actually doing a lot more, by bringing a consistent structure and segmentation and interlinking to all of these books. Still, it was a finite project in my head—not something that was totally unbearable.

I feel like it's often the case that you need outside perspective to push things forward. You need to have enough of a picture of the domain that you're trying to affect to at least have a grasp of what you can and can't do. There's something valuable, also, about having the naive optimism of not knowing how hard a problem is.

There's a common curve that you can see online for startups, where every startup begins with a sense of naive optimism. You just think, "We're going to change the world." Then you hit this moment of the informed pessimism where you learn more about your domain, and you realize, "This is actually really hard—I don't know if we can deliver on all that we were promising before." The success of a project like this comes down to whether you come out of that into an informed optimism—to say, "I recognize there are these real challenges, but we found a path that works, that's still going to be meaningful and helpful." I think, luckily, we were able to emerge on the other side of that coin—and now we're definitely emerging on the informed optimism of the Torah.

Lex Rofeberg: What kinds of resistance has this project been met with?

Brett Lockspeiser: There are some real tensions here that are fascinating, and that we definitely had to grapple with. We are not getting resistance to the idea that making Jewish texts available online is a good thing. Nobody has actually come to us and said, "You shouldn't be putting this text online at all." But, there's definitely concern from educators about the translation, and about how you encourage and motivate language skills when so many translations are available.

The Jewish tradition definitely has tensions around who should be allowed to open up what kind of texts. Should the text be translated or not translated? But the arc of history in the Jewish world is definitely moving towards more openness, more availability to more people.

There was definitely a tension about writing down the Talmud—that the Talmud was this oral tradition. You'll find sources in the Talmud itself and earlier that say that you should never do it—that writing down the Talmud is equivalent to pulling it up by the roots, or burning the Torah, that there's a serious problem with trying to make an oral tradition written. But it happened—there was a decision that if the life of the entire tradition is in jeopardy, then let's write it down.

We definitely believe it's an important first step to give people the opportunity to find something that resonates with them personally in the first place. That's what's going to motivate the desire to develop real skills.

Dan Libenson: What counts as a Jewish text, in general, but specifically for Sefaria? In modern Jewish times, the Jewish texts seem to me at least include all of Yiddish literature, for example, all of American literature in English about the American Jewish experience. It seems like if all of those books could also be made free on the internet, and translated, and linked to all of the sources that they reference . . . wow.

Brett Lockspeiser: I'll say it's already happening currently. Where it's happening is in source sheets. Source sheets are the place where it's your thing—you can add whatever you want to it. We see speeches from Martin Luther King brought in, and Benjamin Franklin, and Shakespeare, and quotes from the Quran. In source sheets, that's happening all the time—and it's becoming connected, too. When you create a source sheet with a particular source in Sefaria, that gets linked to the text. When you click on the text, you can see the sheets that people have made with these other pieces of culture around the world that are already in there.

I should say that I do have a bigger dream for the technology that we're building. Sefaria is an organization that is devoted to Jewish texts—that's in our mission; all of our donors are donating to us because that's what we do in particular. But our software is not particularly Jewish, per se—it models a lot of Torah values, but it's really about interconnected texts. One day, I would love to see a federation of different organizations that each take up the cause of a particular corpus of literature—a particular body of human wisdom. It's not in our skillset to coordinate the body of Islamic texts—we don't know how to do that right. But I would love for the people who do know how to do that right to take our software and build a Sefaria for Islamic texts, Buddhist texts, Shakespeare—everything.

If that happens, then you get the opportunity for the big site that connects to all of them. We'll have to figure out how Sefaria relates to that, because as I say, our mission is about Jewish texts in particular—so we have to figure out how we can do the work of motivating other groups to do that.

Dan Libenson: It sounds like your source sheets app is giving people a platform to ultimately write new texts. That is pretty profoundly democratizing, isn't it?

Brett Lockspeiser: Definitely. Democratizing access to knowledge is one of the big underlying goals of this project. In the Jewish context, text is where the authority comes from. The authority of rabbis in the Jewish tradition is rooted in the text. They're a rabbi because they know the texts well enough that they can navigate them and figure out how to make a decision, and a particular ruling about something.

That expertise is not going to change—but access to the underlying authority becomes more and more open. We like to imagine that there's a student in some classroom somewhere, and their teacher is telling them something, and they're able to do a little search on Sefaria, browse some connections, and find a source that disagrees with what their teacher says. They can express that disagreement in a way that's rooted in authority of the entire tradition—we like that. I think it's more exciting when more people are able to participate because they have the ability to touch into the source of authority in our tradition.

In terms of the new texts being written on Sefaria, it demonstrates that the Torah tradition of text is not over—it's not just the texts of the past. It's still happening today. There is alive today someone who is going to be the Rashi of our generation. 100 years from now, we'll look back and think, "Of course—that's a core part of the Jewish canon." We're always trying to wonder, how is that going to happen?

Aliza Kline

> "If we are designing for a Jewish practice, as opposed to designing for a human need, we will do it differently."

OneTable

Aliza Kline is in the rare position of being the founding executive director of two major innovative Jewish organizations in her career, which she has devoted to re-imagining Jewish ritual and making it open to the full diversity of the Jewish community.

Aliza Kline currently serves as President and CEO of OneTable, an organization focused on helping people make Friday night dinner a central part of their lives. Previously, she served for ten years as founding executive director of Mayyim Hayyim Living Waters Community Mikveh in the Boston area, a mikveh (Jewish ritual bath) whose mission is to reclaim, reinvent, and teach about Jewish ritual immersion for contemporary spiritual use and to make it maximally open and accessible.

Dan Libenson: You are relatively rare in the world of Jewish innovators at this point, because you are now on your second major Jewish innovation. Having spent 10 years building Mayyim Hayyim, you are now the founding director of the OneTable project.

To start, please tell us about the beginning of your work in this area with Mayyim Hayyim—and how you thought about starting a new type of Jewish organization. I'm particularly interested in the idea that you were reaching deep into the Jewish well, into Jewish history, not only to revitalize something that was tired, but to revive something that was, in some ways, dead.

Aliza Kline: Mayyim Hayyim is a mikveh, a gathering of waters. Mikveh is one of our most mysterious and ancient rituals. It comes from the very beginning, literally introduced in the beginning of Genesis, where God gathers up the waters. This primordial water that we can immerse ourselves in gives us a chance to start over.

The idea of creating or recreating a space where people could feel totally comfortable to be their honest, true selves—physically and emotionally and spiritually—was something that people were hungry for and clamoring for, but no one realized that mikveh might be a solution. There was not exactly a groundswell of interest to recreate this mikveh—and yet, in the early 2000s, I was brought in as a partner with Anita Diamant and a small but mighty group of other women—and then eventually men—who really wanted to reclaim and reinvent this mikveh, not by changing the core of what a mikveh is—just a pool of water—but by reframing access to it.

It should be one of the most inclusive and welcoming spaces—it's literally just a pool of water—and instead, over time, mikveh had become mysterious, hidden, interpreted in terribly misogynistic ways. The idea that when you immerse in a mikveh, you go as God created you in your full naked self, can lead to abuse of the space and the power of who controls it.

The idea behind Mayyim Hayyim was to design an entire physical space and program around each person walking in the door or entering into the space. We wanted to make it a desirable place—what happens if you add in windows, if you add in heated floors? If you add in colors and space that are not gendered, but are rather accessible to everybody? What if you add in a lift for someone who can't walk down the stairs? What if the person who welcomes you when you come in reflects who you are? If you are a Jew of color, so might be the person who welcomes you in. If you are healing from a painful illness or injury, so might be the person who welcomes you in. If you are queer and transitioning, converting, celebrating—any of those things—you should be able to be the focus of what happens when you come into a ritual space.

It was an incredible opportunity for me, as a professional, to both dig deep into our Jewish history and ritual well and find the ritual where people could be the most vulnerable. You're literally physically naked when you immerse—and in order to feel safe, and to actually sink, you have to exhale, you have to be calm. You can't do that if you're scared or uncomfortable, or in some way faking who you are. The idea of creating this space meant the bar had to be incredibly high in terms of sensitivity, in terms of thoughtfulness, and in terms of accessibility. That's the very best professional challenge I could ever have—that's the Judaism that I'm looking for, that I am hungry for, and that I firmly believe exists—but it takes a lot of effort and practice to make it happen.

Dan Libenson: Could you walk us through the steps you took, from an innovation standpoint, that potentially could be abstracted and applied to other areas of Jewish life?

Aliza Kline: The initial motivation for Mayyim Hayyim was absolutely articulated by Anita Diamant, who is a writer and a creator and a passionate advocate for accessible Judaism. Her then-fiancé converted to Judaism, and the presto change-o moment before you come out as a Jew is to immerse in a pool of water. She remembers going with him to a mikveh that was clearly not designed for that purpose ... and despite being a guest in a foreign space, he was transformed, and so was she, as his partner.

It sparked a light—can you just imagine what that kind of transition and transformation could be like if it were celebrated and honored and a light shone upon it, as opposed to feeling like an interloper in a different space? That was the beginning—really the kernel—of thinking about what this ritual could be like.

If you approach the creating of a ritual from the perspective of a designer, you want to first know what people need and what they value—what are they looking for, what's missing in their lives, and how are they meeting that gap on their own?

We started talking with people who were looking to mark a transition in their life, which might have the same magnitude even as converting to Judaism, but for which there isn't an obvious ritual. We talked to a lot of people who were dealing with a diagnosis around cancer, or who had become a survivor of it. People who were entering into a new phase of a relationship and people who were changing their bodies and lives because of a major weight loss.

We began designing the space, the program, even the location of Mayyim Hayyim based on what we were learning from them. We spent a lot of time thinking about how do you go through the experience, and how is it done so that you feel like you're the center of the space? We started by designing—thinking very carefully about language and aesthetics.

We built in an art gallery and added music and had original liturgy written for the rituals that were coming. Everything was done with an absolute eye towards *hidur mitzvah*—towards heightening the beauty of the ritual—so that rather than this being an "ichse" kind of experience, it could be an, "Oh, that's beautiful—it's some place I want to go." It meant interviewing several architects and developers and interior designers and writers and so on so that this space could really resonate with as many people as possible, but also reflect the concerns that we heard, and the questions and desires that we heard, from our potential users.

We felt people should walk in and feel like, "This place is designed for me." That, I think, was the most wonderful praise we ever heard from people—that they would come in and say, "I'm coming because I have decided that, while I've been living with my partner for a long time, now we want to get pregnant, and so sex is different. You have a ceremony that absolutely speaks to me—thank you."

Some of these design decisions seemed intuitive to us, but the mikveh itself, creation and design, is actually so counterintuitive that this is not based on market research—it's not about, "Should we build a mikveh—yes or no? Will you pay for it—yes or no?" It was a much bigger question about our spiritual and physical and emotional needs, and how the Jewish community, Jewish resources might respond to them.

Lex Rofeberg: I understand that you had to raise $2 million to create Mayyim Hayyim, and I'm interested in the process of how you take a great idea and prove that it's a great idea that's worth investing in.

Aliza Kline: While there may be hundreds of people converting in each city—and certainly that was the case in Boston when we started—the idea of people lining up to donate money and create resources for a mikveh was totally nonexistent.

There's a lot of conversation about what our community needs, as though we can just declare up high that, "This is what our community needs next." Mayyim Hayyim definitely evolved much more organically than that. There was a particular explicit need that Mayyim Hayyim addresses in its construction and its design—but a lot of what has evolved has been delightfully surprising, and also indicative of other needs.

So, for example, it was created very carefully and politically as a complement to existing organizations in the Boston Jewish community—that was something we worked very hard on, so that we wouldn't be perceived as threatening, but as an added benefit.

A number of individuals, predominantly those who have become our most essential and sacred volunteers—the men and women who become mikveh guides, who really support each individual, and who volunteer several hours a week—for many of them, this has become their community, and this has become the place where they feel the most at home, most safe—they literally become a member of Mayyim Hayyim. It has actually become, for them, not only a place of their personal volunteer work, or their personal spiritual exercises and practices—but also a place of community and belonging.

Dan Libenson: As a transition into your work with OneTable, can you start by telling us what OneTable is?

Aliza Kline: OneTable is an online and in-person hub and platform for young adults to create micro-communities around the Shabbat dinner table, ultimately building a lifelong practice. What that looks like is like an AirBnB for Shabbat dinner—we've created an opportunity for people all over the country to apply, to say, "Shabbat dinner is something I want to try, or is important to me, and this is why."

There's a brief application for hosts, and they create an online posting for their event based on the city they're in and the food they would like to serve, and whether this is a dinner with lots of ritual or a little bit of ritual—but they, as the host, have total control, and can create the environment. They can select whether it's a totally private dinner—they just want to have friends and get together, mostly because they are new to hosting—or whether they're open to having anybody at their table. Most of the dinners that are open for OneTable tend to take place in a public space, in a park or a beach. In smaller towns where the opportunity to go to a Shabbat dinner with other young adults is few and far between, they also tend to be more open and even more welcoming.

Since OneTable started, just two years ago, there have been well over 30,000 seats at the table, well over 2,300 dinners, and each week it grows—literally there's a week over week growth. This says to me that there is a tremendous interest and need. If we provide the platform and the support that hosts need to achieve a gathering, and then get out of the way, we see a tremendous explosion of creativity.

Dan Libenson: I'm really interested in how your innovations are so careful and so thoughtful and take so long. What you are modeling, I think, is a modularization—a tinkering with pieces of Judaism separate from their presence in a larger system.

I'm curious how you feel about this slow and thorough approach. Let's say you spent 10 years on each innovation, you're only going to be able to tinker with five or six things in a lifetime. What are we going to do with everything else?

Aliza Kline: First of all, I personally am a ritualist—if I have a choice between spending a couple hours learning, studying text, versus engaging in a ritual—whether it's meditation or walking or hiking or dancing or praying or singing or immersing or whatever—that's where I go. I have a theory that, for many people, that's more accessible, because it's also universal. Shabbat is my little escape, right now, from the madness of the world—I really need to not look at any news for a while, and I can, because I have to be doing this other ritual, and I can only do one thing at a time.

I will also say there's a broader perspective here. If we are designing for a Jewish practice, as opposed to designing for a human need, we will do it differently. I say this meaning no disrespect for the folks who have created Shabbat alternatives—but I just want to question it.

If you are designing with Shabbat dinner as your goal—and you are asking what are the needs of Shabbat dinner, you might come up with items, like, "Everybody, you need a challah, you need candles and candlesticks. You need wine or juice, and you need a beautiful cup to put it in, because we have this concept of beautifying the mitzvah—so you should have it in a beautiful glass. Let's get them a really beautiful glass, and maybe a nice cover for the challah. And you can put it all in a box—Shabbat in a box. Maybe I'll have a CD with beautiful music." You can think of all the different things that would really enhance and create this experience and pick it up and put it out and now you're done.

However, I'm not designing for that—I'm designing for the person. And if I'm designing for the person, I have a whole other set of questions.

OneTable is really designed to support the population of people between undergraduate education and having children—and obviously, that spans a broad population, and you need to break that down, but let's just say generally 20s and 30s, which is also, because we're in 2016, generally referred to as "millennials," so I'll use those terms somewhat interchangeably—but the idea is, I know what I need on Friday night, but I am not who I'm designing for.

Our first hire at OneTable was Jamie Betesh, who is a market researcher, who was in the target population herself. She could go to dinners on Friday nights—in supper clubs, in restaurants, in people's homes, dinners that were identified as Shabbat, dinners that weren't—and start finding out what are people doing? We ended up identifying a whole team of observers who could fit into the population that they were observing—so if they needed to be Russian-speaking, or gay men, or Upper East Siders—they were able to disappear in, and then would come back and let us know what they learned.

What we found was fascinating. In the early 20s, people live a very similar life to their college years—they might have dinner with friends, maybe with a whole spread from Trader Joe's, and they can even do blessings sometimes—but then they're going to go out. They're not going to have dinner as their whole night—so we want to be sure that we're not getting up a model where you sit down at seven o'clock and then you're there at the table until eleven. In fact, they don't have tables—so ixnay on that, too. We're called OneTable because it's kind of a helpful, catchy term—but to sit around a table with matching plates, it feels like you're playing house, at a certain age.

Then, as people are getting closer to 30, they just kept talking about how tired they were—so tired, exhausted. So when Friday night comes, is there a way to have prepared foods already? And maybe I have just eight or nine people, or maybe five or six, and I have a glass of wine, and that is my night—I'm not going out, no way am I going out afterward.

Then we get into couples, who, as we know, want to be with other couples ... and then people start thinking about whether they're having children and who are they with and what are those needs. It definitely became clear that once you're having kids, Friday night dinner takes on a whole other experience, and becomes clearly beyond our scope.

Then there's this whole world of technology that was not there even three years ago that makes it even easier for people to get together—so let's use it. So for the first year and a half, we built on top of Feastly, which is a social dining platform—which is like AirBnB for food. The technical pieces we can answer.

Your anxiety is a different kind of problem—that one, I think, is going to take a conversation and some coaching. But okay, so we can do that. I think my Shabbat coaches and the dinner hosts are kind of the mikveh guides. In our case, the dinner hosts themselves are volunteers, and they are responsible for creating a beautiful experience for their guests so that their guests feel like, "Oh, this was so good, I want more of it in my life." Ultimately, we're not interested in people doing Shabbat once—we really want this to become a practice in people's lives. That is a whole different design challenge—it's so much more fun.

Dan Libenson: Why do you want it to be a practice in people's lives? You're not coming from a religious denominational organization here—you're just devoted to this one practice of having Shabbat dinners regularly. Why?

Aliza Kline: Every week, there is more research about the epidemic of loneliness and disconnection, particularly among millennials. It's actually higher among millennials right now than any other population. There are a lot of assumptions about how it's probably based on technology and based on how much our faces are in our phones, as opposed to engaging with others. And the loneliness leads to lots of other things, like high stress and pain and suffering.

The desire to connect with other people in real life is important and easily articulated—but for some reason, there is often a barrier between the desire for it and the ability to actually do it.

OneTable, by focusing on Shabbat dinner as a place to have an opportunity to engage in conversation in real life, face-to-face conversation and communication and eating together, has an important value that actually meets the needs of a population who is feeling disconnected from each other. It actually gives them the tools and resources they need to connect. That's one of the deep, ancient values inherent in Shabbat—that it can be a separate, elevated space. That *kedushah*, the holiness, the sanctity of this time, can actually elevate and create community.

I have a long list of the Jewish values behind why OneTable functions and focuses explicitly on Shabbat dinner—but the most fundamental is that interpersonal connection. It comes up every time we do a survey or evaluation or interview—above anything else is the relationship piece, the face-to-face connection piece. It's different than happy hour at a bar, it's different than being in an audience sitting next to somebody and viewing something. It's around the table, and it creates the foundation for a lifelong practice.

The beauty of Shabbat—aside from the fact that it's there, it's ours for our whole lives, and, by the way, every single week, because we need it that much—but it's also an elevated and sanctified time that's beyond our own control. Most of us now time-shift everything. We work when it makes sense to us, we exercise when it makes sense, we eat when it makes sense—we do all these things when it best fits our personal needs. But Shabbat is dictated beyond us—it starts Friday night, whether or not we are in the right place or mind. I think that offers this wonderful relief and humility that we need, that we can actually control all of this—and to just submit for a little while is a relief, and it gives us the opportunity to then replenish our souls and our egos, to start again the next week.

Dan Libenson: I'm fascinated by the interplay of the design thinking process you've described—which inquires deeply into people's needs and experiences right now—and the deep history and traditions that you are working with. I sense you are saying that ultimately this Jewish stuff has to be in the service of people, and at the same time, it is a particular set of things, it does have a past, it does have a perspective.

If you were going to try to create an atmosphere of innovation, of design thinking, what are the factors that you think would contribute to that? Do we need to empower more women innovators? Create projects that bring different generations and populations together? What would you focus on to create an atmosphere where it wouldn't only be Aliza Kline going around from one ritual to another and blowing them up, but that actually there would be a whole cadre of people like that?

Aliza Kline: Well, first of all, we're not reinventing ritual. We did not fundamentally change the ritual of mikveh. We were quite clear, it is a kosher mikveh, and you can use it for the most traditional purposes, or the most contemporary. And when we get to Friday night dinner, we are not reinventing Shabbat. When we asked people what their associations were with it, guess what they said? "Challah." Guess what our logo is? It's a challah. Because it makes people feel good.

I'll probably get in trouble if I say anything around this in terms of the gender piece, but at the beginning I described myself as driven by ritual. I am certainly not anti-intellectual—God forbid. If I'm sitting with a learning partner in *hevruta*, and we have just explored a text, and we come to a new realization—that can get my heart beating fast, but when given the choice, I go to the emotional. I do think that my being a woman is probably connected to that.

Maybe I simply had more permission, growing up, to go to the emotional first. I remember the conversations I had with my mom were different than those with my dad around preparing for Shabbat. My mom was new to Jewish ritual and Jewish practice, and for her, it was incredibly emotional. The work that went into setting the table with a white tablecloth and fresh flowers—that act was just as important as any blessings that were said. She taught me, and I'm the kid who set the table. If you come to my dinner tonight, you will see a white tablecloth with the same Kiddush cup. There are certain of these blessings and rituals and experiences that I think do get passed down in our heritage—and it's fundamentally, though, about the way it feels.

I think that what I and others can bring to this is a willingness to give weight and power to the emotional piece. It's what drives us, what catalyzes our memories, what helps us be creative and curious—it's an emotional thing.

I light candles the way I light candles. You may not light candles at all—that's okay. I think that that permission is also something that I feel is not only my right, but my obligation, to share—that the ritual, our history, our culture, is strong and sturdy and robust and resonant. And because of that, you have permission to make it your own—I want you to own it. I don't know if that's because of my gender or my age or my intuition or my experience, but it's definitely my passion.

I'm a religious person—I'm really comfortable with that language. I really wish more people were. I think that religion provides a framework for my life that helps me know how to respond to the person asking for money on the subway, helps me be a better partner and parent and friend, helps me be more ethical as an employer. It helps me know that I take care of my body. There are just so many places where I, as a person, need guidance. I need history, I need to belong to something. All of those things are pretty fundamental to me—and I'm fairly confident that I'm not the only one.

I've spent my career working for the Jews because that's my religion—that's the place where I can make the most impact, where I am closest to seeing the need, and where I am most connected to people who have these needs but don't yet realize that they have a resource that's right there for them.

I am scared about our world. I'm raising three children, and I don't know how to answer questions for them, a lot. They're scared, and I hate that they're scared. Shabbat is a reprieve, but also I can do my best to pass on ethical teachings to them that were passed on to me. I have the sayings of our ancestors—I have wells. I feel like it's unfair for people who don't have access to those resources—they're on their own. If I can open that up, if I can say, "You have access and you have permission"—that's *dayenu* [enough]. That's pretty good. I think that helps me sleep at night.

Jenna Reback

> "Why are we not instilling people with a pride and an understanding and a love and enthusiasm of what it means to be Jewish?"

Bad Jew Weekly

When we interviewed her, Jenna Reback was the creator and host of the *Bad Jew Weekly* podcast, which ran from 2016 to 2018. Bad Jew Weekly was "an irreverent, inclusive take on Judaism from the baddest Jewess around."

Reback is a Hollywood screenwriter, currently writing a Jewish young adult movie for Steven Spielberg's Reboot Studios.

Dan Libenson: Tell us a little bit about your podcast, *Bad Jew Weekly*.

Jenna Reback: *Bad Jew Weekly* is an irreverent but relevant podcast for Jews who want to engage more deeply with their Judaism. A lot of people feel like, "Oh, I'm a bad Jew, I can't participate, I don't know how to participate, I don't know where to begin," and that's the end of their inquiry. My goal is to move people from feeling like bad Jews, and feeling paralyzed by that, to a state of feeling like badass Jews, where they're very excited and encouraged to learn and grow.

I get mail from all around the world and one of the biggest themes is, "Wow, I really feel so drawn to Judaism, and I really want to connect—but I'm terrified to set foot in a synagogue. I'm terrified that I'm going to go to a rabbi, and he or she is going to laugh at me, or ask me some question about my favorite passage in Ezekiel, and I won't know the answer, and then I'll be thrown out."

I don't pretend to be a rabbi. I think there's obviously so much value to having a real rabbi in your life who can draw on thousands of years of Jewish thought and commentary in a breath, in a way that I am still in the process of learning how to do. I am speaking to the people who are outside the synagogue who want desperately to be in, but are terrified and don't know where to start—because I very much have been that person myself.

The hook of my podcast is that to put an episode together, I have to study a tremendous amount every week. I'm learning alongside my listeners. I am a layperson. I'm a TV writer with degrees in comparative literature. I love study and I love learning, and I love, as a writer, a great story.

Dan Libenson: There are a lot of people that fit into the description that you just gave of yourself, but there's only one *Bad Jew Weekly*. How did you go from having these feelings to having this podcast?

Jenna Reback: When I was growing up, I asked my mother, "Why are you Jewish?" and she could answer me in a sentence. I will never forget it—she said, "I am Jewish because Judaism is a religion that respects and celebrates human nature." That was so deeply moving for me.

I think there's something really beautiful about this idea of us being the people Israel, this idea of *l'dor vador*—we pass Judaism on from one generation to the next. But I think what can sometimes get lost in that process is this idea of intentionality, and this idea of choice. If Judaism is something that you inherit, it can be easy to not ask, "Why is this meaningful to me? Why actually is this something that I bring to the center of my life?

My mom converted to Judaism in the 70s. At the time, Judaism was not, in her words, really set up to embrace converts. Before she found a rabbi who would convert her, she went to two different rabbis who would not. One of them said, "I don't have time," the other one said, "It's the middle of the Vietnam War—why are you doing this?" That really stuck with me. When I look at my mother, I see someone who has contributed so much to the Northern California Jewish community, and to our larger Jewish peoplehood. That really made me think about the things that we do. On the one hand, it's so beautiful that Judaism is not a proselytizing religion—but what are the ways in which we are not welcoming to people who have so much to contribute to Judaism, but don't know how to get in the door?

That made me think about how I can be welcoming to people who feel insecure about stepping into a Jewish space. And how can I be very frank and honest about my feelings, and my doubts, and my gripes, and my insecurities—and also the great passion that I have for the practice of Judaism, and how can I help other people in my position find that as well.

I didn't know what to do with all this until Donald Trump got elected. Then I saw all these friends of mine, these very, very secular Jews, for the first time really having to grapple with what their Jewish identity meant in the face of antisemitism. For the first time, they were saying "People hate me so much because I'm Jewish—but I don't even really know what being Jewish means."

I think it's easy to define Judaism, one's own Judaism, based on otherness and based on what I would call a negative identity—"I'm Jewish because I'm not Christian," "I'm Jewish because I'm different," "I'm Jewish because I know that I'm not like everyone else." To me, that creates this sad feeling of otherness and insecurity, without the positive identity of, "Oh, I'm Jewish because this is a system of thought that allows me to be more compassionate in the world."

I decided to take all these disparate strands of my experience and what I'd observed, and said, "Okay, I'm going to do this and see what happens." A year later, here we are.

Lex Rofeberg: As someone with the ability to communicate awesome things about Judaism to people, do people ever tell you that you should go and become a rabbi?

Jenna Reback: People do say that to me every now and then, and I have a huge amount of admiration and respect for rabbis. But I really, really love my job—I love being a TV writer. It's a compulsion for me to write and to tell stories about characters and about people. I feel very, very fortunate that I get to do that, and that I get to use pop culture to really explore topics and themes that I think are important.

It's also important for me to speak as not-a-rabbi because I think that people assume that rabbis are not like them—they just assume that they're different. I hope that by saying, "Hey guys, I am me, I am a TV writer, I am learning a lot with you every week—I don't have the inherent knowledge base that a rabbi after however, six years of training, has. But I'm here to engage with you as a peer, I'm here to really dig in and learn with you. I'm here to tell you that I always want to get to Shabbat on Saturday morns, I want to get to synagogue—and sometimes I sleep through it. I'm not different than you—I am you." Hopefully in doing that, I'm emboldening people to not feel apologetic about the way they practice Judaism, but to say, "Hey, dive in, and engage as your true self—because that's a contribution that we need."

The other great freedom that I have in not being a rabbi and not having this be my job is that I can say exactly what I think. I talk about politics a lot on my podcast, because I believe very strongly that the Torah is asking us not only to engage with the Torah for the sake of study, but then using that study to go out and take very deliberate political action in the world.

The Torah says . . . disproportionately more than any other commandment is the commandment to remember that you were strangers in the land of Egypt, to remember that we have to love the stranger as ourselves. That means that we have to engage in the world in a very, very specific way. That means it's really so deeply to our detriment culturally, politically, and spiritually that Jewish spaces don't have frank discussions about Israel that lead to thoughtful and nuanced and productive political action.

I believe that politics does belong in Jewish spaces. I'm deeply frustrated by this idea of why can't we all just get along—why can't we just go to a synagogue to pray? Prayer is not just singing a song. If you want to sing a song, go to a concert. Prayer in Judaism is rigorous. Prayer is demanding. Prayer motivates us to go out into the world and, as Heschel said, pray with our feet, or pray with our fingers, or pray with the words that we say out in the world.

I think it is incredibly disappointing when Jewish spaces shy away from that. There's all this talk about how do we bring millennials into Judaism? How do we get them excited? Be sincere—be earnest. Why are we so afraid of intellectual rigor? Why are we so afraid of deep, sincere spirituality? Why are we so afraid of being controversial? Judaism is a subversive religion.

Dan Libenson: What do you think your perspective as a TV writer brings to your take on Judaism?

Jenna Reback: To be a great storyteller, you really have to have compassion, and you have to be able to imagine yourself in somebody else's shoes. The largest takeaway I have about Judaism, the way I bring Judaism into my life, is in doing what we're commanded to do—which is seeing the image of God in every person. Sometimes that's incredibly difficult.

I do also look at the text from the perspective of a writer, and a TV writer. I say, okay, if we assume that all the choices that are made in the writing of the Torah are deliberate—or at least open to inquiry that can help us more deeply explore the themes of the given *parasha*. When it's ambiguous whether an angel is speaking or God is speaking, what does that tell us? Or if we see something happen in the narrative, and then we get one of the participants in the story retelling the entire thing we just saw, so that it's in there twice—as a writer, I would never write that scene. What could be more boring than saying, "Here is this thing you just saw—now let me explain to you what you just saw, verbatim." But if it's there for a reason, then what is it asking us to do?

Listen, there is some really weird stuff in the Torah. We should take the Torah seriously, and it's good that we're encouraged to be. But I think if we're really going to engage with these texts we also should have the freedom to say, "Wow, this is really, really weird, and I'm really, really uncomfortable with it."

That said, as a writer, I am so deeply enamored of the *midrashim*. I think it is such a revolutionary and deeply subversive idea that when the rabbis don't particularly like a passage of the Torah—they write their own Torah fanfiction to try to explain it. This idea that our most sacred text is actually, to some extent, open-source, is incredibly cool. And that's really helped me deepen my own understanding of the Torah, and helped me gain reassurance. Okay, I'm uncomfortable with this parasha—but look, all of our rabbis throughout our tradition are, too. But it's also emboldened me to say, wow, if these rabbis felt that it was important to give these nameless characters names and backstories and motivations, then surely that gives me, as a layperson, freedom to put my own interpretation on what I see in this text.

Dan Libenson: When I hear you talking, I wonder if you are more than just a regular person who takes a leadership role. I feel you are putting out there a very compelling message about what Judaism is all about, what it's meant to do, that could be heard by many institutional leaders—not all—as a critique of the direction in which they're taking their institutions, and that could be heard by a lot of regular Jews as a rallying cry.

It strikes me that that's what the prophets were doing—they were the outsiders, the people who didn't have an official role, who had a vision of what Judaism was meant to be for, and who were screaming at the kings and at the priests and at the leaders, saying, "You have gone wrong."

The prophetic voice became the voice that the rabbis followed most of the time, in terms of their understanding of what Judaism was all about. I think what you've been talking about is one example of the ways in which regular Jews who feel passionately about some aspect of Judaism now have the means at their disposal to learn for themselves and project their prophetic voice.

Jenna Reback: I think my strength is that I have not bought in. I have sat in synagogues and have been really frustrated, and not wanted to come back. I have also gotten ready to go to synagogue, and then been too paralyzed with fear to go because of what people would say about me. Or I've gone, and everyone has looked at me weird, and then I've gone outside and wandered around looking for the coffee.

When you talk about the prophetic voice, I think it's less about being chosen than choosing to speak. There have been things in Jewish institutions that have frustrated me all my life. Throughout my childhood,

I saw this weird adherence to dogma over discourse—especially in the way that Jewish child education says, "We're going to assume that you're not smart enough to debate these issues, so we're just going to tell you how to feel…"

I remember when I was at my Jewish youth group convention, and the leader of the whole youth group gets up and says, "Only date Jews." I got so deeply angry, and I said, "My mother, who converted to Judaism, has done so much more—I guarantee you—for Jewry than probably 95% of the parents of the kids in here. How dare you tell me that my father never should have dated her?"

Why are we not instilling people with a pride and an understanding and a love and enthusiasm of what it means to be Jewish? When we, as the adults, as the elders, adhere to a rote Judaism and we don't know why, when we say, "Okay, you need to go through the steps and do the thing—but we're going to suck the passion out of it. We're not going to demand passion from you because we can't articulate for ourselves why we're passionate about it," then we're lost. We've missed the point.

From what I've studied and observed, I think at every moment in Jewry it's very easy for us to say, "We are in the midst of a crisis about the very soul of our identity." You know what? We better be—we better always be looking at the very soul of who we are. As deeply disappointing as current politics have been, this is an opportunity—and I think a very necessary opportunity—for us to really take stock of what we stand for in the world.

QUESTIONS FOR REFLECTION

- Benay Lappe speaks about SVARA's approach to help students build self-confidence, so that they can learn to "mess with the [Jewish] tradition." Do you feel ready to mess with Jewish tradition yourself? If not, what steps may help you feel more ready to do so? If so, what's one particular direction that you'd like to try out?
- Have you used Sefaria before? How often, and for what purposes? What shifts about Judaism (not just your own experience of Judaism—but Judaism generally) when all of us have the ability to access an entire library of the most canonical Jewish texts, for free, in Hebrew and in English?
- Have you ever referred to yourself as a "bad Jew"—jokingly or less jokingly? Have you heard someone else do so? How would you distill what you (or they) meant with that phrase? How might we normalize the ways in which most Jews (not only "bad" Jews) feel like they haven't learned so much about Jewish text and tradition?

'Regular Jews' Experimenting

Eileen Levinson

> *"There are so many of us who feel like we haven't been included in the mainstream forms of religion and practice as we know it, and yet there's this natural hunger inside us to want to connect to something bigger."*

Haggadot.com

Eileen Levinson is the founder and Executive Director of Recustom, a studio and design lab experimenting with new formats for engaging with ancient traditions. Projects under Recustom's umbrella are *Haggadot.com* and *HighHolidays@Home*, which Levinson also founded. Both platforms enable users to make their own Jewish ritual materials. (Haggadot.com has a comprehensive library of Passover-related texts, from ancient and contemporary sources, so that users can build their own haggadot relevant to their experiences of Passover.)

With the COVID-19 pandemic making clear the widespread need for do-it-yourself (DIY) at-home Jewish materials, Recustom partnered with OneTable (see our interview with OneTable's CEO Aliza Kline earlier in this section) to create the DIY Jewish Network, supported by a $3.8 million "Reset" grant from the Jewish Community Response and Impact Fund, a fund set up by a number of major Jewish foundations.

Dan Libenson: Could we start with the story of the founding of Haggadot.com?

Eileen Levinson: I'm trained as a graphic designer and artist. When I was at CalArts, we had an assignment called "The Future of Publication," which asked us to imagine a new type of publication. This was in 2008 and the big fear was that print was dying. My idea was to create an interactive book where many people could create the story and riff off of the structure. That immediately brought me back to the Haggadah [Passover text including a narrative of the Exodus].

I grew up Reform. There were years in my childhood where my family was very involved in the synagogue and years where we were less involved. We celebrated Passover. By the time I got to my early twenties, I had had experiences where I felt like I maybe didn't fit in the Jewish community. I felt like a little bit of an outsider. I remember going to college and saying, I'm Jewish, but I'm not really that Jewish, or I'm not that kind of Jew.

I had a lot of questions about Judaism. Then I started to think, Okay, I've been very critical about ritual, and about this community engagement—but how do I actually do something productive to facilitate ritual the way that I'd like to have it be?

For this Future of Publication project, I decided to prototype an idea for what an interactive, community-generated Haggadah could look like. Something where you could follow the same structure but interpret it any way that you wanted. After this graduate school project, I applied to ROI, which is a community for young Jewish innovators and social entrepreneurs.

Dan Libenson: What was your early notion of how this was going to work, and what kinds of challenges did you face early on?

Eileen Levinson: The first thing I was grappling with was can we say what the authentic Haggadah text is? Of course, yes, there is the traditional text in Hebrew. It was important to me to put that all on the site. The next question is how much of that actually has to be included for it to be still considered a Haggadah.

What I decided was that I was going to make the rules as simple as possible—give users access to what at least Reform and Conservative movements considered the basic elements of the Haggadah, while still keeping the full traditional text on there if the user wanted it.

It wasn't my job to police usage. If somebody chose to only do a few parts of the seder, I wasn't going to judge whether or not that was a valuable experience—because it's possible that they had never done Passover before, and even doing these three parts of the seder was a great growth experience that was meaningful to them. I wanted to meet people where they are.

The tension between tradition and innovation was something that I was very aware of in the beginning. I felt that I was an outsider Jew, all of a sudden being invited to this space where some very committed Jews were. I felt like I had to explain myself, or I had to make up for some lack of knowledge.

For a few years, I think this made me veer towards more traditional in the sense that the work that I was doing made allowances for more traditional viewpoints without letting my own voice as a maker and a thinker through as much. Over the years, I've tried to insert myself a little bit more—being aware that I want to create this really big tent that is, in some ways, radical in how big a tent it is.

Lex Rofeberg: It sounds like you have come to your own understanding on the question of what counts as being a sufficiently genuine or official or authentic Haggadah—how would you encourage others to approach that question?

Eileen Levinson: I lived with the Jewish writer and thinker Esther Kustanowitz for eight years. She became one of my closest friends and we would go to Ikar together. The music is beautiful, the people are very interesting. But there were many times where I felt like my mind would wander, and I would use that as a meditative space.

Then I brought my husband there for the first time maybe four years ago. He's also Jewish. He grew up Reform. He was like, "There's a lot of Hebrew. There's a lot of stuff that I don't get." I was like, "Well, you know, it's okay. You get most of it, you sit through." He's like, "But why—why should I? Why can't the whole service just be something that I get, or 90% of the service be something that I get?"

I realized how many times I put myself in situations where I accepted that there was something that I didn't get, and it would eventually come to me. Eventually I realized I deserve to get everything. There is a learning curve in Judaism. But I don't have to say that the problem is me or my lack of knowledge or education because I'm not connecting with something.

I'm going to be 40 this summer. I think that that is a main theme in my life right now: If something doesn't feel authentic to me, it's not because of me. It's because it's just not the fit anymore.

Dan Libenson: How do you have the chutzpah to do something like this, when you yourself feel that I don't really know that much? How do you do it?

Eileen Levinson: I don't let perfection get in the way of good enough. I'm okay with building things piece by piece and playing and trying things out. I have, especially when I was younger, a lot of confidence. If somebody says I can't do something, or if I'm not smart enough to do something, or I don't have enough knowledge, I have to do it—because I don't like being told that I can't, or I'm not able to.

Dan Libenson: Do you think that's just a characteristic about you? Or is there some way that we could say to people who are contemplating creating some innovation "Don't worry about it—everybody can do it."

Eileen Levinson: I don't know if I'm saying that anyone can do it, but I'm saying that every viewpoint is relevant in some way. Especially when it comes to Judaism, and I was used to being told that I didn't know enough. There's so much Jew judging that goes on. That was one of the things that turned me off. Even growing up, I remember friends who went to Conservative synagogue or kept kosher, there was a little bit of, Oh, you're eating that?

I wanted to claim that my experience—still being a thoughtful, educated person that cares about tradition and history and connection—that these experiences are valid, and are just as meaningful. Somebody who went to yeshiva growing up, they know the entire Talmud forwards and backwards—but I know art history, and I'm going to bring that to this.

Lex Rofeberg: I'm geeking out because I am a longtime

Haggadot.com user. I'm curious what kinds of people are doing this? When they do, what does it look like?

Eileen Levinson: There are a few types of users. There's obviously the people who are Haggadah fanatics—they've been making Haggadahs for years. We're taking that behavior and we're putting it online, giving them the tools that they always hoped that they would have.

But there are plenty of users who love to browse. They come to the site every year to get a new reading or artwork or something relevant to add to a Seder that they already have, or a Haggadah that they like to do every year, but add a couple new things.

There are those who are just curious. It's the night before Passover, they don't know what they're doing—maybe I should download a Haggadah. Our traffic totally spikes on those two days. I'm totally cool with the last-minute users—because if I weren't making the site, I'd probably be one of them.

We get a lot of college Hillels that are making a Haggadah, which I love. There's also this age of parents with young children, where the kids are getting PJ Library books or they're going to a Jewish preschool. Maybe the parents weren't that intentional about their Jewish practice before, but now Judaism is back in their lives in a surprising way. They're figuring out how they want to do it, because their kids are kind of excited about it.

Lately, there's been a ton of recent retirees reaching out. They have more time; they want to continue Jewish traditions with their family, see what's going on; and they're also a little more tech savvy and this, to them, is a whole new world.

Dan Libenson: What do you see as the needs that your organizations and your design work is meeting for your users?

Eileen Levinson: I think that there's still a feeling of confusion and yet curiosity about religion. I think there are so many of us who feel like we haven't been included in the mainstream forms of religion and practice as we know it, and yet there's this natural hunger inside us to want to connect to something bigger.

I feel that our interest in spirituality is as important as any of our other human needs. Even those of us who say that they're totally atheist or secular, or they don't believe in God but they believe in the universe . . . we're all looking for a way to connect and to mark our transitions and to feel like a human being.

Lex Rofeberg: Can you say a bit more about how people stitch together their own Haggadot? I think if we applied your approach to every Jewish ritual—we would do them better, and they would mean more. It's a simple design idea that you can make a beautiful, meaningful choice with every little second of what you do. Do you share this sense that we should be applying this idea to all sorts of other things?

Eileen Levinson: Yes. That is essentially my ethos, as a designer, and why I do what I do. These basic building blocks of Jewish ritual—not just these content choices, but how you then say it or read it, how are you physically in this space, how are all of your senses engaged—that is what fascinates me.

When somebody comes to Haggadot.com, they can view ready-made Haggadahs, and they can download them. If they want to make their own Haggadah, they can by selecting a template. We have the traditional Haggadah text on there—and then we also have a liberal version, which is by JewishBoston, their Wandering is Over Haggadah.

Then we have a blank template, which is, essentially, no template, for somebody who wants to start from scratch. When they get that template, they then can go through and add additional content, which we call clips, for each section of the seder. Those clips can be a reading, a prayer, a piece of artwork, a video.

We had a lot of user interest in taking this technology, and this idea of mixing and matching to make your own Jewish rituals and taking it to other types of content. That's actually how we arrived at Custom & Craft. We launched Custom & Craft as a partner to Haggadot.com, so that Jews could make their own High Holidays services or Shabbat meals or Tu BiShvat, what have you.

When we launched Custom & Craft, it wasn't like Passover—every single Jewish organization didn't have their High Holiday resources to share in the way that they have their Passover supplements that they were putting out.

We started to partner with organizations to make their content more digestible. Taking their content that they had on their website, or in their programs, and turning it into clips—these digestible modules. We started to build a real brand as being designers for the Jewish community. We received a Cutting Edge Grant from the Jewish Community Foundation of Los Angeles.

Those years were both a huge growth and a huge burden, because we were doing a lot of running around with small client projects, very labor-intensive work that wasn't helping to build the long-term strategic growth of the brand. I got lucky in the middle of 2018 when my husband and I learned that we were going to be moving to Germany. It was perfect timing to take that time abroad to think about how I really wanted to operate as a leader and as an artist.

What's interesting is that this fall I noticed Custom & Craft's audience was growing. The plan for the future is I want as much as possible to take leadership—at least the executive director leadership—off my plate so that I can do as much creative work as possible. It's not like I would totally be stepped out—I just want to focus on continuing to make projects that excite me.

Essentially, Custom & Craft has become a studio to enable Jewish creative seekers to have the tools that they need to make Judaism their own, using technology and media and print products—anything that we need to get Jews, and maybe in the future even more non-Jews, involved in making this all their own.

I think there's an opportunity for us to take the entire High Holiday liturgy and prayer book and turn that into clips—especially the Jewish groups that are popping up around the High Holidays and making their own experiences and their own services. I'm very interested in the possibilities of it.

Lex Rofeberg: Are there moments you think are particularly ripe for experimentation in Jewish services or the Jewish calendar?

Eileen Levinson: This year, I'm very interested in the handwashing, in *urchatz* and *rachtza*. Urchatz being towards the beginning of the seder; *rachtza* being right before we eat the meal. I think that, as the seder was created, it was a brilliant point. They knew that washing your hands is this physical transformation, where you change yourself from one part to the next. We all could think more about those times when we're having a transformation.

I also think that water is very important. We've been taking it for granted—whether it's thinking about Flint, Michigan, or the Dakota Pipeline, or climate change. I am making a push for those two moments in the seder. Washing the hands is a very simple but powerful moment.

Another moment in the Jewish calendar which I think is not yet popular but deserves to be is *tashlich*. *Tashlich* is the experience where, traditionally, you would take pieces of bread and throw them into a large moving body of water as a way of casting off your sins before Yom Kippur. East Side Jews put together a great event called Down to the River, where part of that was a community tashlich ritual. They invited me to produce a piece at this event.

What I found very interesting about *tashlich* is that it's so independent. You're never stating what you're apologizing for, or why. You're in your own head. It is quite beautiful, because you are doing it as a group. I think that the original practice of tashlich, on its own, is very meaningful. I hope that it continues to grow.

I also created another way of considering tashlich, where visitors can come to an apologies booth, and take rice paper that will dissolve in water and write their own apologies on in this booth. It's anonymous. Post it on a wall. The next person who comes in can then read these anonymous apologies off the wall, take one down, and replace it with their own. Then, when they leave, they take that note card and drop it in water. The cards start to dissolve, and the words dissolve. That's tashlich.

I think Sukkot is also really cool. Sukkot is the holiday where we build these huts in our backyard, and if you are observant would even sleep or dine in the [*sukkah*] hut. There is a set of instructions for how you build this hut—essentially, it's a design brief—that you have to be able to see the stars, it has to have natural materials. There's something very magical. I remember this, also, as a kid, going to the temple's sukkah, and sitting out and having dinner under the stars with these handmade decorations in this funny building. I just see a lot more people embracing it.

Dan Libenson: How do you think about designing events that work and are comfortable for both religious and observant folks and for more secular or newly exploring folks?

Eileen Levinson: I'll back into this and say that for so many years, I focused on making other people comfortable. If I am going to host, I want to make sure that everyone is comfortable, to the point of making myself feel too stressed and not able to fully be present in the moment.

We all would like to think of ourselves as welcoming and inclusive. In addition to being radically welcoming, I want to be transparent about my perspective and needs as the creator of the site. I encourage you to be transparent about your needs as the host. I think being clear about [your needs] from the beginning gives people an opportunity to respectfully bow out.

If you invite somebody to a seder, or any circumstance where you know that something might happen that makes them uncomfortable, give them a heads-up beforehand. But remember it's also not your primary responsibility to elevate their needs over everybody else. The trick is to find that line between understanding your needs and being true to yourself, while also making space for that which makes you uncomfortable, too, in the service of learning.

Tiffany Shlain

> "I think we've created a society where there's no separation between anything—and I don't think that's healthy, I don't think that's good."

Six Days a Week

Tiffany Shlain is an artist and Emmy-nominated filmmaker. She is the founder of the Webby Awards and the cofounder and executive director of Let It Ripple Film Studio, a nonprofit film and idea studio that produces films, original series, and live and virtual experiences that inspire audiences to think about what it means to be human in today's world.

Shlain is best known in the Jewish community for *The Tribe*, an 18-minute short film that calls itself an "unorthodox, unauthorized history of the Jewish people and the Barbie doll." She has also made many other fascinating films, including one on the science of character, with a Jewish take, called *Making of a Mensch*, around which she built Character Day, an annual event that ran from 2014-2019 in which hundreds of thousands of people all over the world gathered together to learn the science of character and to develop and deepen their own.

Her art has been shown at the Museum of Modern Art, the National Mall in DC and will be part of the Getty Museum's Pacific Standard Time *Art & Science Collide* at the Skirball Cultural Center. She is also the author of *24/6: The Power of Unplugging One Day A Week*. It's the story about how she and her family have been experimenting, over the last decade, with a tech-free Shabbat—the idea that on Shabbat, from Friday night to Saturday night, their family doesn't use any devices with screens.

Dan Libenson: We're always speculating, on this podcast, about what it might be like if people took more ownership over their Jewish experience, played around with Jewish content, and reimagined things. It's exciting to actually talk to somebody who's doing that! Can you start by describing for us what your Shabbat looks like?

Tiffany Shlain: We do what my family calls a technology Shabbat, because it integrates the practice of no screens, which is life-changing in our modern 24/7 screen-addicted world. We invite friends and family over. It's always a great, boisterous group. We have screens off—they're all shut down, usually, right before the guests arrive, and guests are told not to bring them. We make fresh challah every Friday. We bring the table together. We do the blessings, and we have musical instruments around. It's a beautiful night of engagement.

The next day is much more still. My husband and I usually get up before the kids, and we journal, we read articles. When the kids get up, we make art, we go out in nature, we nap, we read, we do nothing. We play board games. Then we don't wait for the three stars in the sky, but at five pm, our tech Shabbat ends—and the kids go back online, and Ken and I go out for our own date. I get reenergized thinking about the potential of technology again. I'm so happy to have had a day without it, one day every week. We've done that for 10 years, and it's been the best thing that we've ever done.

Dan Libenson: Can you describe how this all started—this idea of the tech Shabbat?

Tiffany Shlain: I'm Jewish. I did not grow up with Shabbat. I grew up really wrestling with a lot of ideas of Shabbat. I met my husband Ken, who is Jewish, and he did grow up with Shabbat. By that I mean that he grew up with Friday night dinners—which I think most of my friends would call Shabbat, but now that I understand the full day off as the full megillah of Shabbat, that seems like one-third of it to me now. For years we did various permutations of Shabbat, but usually, at most, it was a dinner.

I'm part of the first class of Reboot, which is a group of Jews who are kind of a punk rock band of creative types who come together and rethink things. Ten years ago, we did a national day of unplugging, and it was one ceremonial day, no screens. It was a pretty traumatic period in my life—within weeks of each other I had just lost my father, and my husband and I had just had our daughter. One thing I knew for sure about these life events happening was I wanted to be more focused with the people I loved.

So, we did this national day of unplugging, and we just never stopped. I think we were the only ones. It was like, "Oh my gosh, this feels so good." To me the big epiphany came from the stillness and the quiet of the day after the dinner. The thinking, the reflection, that was huge for me. I don't think we get that anymore with just the way we're living.

Our teenage daughter loves it. Our 10-year-old loves it. It is our favorite day of the week. I never thought I'd write a book about it, but the longer we did it, the deeper it got, and the more crazy our society became. Rereading the wisdom of Shabbat, and really thinking about it for the modern era, has been really exciting.

Dan Libenson: Can you give us the whole picture of what you do and don't do in terms of screens on Shabbat? You're not a traditional Jew in the way that we think of religious practice—but you're really religious about this.

Tiffany Shlain: Most people just assume—because they maybe know I do the tech Shabbat—that I'm very religious, which is always an interesting place for people to meet me, because I'm not religious. I actually thought that the only people who took a full day off for Shabbat were Orthodox Jews. I didn't really think I could engage with it this way.

To get down to the nitty-gritty—It's a day about no phones. No TV, no laptop, no iPad—yes, no screens. Life is beautiful without screens—we've forgotten that. I think Shabbat is a wonderful framework to bring that back in.

We have a landline, for real. It's good for emergencies too, but that's what we use if we want to call someone. We have a record player—we play music on that. We also use the Alexa for a timer, because that doesn't have a screen. For us, the key is to avoid the rabbit hole of the screen that takes people out of the moment.

I use a Sharpie and a big white pad of paper to write down any thoughts I have. When we make plans with people, they know they're not going to be texting us every waking moment—"I'll be there, I'm parking," who cares. We'll either be there or we won't. We've done it with two kids and soccer—a lot of people want to know that.

I reread so much Heschel during this whole process, and he talks about building a palace in time. That's what I feel like we do to our home every week. It's really like I'm living in the seventies or eighties—that's what it's like. It's like you're back in your home in the eighties when your phone was stuck to the wall, and you listened to music different ways, and you weren't available to the whole world every second, and the whole world wasn't available to you every second.

I think we don't realize how much that changes our every movement, where we're responding to everything and everyone else, instead of ourselves. I think Shabbat is about quieting the wind on the water—which is actually a Buddhist expression—you can't see in the water if there's wind blowing across it, and it's reflecting everything else. How do we quiet the wind on the water? That's what I feel like I do every week.

Lex Rofeberg: I'm curious—to what extent do you conceptualize this as an old practice? To what extent do you see it, really, as a new practice—something that is powerful because it is of our time?

Tiffany Shlain: My favorite things to do involves both great respect for the old and rethinking for modern times. I think if you look at all of my work, so much is about holding both.

I've heard of people making lots of different rules for their phones—maybe they don't bring it on vacation, maybe not before bed, all this stuff—and that's great. But I actually think we need the strictness of a boundary, because the wisdom of Shabbat is that you need a day that feels different—you need a day that is protected, and that is a space different from all other days. I think in these modern times it is about the technology.

I'm happy and excited to have people try this in a strict way. I think we don't even realize how much we're influenced by the smartphone. We wake up to it, we go to bed to it, we're pinged... I'm like a marionette doll responding to it. I have turned off every notification on my phone, except for from my family, which has been really wonderful. I don't wake up to it anymore. I do all these things throughout the week, too.

Really, the Shabbat part, and really being strict around the screen technology that can take you out of being present—I think is really important to discuss right now.

Dan Libenson: The way that Shabbat practices evolved is basically, the Torah says you should rest on Shabbat. Then the Talmud says, "What does rest mean?" And they say there were these 39 activities that were part of the building of the Tabernacle, and anything that looks like one of those activities, we're not going to do on Shabbat—that's how we're going to define rest.

It feels to me like what you're saying is that, in our modern time, there's something that's missing from that list of 39. And in some ways, it is the most important thing—the thing that's really driving us, the thing that really feels like work all the time. You're not saying, "Let me add a 40th." You're saying, "Let me just do this one."

But then at the same time, you're saying, "I'm going to take this so seriously." A lot of people who don't observe Shabbat traditionally don't really have a critique of the practices of Shabbat—they're just like, "Oh, it's too much, it's too hard to do it in this very serious, religious way." You're saying, "No, we're going to keep that part—we're going to be super-religious about it, super-serious about it."

Tiffany Shlain: I love that you're bringing up the Tabernacle and the 39 things. So, what's the modern Tabernacle of our time? What is the thing? This smartphone is a conduit to absolutely everything. Even leisure looks like work these days, when you have to post it and write something about it and check it. It has framed everything, on some level, as work and being on.

I have a chapter in the book about the history of being on and being off. I think that's an important distinction—what makes us feel like we have to be on? We need to have a serious conversation about when is it good to be on, and when is it good to be off. When should we be on our screens, and when should we be present with the people we love? When should we have time for reflection and writing and big-picture thinking that drives culture forward? I don't think we have any time for it anymore. I think that's why we have the president we have. I think that we are distracted to the point where we can't have a big idea anymore.

I am being strict. I think we need it. Sometimes people need to really think of something in a strict way to even pull them a little bit closer to it. It's been too loosey-goosey. I think the phone has infiltrated our beds, our tables, our everything, our workspaces. We really need to really think about this really powerful object we've created.

You have to know, I founded the Webby Awards, I'm not anti-tech. I do these global days of discussion, which I could never do without modern technology. I love it—just not all the time. I love it six days of the week.

Lex Rofeberg: As you know, I spend a lot of my time arguing that we should experiment with ways to use technology on Shabbat and otherwise—on holidays, et cetera—to amplify forms of Jewish practice.

I appreciate the idea that the problem with screens, and why we should take a day off from them, is that they take us out of the world and encourage us not to be present. But, if the issue is that we retreat into our own universes, and screens take us out of the moment, my argument would be that then you shouldn't read books—especially fiction—on your Shabbat, because books do the exact same thing.

Tiffany Shlain: I hear you that if we're talking about being present, a book takes you out of being present. I hear you. But I would say that a book is a beautiful way to walk in someone else's footsteps. Angela Duckworth, who wrote the book Grit and is a professor at UPenn, just released this research about how much reading builds empathy. On your smartphone, you're guided to sensational headlines, you're guided to FOMO [fear of missing out]—and the list goes on. I would say that you can experience great empathy reading a book.

When my family is all in the living room and everyone's reading, I find that to be a beautiful time. To be parallel reading, instead of parallel scrolling, is a much more beautiful way to have a moment together. I wish we had more time for undistracted reading. Shabbat, for me, is this space to think deeply about things, where I know I'm not going to be distracted. That's a very different reading practice than how most of us read in our everyday lives. We're reading more than ever, but we're skimming. We're living in a skimming, scrolling culture. On Shabbat, I put aside the New Yorker article, the New York Times article, and focus on a thing I really want to be focused on. I don't know if we have time like that anymore.

Dan Libenson: I love that the conversation we're having now sounds a lot like the conversations that there are in the Talmud in which everyone agrees about a certain principle, but then we start poking at the edges of it to say, "But is this really consistent with that? Is this really necessary, is this going too far, is this not going far enough?"

Another place to probe might be why you advocate no screens versus no phones, or some other variant of that.

Tiffany Shlain: That's a good question. The majority of people I know don't even watch films on their TV anymore—it's on their laptop. How many times have you watched a Netflix show or something, and you're being pinged by five different things bouncing at the bottom of your screen to get your attention? As a filmmaker, I think, "The horror."

For us, no screens is really about how it's no laptop, no iPad, no TV, though we barely watch things on the TV anymore. It just is a clean line. I think it's helpful for today.

Lex Rofeberg: The way you spoke about the experience of notifications popping up while you are watching Netflix makes me think about a Talmudic principle. There's this whole idea that you have certain rules that are enshrined as rules, but then you have some rules that are there to protect you from breaking a different rule.

I wonder if this is the case with the Netflix example—it's not so much that, on its own, watching a movie is so bad—it's that when you do so, there's this potential of all these notifications coming in.

Tiffany Shlain: Yes. That's exactly right. It's the adjacency of so much other of our lives and distractions and work. Is the outside world getting into your palace in time? How do you create a real palace and protect its space? How permeable is your space? I think we've created a society where there's no separation between anything—and I don't think that's healthy, I don't think that's good. I think that that's what Shabbat was originally about—a day of rest.

I wrote an op-ed for the *Boston Globe* all about rethinking Labor Day in our 24/7 society. The labor movement fought for the weekend—there were bloody battles in the streets of Chicago in the fight for a weekend. Now we've just given it away. We're available to everyone all the time. There was some study that 63% of people feel like they need to respond to their boss on the weekend. What is that? It's not healthy.

This extends even to family and friends. I love my family and friends, but on Friday night, unless they're coming over for Shabbat—which a lot of them do—I say, "I'll talk to you on Sunday." It's good. It's good to have, every week, to have a little space for yourself. If you're single, to have a little self-reflection; if you're in a [relationship], time for your relationship; if you're in a family, time for your family. It's good to create and not let the whole world into that.

Lex Rofeberg: What's interesting is, as much as I described that I do consciously and purposely use my phone on Shabbat, you and I share as a foundational goal that Shabbat will be a time of rest from work, a time focused on family time and friends and relationships, and a time that is different from the rest of the week.

Tiffany Shlain: As a non-religious cultural Jew, the crazy thing is that I think, at the core, we're talking about the same thing, and I think, at the core, I'm talking about the same thing as Orthodox Jews. The core is about a day different from other days, a day of rest, and presence and gratitude.

We haven't talked about gratitude, but that feels like very much a part of my practice, too. I really stop the hustle and bustle. My husband and I lead very busy lives, and this is a day that I feel like we focus on the best parts of ourselves. We're with each other in a very different way. I agree with you—it's a day different. I make challah on Shabbat with my girls, and I don't do that any other day of the week.

My invitation to people reading the book 24/6 is that there's so many beautiful ideas here, and you might do them slightly differently for yourself and your family. I would really love for people to rethink what that phone means to them, and I even invite you to rethink that.

I think you should get a landline, because in any natural disaster, it's super important, and people have forgotten that. I live in earthquake town—we need landlines.

I also think people don't realize how much they associate with that phone. Just thinking about that, I think, is an important thing to be doing right now. There are so many good things—obviously, connecting with family and friends. But it is also manipulating us in all sorts of ways. There's a lot of things happening with our data—we've given it away for free because we use all these tools for free. People are buying and selling information about us to manipulate us. We need to be aware of that, too.

There's a lot of good that comes from it, but if we really took a true day away from it, we'd have the time to think about what it's doing more. I think people do not have their arms or their heads around how much it is manipulating us.

Dan Libenson: I think that what I hear from you is this idea of grappling towards what we might call a new Jewish *halachah*. Halachah is generally translated as "Jewish law," but it actually means "a path," or, "a way," and it doesn't have to be law.

I think many people share the sense that "If I'm going to be strict about my practices, I have to be really sure that they're going to do the work that I'm trying to do in my life, and I don't know that these ancient practices all do that." We need to go through a process of reimaging what the practices of Judaism ought to be. Once we've done that, we should be really strict about it.

I want to invite you to bring in your other work on character and musar and habits, because I think that the whole question of habits is really what's at play here. Judaism has focused on the idea that it's not enough to have values; in fact, having values is not that significant. What's significant is how you put those values into play. And traditionally, Judaism has had a very particular way of doing that through almost automaton-like habitual behaviors.

What does your work on habits suggest about this?

Tiffany Shlain: What I love about Judaism, I would say, are the rituals, practices, and ethics. I don't believe in God. I'm saying that here. I don't like the word "god." I don't like the patriarchal framework. It really bothers me. I think we're perpetuating very patriarchal, angry structures. The framing of God does not work for me—it shuts me down. I don't want to engage with that. That's not my story.

That being said, I do believe in something greater than ourselves. Albert Einstein spoke the most clearly. What he said articulated the most how I feel. It's in nature. What he said was, "I have a humility for the complexity that I don't understand." Boom. That is very similar to how I feel—but I don't frame it in the language of God. I have great respect for the history of these stories, but I really look for the essence of what that story is about, and I like to rethink it. My project has been to rethink Shabbat for me and for today, and I'm not saying God has mandated it for me at all.

It's funny that people say I'm really religious about the practice, because that word is so loaded for me. I think a lot of ideas around Judaism—Shabbat, taking a day that's different with family and friends and for reflection—is a good way to lead a meaningful and purposeful life. Thinking about slavery and freedom is a good way to live a meaningful and purposeful life.

I just don't frame these things in terms of God, I frame them around meaning and purpose. When we started doing full-day Shabbat, I was like, "Not only can we do this—I think everybody should do this. It's changed my life—it's brought so much meaning and purpose. It's grounded me. It's reframed my week, it's reframed my family. We have this one day that's so solid and so present, and it keeps us going the other six days."

Kristin Eriko Posner

> *"No matter what culture you come from, our ancestors have been updating our traditions from the beginning of time."*

Nourish Co.

We initially wanted to speak to our guest, Kristin Eriko Posner, because she was starting to get a lot of media exposure about some of the things that she was doing, relating to food and creating new rituals and creating new ritual objects, that were coming from a connection between her Jewish identity and her identity as a Japanese American.

We thought that was extremely intriguing, in terms of the things that we talk about here on *Judaism Unbound* all the time, where we really embrace the idea that Judaism has always been a mixture of things that have come from all kinds of different cultures, and that have been remixed with things that might have had a Jewish origin—whatever that means—or maybe Judaism has always been a mixture of things that none of which had a Jewish origin, so to speak. We really wanted to start to explore that, particularly in the context of Passover. That's what we're going to do on this episode.

Let me give a few words of introduction for our guest. Kristin Eriko Posner is the founder of Nourish Co., a lifestyle brand that helps multiethnic people and families create nourishing new rituals drawn from time-honored wisdom. She does that through her writing about her experience as a Japanese American Jew, the rituals that mark time and the cycles of our lives, and through new modern heirlooms which she is creating and selling on her web shop.

You can find Kristin online at nourish-co.com, and at Instagram at @bynourishco. You can become a member of the Nourish Co. community by signing up for her monthly newsletter at nourish-co.com/community. If you subscribe, you'll receive a personal letter each month with resources and announcements.

We love the idea of Jews out there that are creating and playing around with one small aspect of Judaism. We think that Kristin Eriko Posner is another example, like Tiffany Shlain, of somebody who is doing exactly what *Judaism Unbound* is all about.

Dan Libenson: I think a good place to start might be just to give us a little bit of your Jewish story, and tell us how you got to where you are right now.

Kristin Eriko Posner: All of my ancestors were Shinto and Buddhists from Japan. My parents were atheists, and I wasn't really raised in any sort of tradition. My mom tried really hard to make sure that I had a connection to Japan by sending me to Japan in the summers and by sending me to Japanese school. But I was born and raised in Southern California.

I started searching for spiritual guidance in churches in high school, even in yoga classes or religious studies classes. I never felt like I could find what I was looking for. I often felt like my heritage was slipping away from me.

I spent a few years after college teaching English in a rural area of Japan, but I left feeling depressed. I went to Japan thinking I would find this part of myself, but I left with a deep sense of grief, feeling that I didn't belong in the US but I also didn't belong in Japan.

Fast-forward a few years. I met my very secular Ashkenazi husband, Bryan, in San Francisco. Because he's so secular, and his family is very secular, I felt that if we were going to pass down our Jewish and Japanese American cultures to our future children one day, it was going to be up to me to do that.

We started taking classes, and I totally fell in love with Judaism—its traditions, its rituals, all of these things to support us during both difficult times and celebratory times. Unexpectedly, I found the sense of belonging I'd been seeking in Judaism.

Then I had another identity crisis. I worried that, by converting to Judaism, I would lose parts of my Japanese American heritage. A few days before my conversion I went to my rabbi, Rabbi Bauer, at Emanu-El, and I said, "I don't think I can do this. I'm really scared." He just looked at me and said, "I don't understand. Why can't there be room for both?" That was something that I hadn't even considered. The decision had felt very polar, that I had to choose one or the other.

I had this whole honeymoon phase with Judaism after I converted, where I loved everything about it. A few years later, I started to become painfully aware that I was one of very few Jews of Color in the room. I thought if I just studied hard and knew more, I would make sure that no one would ever see me make a mistake. If anyone ever saw me make a mistake, in my mind I thought that would prove that I didn't belong here. This is all subconscious, but looking back on it now I can kind of see this.

That was when I met Rabbi Benay Lappe. When I heard her speak, I literally ran down the aisle with tears streaming down my face and hugged her. Just listening to her and her message really helped me feel seen, which is so incredible. I know that she really helps to empower Jews in the LGBTQ community, which I don't identify with, but yet I do feel like someone who is different than most Jews here in America. I felt like she really saw me. It was the first time, I think, that I realized that I could have an impact, and that I had a voice.

Dan Libenson: Let's talk a little bit about your work, now, with Nourish Co., and particularly the Jewish side of it. How did Nourish get started and what's your philosophy?

Kristin Eriko Posner: Really, I just started by hosting a dinner party with some friends. I served a couple of dishes that I made up. I did a donabe, which is a Japanese hot pot that I had cooked rice in. For my Ashkenazi Jewish husband I put in some smoked salmon and some everything bagel mix and dill. That was the most popular dish of the night. I don't even know if people remember anything else from the night, but they still talk about this one dish that I made. I thought, Okay, maybe I'm on to something.

Then, when we were getting married, I was looking online for examples of other Japanese and Jewish weddings and I couldn't find anything that really resonated with me. I did a post for Smashing the Glass about our Japanese and Jewish wedding, just in hopes that other people would see it and maybe get some ideas.

My husband is a mechanical engineer, and I'm an interior designer, and so quality is really important to us. We can tell when something has been really well made. I always knew that part of Nourish would be designing something. I wanted to design product, which I eventually did.

Neither of us had a lot of heirlooms that were passed down through our own families, and when we were registering for our wedding we were really disappointed by the quality of what was out there on the market, in terms of both Japanese and Jewish ritual objects.

Also, I was talking to friends from other cultures—not just Japanese and Jewish—and they also felt like they couldn't find quality ritual products. For example, I have a friend who is Chinese, and she wanted to get a moon cake mold for Lunar New Year. She wanted to find one that was really beautiful, like how they used to make them, but she couldn't find one that wasn't made of plastic.

I realized that it's not just a Japanese and Jewish thing, that heirlooms are really anchors that help us to connect to our cultures, and yet these things that I kept seeing were not what I felt like were heirloom quality.

Then there's the total other end of the spectrum, where there are these artisans making these beautiful Judaica objects. For most newlyweds, though, they're totally inaccessible—they cost thousands of dollars.

Dan Libenson: As someone who converted to Judaism can you talk a bit about how you feel about being part of the project of reimagining Judaism?

Kristin Eriko Posner: There are a couple different pieces. Yes, I fell in love with Judaism, and, yes, I see that it is crashing. I spent my whole life feeling like my own heritage was slipping away from me and I've seen the damage that that can do. Our rituals are what our ancestors used, across time, to heal and to celebrate. Being able to do those things is so important, especially now when we're moving so quickly.

There is this chapter in Michael Twitty's book *The Cooking Gene* called "Sankofa." He explains that sankofa is a word and a symbol in the Twi language of Ghana. He translates it to, "it's no sin to go to your past and fetch what you need to go forward into the future in a positive way. The seed for the next generation is rescued from the past." I've returned to this so many times. Every time I hear it, I get full-body chills.

No matter what culture you come from, our ancestors have been updating our traditions from the beginning of time. That is a way that I give myself some permission and grace to update things. Fraud syndrome is a very real thing, that it can be really debilitating for people. It's very scary to update traditions—especially if it's not your own. I like to think that Judaism is my own, now that I am Jewish, but it still . . . it doesn't make it less scary.

Lex Rofeberg: I'm curious to talk about the word "fusion." It comes up for us in a number of contexts—especially when we're talking about the intersections, or collisions, of two ethnic or religious things. With your ritual objects you've blurred the line between things that we classify in our heads as Jewish, and things that we classify in our heads as Japanese. I'd love to hear what your thinking is behind that, and if you're making a bigger claim, or crafting a different kind of Jewish world, in the very creation of those kinds of objects.

Kristin Eriko Posner: Of course this has been done from the beginning of time. A lot of people have reached out to me asking if I will develop a recipe that is Japanese and Jewish. In some ways, I feel like it's something that people are really intrigued by and curious about, and that's wonderful. At the same time, I don't actually feel like it's that different from what people have been doing from the beginning of time.

When I think about the ritual objects, I think we are the ones who make it Jewish. Just because something looks traditionally or authentically Jewish doesn't make it more Jewish than something else.

When people go to an "ethnic" restaurant, they will often measure how "authentic" the food was. I think often about who gets to lay the claim to what's authentic and what's not authentic.

I looked it up in the dictionary. Authentic is defined in the dictionary as having been made or done in the same way as an original. If I practiced a Japanese holiday in the same exact way that my great-great-grandmother in Japan, for example, would have practiced it, it would probably be, a, impossible, and, b, really not resonate with me that much.

Japanese Americans all have very different ways of celebrating Japanese New Year, based on how their families came here, where in the US they live, if they lived somewhere else before. If I were to go to a Japanese New Year party, and it was really different from how my family celebrates it—just as if I were to go to a Jewish seder, and it was really different than the way my family does a seder—I would never say to anyone, "What you're doing is inauthentic." I think that every family and person has a totally different way of celebrating. The objects that they fill their home with, the food that they eat, the holiday, the ritual . . . it's all very different, based on the story of their family.

I've been so lucky to have developed my Judaism here in California, where it really feels like anything goes, and it feels safe for us to reinterpret, for example, our Passover seder.

I've hosted, I think, three Passover seders. The most recent one was the racial justice Passover seder, which I hosted a few years ago with Annette Blum from Shalon. We took the entire seder apart, and really dissected everything, and tried to make sure that we were involving everyone who we had invited. We wanted to really make sure that we included a wide variety of Jewish stories and cultures.

One of the first dishes that we served was *tsukune*, which is Japanese for chicken meatball matzah ball soup. That was my contribution. Then there was a woman who taught us about this tradition of hitting your neighbors with a scallion. Racial justice seems like this really heavy, depressing thing to talk about sometimes. It can be overwhelming. And yet this dinner was such a celebration of cultures, and an opportunity to shine some light on what so many people of color in our country and across the world have to deal with on a day-to-day basis.

Dan Libenson: What is food supposed to do in a ritual setting? Are there ways in which thinking about food in a more powerful way could open new possibilities or directions for Jewish practice?

Kristin Eriko Posner: People have actually asked me—this is a separate question—but people have asked me, "Do you think that food is enough of a way to practice being Jewish?" which I think is a very layered question. Often people say it's not enough, there has to be more, but I think that that question really discredits how powerful food can really be.

For me, food was one of the only things that helped remind me of my Japanese American heritage. I think that's true for many Japanese Americans who have lost so much of their culture in the past 70 years. But I think it is also true for so many other cultures who have been marginalized, especially here in the US. Food is the one thing that we have left.

I think that food is one of the most accessible ways to learn about a culture, because we all have to eat. We have to eat three times a day. It's the easiest gateway into a culture, in some ways. I think that the other thing is that food has been how the people in our lives have shown us their love.

My dad grew up during a time when it wasn't really accepted to be proudly Japanese American. When I make him a Japanese dish that his mom, or my grandmother, made for him, that is really an act of cultural preservation and reclamation—even if my dish isn't made with the exact same ingredients that she would have made it with.

When I think about Passover, I think about dishes that have adapted over time. One example is a gefilte fish dish that I've made for Passover that's inspired by a Japanese fish cake called kamaboko, which is delicious. You talk to any Japanese person, and they'll say, Kamaboko is delicious. But then you ask a Jewish person about our Ashkenazi version of a fish cake, gefilte fish, and I don't know a lot of people who would say, "It's so delicious."

I'm talking in terms of food, but when you're updating something, I don't think you have to get rid of one thing and replace it with another thing—I think that you can have both of those things. Or you can replace it with a new thing, and then come back to the old thing the next year. I don't think anything has to be so rigid.

Dan Libenson: As you think of yourself as what Benay Lappe calls "a player in this next era of Judaism," I'm wondering if there's wisdom you can share with us about the experience of your having stepped into the space of the Crash with your own small-scale project for enriching Jewish experience.

Kristin Eriko Posner: When I approach things from a perspective of how is this going to bring in income, or how can I make it grow even more ... when I think about it from a numbers standpoint, I get really drained thinking about that.

But when I think about my purpose and the purpose of Nourish ... just thinking about it makes me feel teary. People have emailed me and said, "Thank you for existing." I know how that feels, because I remember when I first heard about Rabbi Angela Buchdahl in New York. She's one of the first Asian American women to be ordained as a cantor and as a rabbi. I felt that way when I learned about her story. To think that I'm doing that for other people is so amazing and so energizing. That is what helps me move forward every day.

Like you said, Dan, there's this ... I wouldn't call it smallness, because to me it feels very big. But it is more grassroots—not coming from large organizations and funders and philanthropists. I think that when you are working in this way it's really important to remember what your purpose is. That is what's going to give you the most impact, in the long term.

QUESTIONS FOR REFLECTION

- We receive an important question from Eileen Levinson: "Why can't the whole service just be something that I get (understand), or 90% of the service be something that I get?" Should each of us be able to understand the fullness of our Jewish rituals, in whatever language? If so, how might we strive to achieve that reality without simply saying "more Jews should have more Jewish education?" If not, why not?
- Tiffany Shlain's approach to Shabbat is in certain senses quite unorthodox, and in other senses quite traditional. What's one experiment you might try with Shabbat, to enhance your experience of it on a week-by-week basis?
- Kristin Eriko Posner's understanding of Jewish food, and Jewish objects, is that "We are the ones who make it Jewish. Just because something looks traditionally or authentically Jewish, [that] doesn't make it more Jewish than something else." What is a food, or object in your home, that you have never thought of before as "Jewish"—but which you could understand as Jewish moving forward?

Afterword

From its beginnings, the *Judaism Unbound* podcast was an experiment. What might come of a series of thoughtful, open, probing, provocative conversations about the past, present, and future of Judaism, peppered with periodic analysis from its co-hosts? In a sense, the podcast was Dan's and Lex's own learning journey, and they invited the rest of us to come along. Might such conversations widen the sense of what might be possible? Could they draw more people into the process of thinking creatively about the Jewish future?

After eight years and nearly 500 conversations with deep thinkers and creative practitioners, the experiment continues, and yet *Judaism Unbound* has turned into something more than a bank of interesting ideas and inspiring examples. A community has formed around the podcast and its ideas. According to scholar Steven Kaplin, the podcast has played a particularly significant role in digital Judaism by putting forth a "theory of tradition as a methodology, or discursive strategy, through which new forms of Judaism, particularly digital forms, can become recognized and legitimized as Jewish." One might think of the podcast as a collaborative, non-hierarchical think tank of those actively seeking to innovate Jewish lives and communities.

In the following bonus chaper, first published in *American Examples: New Conversations About Religion* by the University of Alabama Press, author Steven Kaplin argues that *Judaism Unbound* not only proposes a theory of change in which we must connect with tradition in order to reimagine it, but also serves as an example of that very theory. Consider this chapter an effort to study *Judaism Unbound* itself as one of the bold contributions to the future of Judaism that the podcast is devoted to studying, the kind of organization that might land its leaders a guest spot on *Judaism Unbound*.

Steven Kaplin

Podcasting Judaism: *Judaism Unbound* and the Method of Jewish Tradition

Introduction

Though overshadowed by other forms of online digital media (e.g., streaming services and social media platforms), podcasts have become a popular and influential form of contemporary media. As the authors of *Podcasting: The Audio Media Revolution* note, top podcasts have download and subscriber numbers well into the millions: *Serial*, for instance, had four million downloads per episode in 2014, while 2017's *S-Town* had ten million downloads in just its first four days.[1] In the years since *S-Town*'s release, podcasts have only become more present in popular culture. Eric Hoyt and Jeremy Wade Morris add that "By many measurements, the medium is flourishing—with the quantity of podcasts, listeners, advertising revenue, and nonprofit funding increasing sharply year after year, including an 'explosive' 2018, which saw the number of US people over the age of twelve who have ever listened to

---

[1] Martin Spinelli and Lance Dann, *Podcasting: The Audio Media Revolution* (New York, NY: Bloomsbury Publishing, 2019), 1.

a podcast climb above 50 percent for the first time."[2] In an era when celebrities, journalists, and even presidential candidates host and appear on podcasts, it has become necessary for scholars to take the medium seriously as a space of public social and intellectual engagement.

While Jewish podcasting obviously functions at a far smaller scale than the major podcast productions, the popularity of podcasts has nevertheless trickled down into the Jewish world as well. There are podcasts about Jewish parenting, Jewish politics, Jewish pop culture and lifestyle, Jewish texts, Jewish women, Jewish humor, Jewish Studies. It is clear from the proliferation of Jewish podcasting that there are both producers and audiences for such projects: People want to create Jewish content in podcast form, and people want to engage with Jewish content in podcast form. Jewish podcasts, then, are also sites of public Jewish expression and thought, sites in which Jews grapple with the big questions and concerns of Jewishness and Judaism. As such, Jewish podcasts and other forms of Jewish digital media have become indispensable platforms for the study of contemporary Judaism and, by extension, religion in the internet age.

I view the podcast *Judaism Unbound* as a digital case study through which to analyze contemporary American Jewish thinking and the methods that inform it. I contend that Dan Libenson and Lex Rofeberg, the hosts of *Judaism Unbound*, leverage the podcast medium toward the presentation of a vision for American Judaism in the digital age. Libenson and Rofeberg put forth the seemingly contradictory notions that podcasting represents a new way of expressing Jewish thinking and doing *and* that their podcast lies within a much longer tradition of Judaism. By claiming that *Judaism Unbound* is simultaneously an instance of both innovation and tradition, the two hosts have constructed, I argue, a theory of *tradition* as a *methodology*, or discursive strategy, through which new forms of Judaism, particularly digital forms, can become recognized and legitimized as Jewish.

Jewish tradition is often understood and mythologized by Jewish

---

[2] Eric Hoyt and Jeremy Wade Morris, *Saving New Sounds: Podcast Preservation and Historiography* (Ann Arbor: University of Michigan Press, 2021), 2.

practitioners as ancient and intentionally unchanging—see, for instance, *The Fiddler on the Roof*—and it is against this conception that Libenson and Rofeberg present their alternative approach. For Libenson and Rofeberg, Jewish tradition is neither ancient nor unchanging; instead, it is an intellectual and rhetorical strategy by which contemporary Jews selectively construct the boundaries of Judaism to grant authority to their own forms of Judaism. This type of tradition-as-methodology is not, according to the hosts of *Judaism Unbound*, a cynical, selfish, or insincere attempt to artificially shape Judaism toward one's own ends but is rather the process by which Judaism can, and should, adapt and survive in an ever-changing world. Moreover, they argue that it is what Jewish tradition has always meant.

To a large extent, Libenson and Rofeberg's claim that Jewish tradition is a method by which contemporary people discursively make and remake their collective pasts, presents, and futures mirrors widely accepted scholarly analysis of tradition. In terms of Jewish tradition, Gershom Scholem, the Israeli scholar of Jewish mysticism, theorized that Jewish tradition is the process of an original revelation (in this case, that described in the Hebrew Bible) persevering from one generation to another as each undergoes extensive changes to their circumstances.[3] For Scholem, "the true carriers of tradition" are not those who simply memorize the past for its repetition in the present but those who can interpret the memories of the past and their repetition in new, ever-changing contexts. Because tradition, according to Scholem, "perceives, receives, and unfolds," it is, by necessity, a creative, even innovative, endeavor.[4]

Like Scholem, influential folklore scholar Henry Glassie argues that tradition is a mode of creativity and innovation. For Glassie, tradition is a process of drawing from the resources, the "accessible raw materials," of the past to shape present selves. Opposed to the "problematic notion

---

[3] Gershom Scholem, "Revelation and Tradition as Religious Categories in Judaism," in *The Messianic Idea in Judaism and Other Essays on Jewish Spirituality*, trans. Michael A. Meyer (New York: Schocken Books, 1971), 284-5.
[4] Scholem, "Revelation and Tradition," 297.

that any alteration ... amounts to tradition-breaking apostasy," Glassie contends that genuine tradition necessarily includes creativity, change, variation, and innovation.[5] As Glassie writes, "Such a formulation foregrounds the agency of the individual and frees the notion of tradition from its associations with stasis. The antonym of neither change nor creativity, tradition as process depends on both and flowers in variation and innovation."[6]

The theorization of tradition as more than the simple handing down of the unchanged has been replicated in recent years by scholars within other disciplines, including Seth Lerer, who writes in his study of tradition in literature that "tradition, in my view, is not a thing, it is an activity. To work within tradition is to make anew, not just to curate," and Vaia Touna, who argues through her work on contemporary conceptions of the "traditional Greek village" that tradition is always constructed, or fabricated, through contemporary discourses of religion and identity.[7] In line with such academic studies on tradition, *Judaism Unbound* presents a notion of tradition in which Judaism is constantly constructed anew through the discursive method of tradition-making. What makes Libenson and Rofeberg's work on the podcast interesting, however, is that they are self-aware and explicit about their use of tradition in this way. Although scholars have long been aware that tradition is a method of religious construction and authorization, it is not necessarily the case that constructors of religious tradition understood the process in such a way. Tracing the ways in which the hosts of *Judaism Unbound* explicitly think through this process for themselves grants us additional insight into how tradition-as-methodology might

---

[5] Ray Cashman, Tom Mould, and Pravina Shukla, "Introduction: The Individual and Tradition," in *Individual and Tradition: Folkloristic Perspectives*, ed. Ray Cashman, Tom Mould, and Pravina Shukla (Bloomington: Indiana University Press, 2011), 2-3.

[6] Henry Glassie, *Turkish Traditional Art Today* (Bloomington: Indiana University Press, 1993), 9. Also cited in Cashman, Mould, and Shukla, "Introduction," 2.

[7] Seth Lerer, *Tradition: A Feeling for the Literary Past* (Oxford: Oxford University Press, 2016), vii. Vaia Touna, *Fabrications of the Greek Past: Religion, Tradition, and the Making of Modern Identities* (Leiden, The Netherlands: Brill, 2017).

function as an *intentional* discursive strategy.⁸

Judaism Unbound, then, is a compelling instance of Jewish thinking for several interrelated reasons. First, it is a podcast that thinks a lot about being a podcast. While many forms of religious digital media attempt to replicate offline religiosity online—a livestream of a religious service, for example—*Judaism Unbound* does not necessarily attempt to replicate an offline Jewish experience. Instead, its hosts often conceptualize the podcast as a new form of Jewish religiosity, one designed by and for Jews who have brought much of their lives onto the internet and want their Judaism to live there, at least in part, as well.⁹ It is not obviously or inherently the case that listening to a Jewish podcast conversation is a form of "doing Judaism," as the co-hosts like to say, but the hosts' theorizing of *Judaism Unbound* as such makes the podcast an analytically interesting occurrence of contemporary Judaism.

Secondly, *Judaism Unbound* rarely features conversations about normative forms of Judaism. Instead, the podcast highlights new, creative, innovative, and otherwise non-normative forms of Jewish thought and practice. In just the few months prior to this writing, the podcast has featured episodes on a non-profit community farm, the Netflix series *Russian Doll*, a new book about Bob Dylan, and vegan prosciutto. Not only does *Judaism Unbound* attempt a new form of Judaism through its medium, it also attempts to use its new medium toward the creation of many further new ideas and practices for future Judaism. The newness of the podcast allows for additional Jewish newness. *Judaism Unbound* is therefore expansive in its conception of Judaism in both form and

---

⁸ My use of discursive tradition here is aware of and, to some extent, in conversation with Talal Asad's well-known work, particularly his theorization of tradition in "Thinking about Tradition, Religion, and Politics in Egypt Today," *Critical Inquiry* 42, no. 1 (Autumn 2015). Asad, however, is primarily concerned with how scholars might recognize and define tradition, while I focus instead on the ways in which practitioners, like Libenson and Rofeberg, understand and utilize tradition for themselves.

⁹ This is a frequent theme of the podcast, but it is especially the case in Dan Libenson and Lex Rofeberg, "Episode 310: Judaism Unbound, Director's Cut," *Judaism Unbound* (podcast), Jan. 21, 2022.

content—the medium, the methodology, and the ideology align.

Finally, the thinking exhibited by the hosts of *Judaism Unbound* parallels significant Jewish intellectual trends about Judaism and the United States a generation earlier. In the postwar period, particularly after the destruction of European Judaism in the Holocaust, American Jewish thinking has largely revolved around the difficulty of maintaining Jewish tradition, Jewishness (i.e., Jewish distinctiveness in relation to other Americans), and Judaism in a new American environment. The internet, interestingly, has inspired similar questions among Jews. As people increasingly spend time online, how might Jews maintain Jewish tradition, Jewishness, and Judaism in this new online environment? Within this context, *Judaism Unbound*, in both its podcast form and the questions it asks, is more a new iteration of a longer intellectual trend with American Judaism than an entirely new form of Judaism. *Judaism Unbound*, in these ways, presents a significant opportunity for exploring the most pressing concerns within American Judaism.

Judaism Unbound as Digital Religion

The internet and other forms of digital media have taken on an outsized influence in nearly every segment of American society, and conversation about the relationship between digital media and religion has become increasingly active as well. In the Jewish world, both within religious communities and from outside observers, much of this conversation has focused on the potentially destructive nature of digital media regarding religion. Many Jewish leaders and practitioners have theorized that the accessibility and democratization, the radical expansion of religious "voices" from widely varying backgrounds and perspectives, offered by the internet would make religious norms, institutions, leadership structures, and codes of behavior nearly impossible to uphold in the new, digitally infused world. Scholarship on Judaism and the internet overwhelmingly focuses on Haredi ("ultra-Orthodox) Jewish communities and the trend among its leadership to reject as much as possible modern American trends in the hope of retaining communal insularity and adherence to notions of pre-modern tradition.[10] As Heidi Campbell writes, "To date most research on Judaism and new media has focused on Orthodox Judaism, and specifically ultra-Orthodox groups' negotiations with such platforms. Within this work most studies have centered on a few select themes, namely, (a) ultra-Orthodox engagement online and particularly (b) female use of the internet, allowing them to bypass or negotiate with traditional authority structures."[11] The proliferation of scholarship of this kind is exciting, in part, because it signals that the relationship of digital media and religion is significant enough to support numerous studies, but the near-complete emphasis on Haredi Judaism gives the mistaken impression that digital media primarily functions as a problem to be solved for Jews.[12]

As I show here through the *Judaism Unbound* podcast, an expansion of online Jewish sources reveals that disruption to religious authority and normativity is not the sole impact of digital media on religion. That digital media, and the internet in particular, has transformed the functioning of religion by changing the nature of how and where religion is practiced, who can speak on its behalf, and what tools are available for religious use, does not imply to the hosts of *Judaism Unbound* that Judaism has been undermined by digital media. Instead, they theorize digital media as a contributor toward the *preservation* of

---

[10] For just a few recent examples, see Ayala Fader, *Hidden Heretics: Jewish Doubt in the Digital Age* (Princeton: Princeton University Press, 2020), Hananel Rosenberg, Menahem Blondheim, and Elihu Katz, "It's the Text, Stupid! Mobile Phones, Religious Communities, and the Silent Threat of Text Messages," *New Media & Society* 21, no. 11–12 (November 2019), Rivka Neriya-Ben Shahar, "Negotiating Agency: Amish and Ultra-Orthodox Women's Responses to the Internet," *New Media & Society* 19, no. 1 (January 2017), and Jeremy Stolow, *Orthodox by Design: Judaism, Print Politics, and the ArtScroll Revolution* (Berkeley: University of California Press, 2010).

[11] Campbell, "Introduction," in *Digital Judaism: Jewish Negotiations with Digital Media and Culture*, ed. Heidi Campbell (New York, NY: Routledge, 2015), 5.

[12] See Campbell, "Introduction," 2 and Nathan Abrams, "Appropriation and Innovation: Facebook, Grassroots Jews and Offline Post-Denominational Judaism," in *Digital Judaism: Jewish Negotiations with Digital Media and Culture*, ed. Heidi Campbell (New York, NY: Routledge, 2015), 40.

Judaism and Jewish tradition in the contemporary world. Moreover, *Judaism Unbound* places the internet into a tradition of sustaining technological innovations, such as the printing press or the pen, which make Judaism—its theologies, rituals, texts, literature and music, arts and material cultures, etc.—more widely and easily accessible and its communities more vibrant.[13] In this way, the transformations brought by the internet are theorized by the hosts of *Judaism Unbound* to function as *traditional innovations*, changes that fit within the overarching method of Jewish tradition to remake Judaism according to the needs of its practitioners. With *Judaism Unbound*, I seek to move beyond the idea that digital media (and modernity more broadly) has crash landed into Judaism and forced dramatic and damaging transformation.

Scholarship on digital media and religion outside of Jewish communities provides a roadmap for such thinking. In *Digital Creatives and the Rethinking of Religious Authority* Heidi Campbell identifies a new type of religious authority, the group of people she terms "religious digital creatives" (RDCs), who produce religious content through digital media but are not, typically, normative religious professionals (they are, rather, media professionals).[14] RDCs serve an interesting role in the religious landscape because on the one hand, they produce religious content, sometimes in conjunction with normative religious institutions, but on the other, they have become a new type of religious authority, often in ways that make normative authorities uncomfortable. Campbell's RDC language is useful when applied to Libenson and Rofeberg: in putting forth their ideas and imaginings about Judaism through *Judaism Unbound*, the two hosts place themselves into a complex hybrid model of religious authority, in which they simultaneously have little normative authority but are nevertheless publicly influential. As will become evident in the "Ten New Commandments" case study, Libenson and

---

[13] See, for example, "*Judaism Unbound*, Director's Cut," in which Libenson and Rofeberg conceptualize their podcast, and other Jewish podcasts, as contemporary versions of both the Talmud and Jewish newspapers, each of which, in their respective eras, functioned as new forms of media through which greater numbers of Jews could engage seriously with Judaism.

[14] Heidi Campbell, *Digital Creatives and the Rethinking of Religious Authority* (New York, NY: Routledge, 2020), 4-5.

Rofeberg recognize this hybrid positionality and incorporate it into their understanding of Jewish innovation and tradition.

Judaism Unbound as American Judaism

Although the online nature of a podcast allows *Judaism Unbound* to reach audiences outside national boundaries, Libenson and Rofeberg are primarily concerned with Judaism in the context of the cultural, political, economic, legal, and religious norms of the United States. American models of religion-skeptical spirituality are particularly relevant to *Judaism Unbound*: a general discomfort with normative religious leaders and institutions, a strong inclination toward diversity (e.g., racial, sexual), and a willingness to converse with and borrow from a wide variety of religious and religion-adjacent communities are common features of *Judaism Unbound* episodes.[15] Moreover, American modes of Judaism and Jewish thinking serve as the springboard from which the hosts level their critiques and proposals. The co-hosts frequently describe their frustrations with American Jewish settings, both in Orthodox and liberal Jewish communities, and along with their weekly guests, most of whom are American as well, use the podcast as a think tank for new possibilities for Judaism in the U.S. Over the years, the podcast has explored un-orthodox (and un-Orthodox) perspectives on a wide range of Jewish themes, including, theology, Israel/Palestine, Jewish texts, gender and sexuality, race, Jewish institutions and communities, and ritual and holiday observance, but each of these topics—even Israel/Palestine—is conducted through the lens of American Jewry. In using their podcast to question the

---

[15] There is an extensive body of academic literature on the American turn toward spirituality and its relationship to normative conceptions of religion; in addition to Turner's *Counterculture to Cyberculture*, see Robert C. Fuller, *Spiritual, but Not Religious: Understanding Unchurched America* (Oxford: Oxford University Press, 2001), Wade Clark Roof, *Spiritual Marketplace: Baby Boomers and the Remaking of American Religion* (Princeton, NJ: Princeton University Press, 1999), and Robert Wuthnow, *After Heaven: Spirituality In America Since the 1950s* (Berkeley: University of California Press, 1998).

normative forms and ideologies of American Judaism, the hosts of *Judaism Unbound* are working within an extensive American tradition of leveraging spirituality, and technology, toward an internal critique of religion.[16]

Such American-style spirituality has been of particular importance to American Judaism in recent decades. In the immediate aftermath of the Holocaust in the 1930s and 1940s, much Jewish thinking, in all national contexts, centered around the issue of how to ensure the preservation and continuity of Judaism into the future. In the United States, two general trends of thought emerged in this regard. The first, endorsed by the major Jewish denominations, was that the post-Holocaust rebuilding of Judaism ought to involve the widespread return to longstanding Jewish norms and traditions. Unlike in Eastern Europe, where Jews were, to some extent, separate from the dominant culture, American Jews—particularly in the Protestant-Catholic-Jew triad of postwar American religion—were largely integrated into American society, and many Jewish leaders, fearing that intermarriage and widespread adoption of American culture would diminish engagement with Judaism, argued that traditional communal norms would serve as a barricade against extinction by assimilation.[17] Although the various denominations oriented themselves toward differing norms and differing historical traditions, they remained in general agreement that adherence to collective normativity—and to American norms of religious decorum—was important to the continuity of Judaism in

---

[16] As several recent scholars have described, spirituality indeed represents a long-running American tradition; see Catherine L. Albanese, *A Republic of Mind and Spirit: A Cultural History of American Metaphysical Religion* (New Haven: Yale University Press, 2007), Courtney Bender, *The New Metaphysicals: Spirituality and the American Religious Imagination* (University of Chicago Press, 2010), and Leigh Eric Schmidt, *Restless Souls: The Making of American Spirituality* (Berkeley: University of California Press, 2012).

[17] For a general discussion, and critique, of Jewish continuity in the postwar period see: Lila Corwin Berman, Kate Rosenblatt, and Ronit Y. Stahl, "Continuity Crisis: The History and Sexual Politics of an American Jewish Communal Project," *American Jewish History* 104, no. 2 (2020). See also chapter 7 of Michael E. Staub, *Torn at the Roots: The Crisis of Jewish Liberalism in Postwar America* (New York: Columbia University Press, 2002).

the United States.

The second trend, largely an oppositional response to the first, was the idea that the post-Holocaust era provided a unique opportunity to address long-running problems in normative Jewish life (e.g., sexism, empty ritualism, lack of engagement). This ideology posited normative forms of Judaism in the United States, like other normative forms of American religiosity, to have long been in decline, even before the Holocaust, so the proposed adherence to such norms would not, in fact, promote the continuity of American Judaism. Instead, Jewish continuity would best be achieved through intentional transformations that addressed the ongoing problems from pre-war American Judaism. Inspired in large part by the spiritual trends of the American counterculture, this approach was endorsed by many countercultural Jews of the 1960s-90s, including Jewish feminists, secular Jews, Jewish leftists, and other such non-normative groups.[18] These two competing orientations to Jewish continuity—traditional norms versus religious transformation—played a crucial part in the much broader conversation about the role that America should play in the construction of Judaism in the United States.

Judaism Unbound and its approach to Judaism are directly descended intellectually from this second trend in post-Holocaust American Jewish thinking. Transformation as a means of continuity is a key theme in the project of *Judaism Unbound*, and Libenson and Rofeberg's inclination toward creativity, expansion, and innovation in Judaism are obviously in line with the countercultural and anti-normative ideologies of the generation prior. In one of their very earliest episodes, even, Libenson and Rofeberg interviewed scholar Shaul Magid and used his book on innovative American Jewish thinking in the 20th century, *American Post-Judaism*, as a jumping off point for imagining further innovation, through methods shared with the prior generation, in the

---

[18] There are many histories of Jewish thinking in this era; as just two examples, see Rachel Kranson, *Ambivalent Embrace: Jewish Upward Mobility in Postwar America* (Chapel Hill: University of North Carolina Press, 2017) and Riv-Ellen Prell, *Prayer and Community: The Havurah in American Judaism* (Detroit: Wayne State University Press, 1989).

new century, thus situating the podcast within a tradition of innovative thinking.[19] By embracing the internet as an exciting and, in some sense, traditional new space, culture, and environment for Judaism, rather than as dangerous and destabilizing, *Judaism Unbound*'s methodology and conception of tradition is reminiscent of the earlier generation's embrace, rather than fear, of America. As Rofeberg pithily argues, the address of future Jewish communities "ends in .com or .org instead of avenue or road," but in either case, Judaism—and, here, its American outlook—nevertheless remains.[20]

Judaism Unbound: The Ten New Commandments

I turn now to "The Ten New Commandments," a case study episode of *Judaism Unbound* that reveals clearly Libenson and Rofeberg's collective understanding and utilization of Jewish tradition as a method for the remaking, and authorizing, of American Judaism.[21] In this episode in particular, the co-hosts construct a concept of Jewish tradition in which it is not a given *thing*, not a stable and normalized category, but a method, or process, of development that Jews use to adapt and transform Judaism in new and unforeseen circumstances. Whereas many American Jews and Jewish organizations prefer to imagine tradition, and by extension Judaism, as maintaining itself with as little disruption or change as possible, Libenson and Rofeberg use *Judaism Unbound* to suggest that Judaism in the contemporary United States needs disruption, particularly in regard to the internet. And most importantly, that it is through the methodology of tradition that this

---

[19] Dan Libenson and Lex Rofes, "Episode 13: American Post-Judaism - Shaul Magid," *Judaism Unbound* (podcast), May 13, 2016. Shaul Magid, *American Post-Judaism: Identity and Renewal in a Postethnic Society* (Bloomington: Indiana University Press, 2013).

[20] Dan Libenson and Lex Rofes, "Bonus Episode: Lex's ELI Talk (Migrating Judaism: The Internet Movement)," *Judaism Unbound* (podcast), May 2, 2017.

[21] Dan Libenson and Lex Rofeberg, "Episode 154: Ten New Commandments," *Judaism Unbound* (podcast), January 25, 2019.

disruption can be discursively normalized as "truly" or "authentically" Jewish.

In this episode, Libenson presents his idea for a renewed Ten Commandments that might contribute to the creation of new forms of Judaism and talks them through with Rofeberg. In line with the experimental and dynamic nature of *Judaism Unbound*, the ten new commandments are not given "official" language, so the list I present below uses Libenson's words but are edited by me for clarity:

Dan Libenson's Ten New Commandments

1. We [Jews] should stop doing the things that do not work.
2. In remembering our collective Jewish past, we should elicit help from people who did not grow up Jewish.
3. We should grieve properly for what is left behind.
4. We should forever study even the things we no longer do.
5. In order to keep alive the things we no longer do, we should develop practices that help us to remember (e.g., holidays).
6. We should give new innovations time to develop without immediate comparison to already-existing Judaism.
7. We should "modularize and democratize" the creation of Judaism by encouraging a wide range of people to develop and test individual ideas and practices.
8. We should recruit non-Jewish friends to help us develop Judaism.
9. We should be wildly experimental.
10. We should center artists and innovators as leaders.

As Libenson notes, the commandments are split into two categories: the first five commandments deal with "mourning" and "honoring" the past, while the final five commandments are concerned with constructing Jewish futurity. Together, these ten commandments, and their combined concern with both tradition (commandments 1-5) and innovation (commandments 6-10), present *Judaism Unbound*'s method for a new American Judaism.

I begin with commandments 6-10, which best exemplify *Judaism Unbound*'s general inclination toward religious innovation. In opposition to the "conserving impulse" exemplified in normative forms of Judaism and re-imagined by Libenson's first five commandments, these final five commandments argue for increased emphasis on the "creative impulse," in which American Jews try as many new things as possible to see what sticks. With commandment 7, Libenson imagines a process in which new experiments in Judaism will be constructed, tested, and reconstructed across Jewish groups—a "modularized and democratized" approach to Jewish creativity. The same theory holds in commandments 8, 9, and 10, which each call for further experimentation and innovation, not only regarding what Jews do and think but in terms of what kinds of people are engaging in the process as well.

Libenson's call for Jewish innovation is modeled by Rofeberg and himself on *Judaism Unbound* and also by the many guests on the podcast: Nearly every episode features an individual or community representative who has created some new form of Judaism and is trying to make it work within their own community. *Judaism Unbound* also features conversations oriented toward creativity in the realms of Jewish theology, gender and racial constructions, community building, education models, and artistic creations. No individual innovation modeled by a guest can alone represent a "new Judaism," but grouped together under the *Judaism Unbound* umbrella, the podcast serves as a digital hub for the innovative process.

It is commandment 6, however, that is best reveals Libenson and Rofeberg's thinking on Jewish innovation. By arguing, explicitly and at the beginning of the innovation process, that new innovations should not be compared to already-existing modes of Judaism until they have had time to develop, the hosts anticipate the "but is it Jewish?" question/critique that often accompanies changes in Jewish life. In the episode, and in many others, Libenson and Rofeberg reflect upon the question of what makes an innovation in Jewish life as "truly Jewish" as elements that have long been legitimized, rather than something else altogether (i.e., not Jewish). While scholars rightfully refrain from weighing in on authenticity disputes, such questions about "true Judaism" remain of utmost significance to many Jewish practitioners, including Libenson and Rofeberg, and it is through their grappling with authenticity and legitimacy that the hosts' thinking about tradition and innovation is revealed.

I turn now to the first five of the new commandments, which use notions of tradition, I argue, to legitimize the innovations resulting from the second five commandments. In commandments 1-5, Libenson rethinks the "conserving impulse" of normative Judaism, which seeks to preserve Jewish ideologies and practices in order to continue them into the future. As described above, such conservation is a widely held ideal among American Jews, particularly Jewish institutions, but the for the co-hosts of *Judaism Unbound*, the American Jewish attachment to the past bogs Judaism down with religious expressions that many modern Jews do not value. Modeling the second new commandment, which calls for eliciting the help of non-Jews in remembering the Jewish past, Libenson turns to Marie Kondo, the Japanese author and television personality, for a new method of thinking about and preserving the past.

When the "Ten New Commandments" episode of *Judaism Unbound* was released in January of 2019, Libenson was in the midst of watching *Tidying Up with Marie Kondo*, the newly released Netflix show in which Kondo helps people to tidy up their homes, and their lives, by sorting through every one of their items before either keeping or throwing them away. For Libenson, many Jews are like the participants in *Tidying Up*: they are overly fearful of letting go of even undesired elements of Jewish tradition and therefore become destructively inclined to conserve everything. The American Jewish fear that Judaism will be lost if unwanted aspects of Jewish tradition are put aside, Libenson argues, creates a Judaism that retains harmful ideas and practices of prior eras and, as a result, fails to adopt useful ideas and practices in the new era. Libenson suggests that Jews instead adopt the "KonMari Method": take inventory of each element of Judaism, assess its current usefulness, and let go, with honor, those elements that no longer "spark joy."[22]

---

[22] As the KonMari Method website says, "Keep only those things that speak to the heart, and discard items that no longer spark joy. Thank them for their service—then let them go" ("Overview," KonMari, accessed July 27, 2022, konmari.com/about-the-konmari-method). The television show is based on the bestselling book by Marie Kondo and Cathy Hirano, *The Life-Changing Magic of Tidying Up: The Japanese Art of Decluttering and*

The method behind Libenson's Kondo-like process for Jewish tradition is expressed in commandments 1, 3, 4, and 5, which respectively argue that Jews should "stop doing the things that don't work" but should nevertheless grieve for the things that are left behind, remember them forever, and keep them alive, albeit changed, through ongoing ritual enactment. With these commandments, Libenson argues that the conserving impulse in Judaism is valuable and necessary to the project of Jewish creativity, even in cases where the things that have been conserved are not, because they remind contemporary Jews of both that which came before and the process of constructing what now is. Libenson and Rofeberg wish to leave behind, for instance, misogynistic practices prescribed in Jewish texts, but they do not wish to leave behind historical mention of such practices, the texts themselves, or, most importantly, the method by which such practices have been reimagined from one era to the next. Rather, they argue that such no-longer-useful elements of the Jewish past can be studied with transformation in mind, that such study serves as a method for imagining the possibilities of a better Judaism, whether as examples of what not to do, as frameworks for reworked or renewed practices or ideas, or as models of creative process and authorization. Libenson's general call to leave behind unwanted aspects of Judaism in favor of desired innovation is thereby revealed as a theory of *traditional* innovation, in which Jewish creativity is not a replacement of the old with the new but a recognition that the new is always already based in what came before. For Libenson and Rofeberg, "tradition" is therefore the method that allows Jewish innovations to be recognized and legitimized as Jewish.

This process of Judaism-building, in which tradition is conceptualized as a methodological approach to Jewish innovation, can be seen in nearly every episode of *Judaism Unbound*. One particularly clear example is from the episode "jOS 4.0 - A New Jewish Operating System," in which the hosts theorize that Judaism might best be understood as a computer operating system that stores the many

---

Organizing (Berkeley: Ten Speed Press, 2014).

components of Judaism in one widely accessible digital location.[23] According to Libenson and Rofeberg, "jOS" is not a set of standardized ideas and practices—that is, Judaism as we typically understand it—but a broader system through which people and communities can access a wide variety of ideas and practices. Innovations, in this model, exist alongside old, no-longer-needed forms of Judaism and, moreover, can be discursively shown to be continuous with them, thus legitimizing them as "truly" Jewish.

From this perspective, *Judaism Unbound* itself functions as a digital archival expansion and reiteration system; it holds within its many episodes a huge range of Jewish practices and ideas that allow creators of new Jewish forms to make connections to other Jewish forms, especially those that are already recognized as Jewish. Moreover, it holds within it other digital archival expansion and reiteration systems. In "The Future of Torah," for instance, Libenson and Rofeberg interview Brett Lockspeiser, the co-founder of an online Torah library called Sefaria, which attempts to catalog and display for free as many Jewish religious texts as possible.[24] Libenson, Rofeberg, and Lockspeiser share their excitement for both Sefaria's large database, of texts popular and obscure, and social media component, which allows users to collect and publicly share lists of texts with commentary. What makes Sefaria such an exciting project for Libenson and Rofeberg is not necessarily that *Judaism Unbound* listeners are likely to read most of these texts as sources of prescriptive religiosity but that they may be interested in those texts as part of a larger Jewish archival system that can be mined for legitimization purposes and easily shared among Jews in various communities. Even if almost no one is persuaded by the texts themselves, they can be read, memorialized, and potentially transformed for future Jewish use, including in ways that go against normative readings of the text. In the schema of Libenson's commandments, the claims and content of Sefaria's texts matter far less than their place within

---

[23] Dan Libenson and Lex Rofes, "Episode 21: jOS 4.0 - A New Jewish Operating System?," *Judaism Unbound* (podcast), July 7, 2016.
[24] Dan Libenson and Lex Rofes, "Episode 98: The Future of Torah - Brett Lockspeiser," *Judaism Unbound* (podcast), December 29, 2017.

the Jewish textual tradition and their accessibility within an archival system that allows Libenson's notion of Jewish tradition to function as a discursive method of Jewish creation.

For Libenson and Rofeberg, digital resources like Sefaria are exemplary of projects they hope many Jews will develop across varying contexts and online platforms. We can see other examples of such projects in those that Libenson and Rofeberg have created themselves. Libenson, for instance, co-hosts with Rabbi Benay Lappe an online streaming show called "The Oral Talmud," which originally debuted in April 2020, during widespread lockdowns in response to COVID-19.[25] In the show, Libenson and Lappe discuss selected passages from the Talmud, the foundational Jewish commentary on the Torah, and attempt to relate its themes—though rarely its prescriptions—to issues in American Jewish life. The central theme of many of the early videos is that the Talmud is a perfect text to study during a catastrophe (immediately, COVID-19; more generally, American Judaism) because it represents a historical example of Jews re-creating Jewish norms in response to catastrophe. To begin the first episode Libenson asks Lappe what the Talmud means to her, to which she replies:

> The Talmud is ... a handbook for how to respond to crashes. How to take a system that you live in, that you inherited, that's no longer working in this element or that element and make it better ... [after the fall of the Second Temple in Jerusalem] the rabbis were putting together this handbook to say to those who came after them, "this is going to happen to you. This is not a once in history event, it's going to happen in the future. Be prepared, know that it has already happened, that we survived, here's how we survived,

---

[25] See JewishLive.org/OralTalmud. In addition to being a frequent collaborator with Libenson and Rofeberg, Lappe is the founder and Rosh Yeshiva of Svara: A Traditionally Radical Yeshiva, frequently cited by Libenson and Rofeberg as exemplary of using tradition—in this case Talmud study—as a method toward the remaking of American Judaism.

and you can stand on our shoulders and know that, even with the radical changes you're going to need to make to your system, you'll know that that's traditional, you'll have lots of precedent to stand on, and the learning of this document will help you become the type of person you'll need to be in order to be . . . resilient, creative, bold, courageous, and willing to take chances to create a system that might have been unrecognizable to those in the past but might work better to do what we're ultimately in business to do.'[26]

Lappe's notion that the rabbis of antiquity recognized that there will be a future need to change Judaism, just as they themselves were changing Judaism in their own time, presents a method of Jewish tradition-making in which changing "the tradition" is a traditional thing to do. Libenson, trained as a lawyer, builds upon Lappe's logic by comparing the Talmud to a law school textbook: If the textbook is designed not only to teach students the law but to think like lawyers, the point of the Talmud, for contemporary Jews, should be to learn to think in the method of the ancient rabbis, not to simply follow the teachings of the rabbis.[27] By framing "the Oral Talmud" show as both a new way of doing Judaism and as methodologically continuous with the ancient rabbinical construction of the Talmud, Libenson and Lappe are making the argument that Jewish tradition functions as a way to authenticate innovations as within the category of Judaism.

In the process modeled by "The Oral Talmud," the "Ten New Commandments," and the broader *Judaism Unbound* project, the nature of Jewish tradition is re-theorized from a normative notion of Judaism that is handed down across generations to a Judaism that is always in the process of re-creation through the discursive use of "tradition." In such an understanding of tradition, which, again, mirrors those

---

[26] Benay Lappe, "Talking Talmud with Benay Lappe and Dan Libenson, Episode 1," *The Oral Talmud* (livestream), Apr. 2, 2020. "The Oral Talmud" is unscripted, so I have edited Lappe's words slightly for clarity.
[27] Dan Libenson, "Talking Talmud," *The Oral Talmud*.

posited by scholars of tradition, Jews can honor but ultimately leave behind the specific teachings of Jewish tradition while simultaneously retaining Jewish tradition as a methodology. While the recognition by Libenson and Rofeberg that Jewish tradition is not the preservation of Judaism as much as the preservation of its creative process is not new, their explicit understanding and use of it for further innovation does reveal the ideology and methodology behind their podcasting project.

Conclusion: The Ten New Commandments and the Internet

As hosts of the *Judaism Unbound* podcast, Dan Libenson and Lex Rofeberg conceptualize Jewish tradition as a method for remaking Judaism in the contemporary United States. As such, they theorize Judaism as *traditionally* experimental, creative, and in a process of ongoing transformation. This, as described above, is not a new theory of tradition but one that is common both in Jewish history and among scholars of tradition. Unlike earlier Jewish iterations of this tradition, however, the hosts of *Judaism Unbound* have access to digital technologies and the expanded access to information and practices allowed by the internet. By way of conclusion, I consider more carefully the importance of the internet to *Judaism Unbound*'s notion of tradition as a method.

To some extent, what makes the internet a perfect platform for *Judaism Unbound*'s Judaism is that it has unique tools for traditional innovation. As Libenson's ten new commandments exemplify, the process for Libenson and Rofeberg's Jewish creation requires both the conserving impulse and the creative impulse, each of which is bolstered, at times radically, by the functions of internet technology. The internet, for instance, allows for a near-infinite archive of Jewish traditions from which Libenson, Rofeberg, and their many collaborators might pull. As shown above through examples from podcast guests, the internet can store and provide immediate access to Jewish texts, rituals, religious objects, languages, art, liturgies, and community structures that have been "excavated" from the Jewish past for use by anyone, at any time, for any purpose. Jews of prior eras, even Jews of just one generation prior, did not have such radical access to Jewish traditions in their many varieties, which, in comparison, limited their abilities to utilize tradition as a method for Judaism.

In this way, the internet acts as a "long tail," to borrow (somewhat outdated) terminology from the business world, for Judaism and Jewish innovation. Just as the internet allows online sellers to host a much larger inventory of goods than do traditional brick-and-mortar stores, online databases of Jewish "goods" provide access to aspects of Jewish tradition that have not been popular enough for widespread use among offline Jewish communities.[28] Rofeberg, who lives in Providence, Rhode Island and has spent time in other areas with low Jewish populations, frequently expresses particular excitement about this aspect of the internet: In his experience, the niche Jewish resources provided by the internet are crucial for Jews who have limited offline Jewish options in their geographic areas. The access the internet provides allows, in the ideology of *Judaism Unbound*, further study of the past and, potentially, further innovation for the future.

The compatibility of the form and content of *Judaism Unbound* is also obvious when we broaden our definition of *Judaism Unbound*'s thought to include the guests Libenson and Rofeberg bring onto the show. Many of the guests are creating the types of innovations that Libenson and Rofeberg are calling for, particularly through the internet, and each of the guests and the projects they represent fulfill a small part, each in their own way and in their own area, of Libenson and Rofeberg's overall mission of an innovative, experimental Judaism, all relying on the resources of the internet to do so. When brought together by *Judaism Unbound*, such projects collectively represent the confluence of *Judaism Unbound*'s tradition-as-method ideology and the many possibilities of *Judaism Unbound*'s online format. Moreover, *Judaism Unbound*'s method of tradition-making serves to discursively authorize such projects as "authentically" Jewish.

---

[28] See Chris Anderson, "The Long Tail," *Wired*, October 1, 2004 and Chris Anderson, *The Long Tail: Why the Future of Business Is Selling Less of More* (New York: Hyperion, 2006).

Judaism Unbound suggests to me that contemporary American Jewish thinking has taken on methods that are foundational to digital media, much the way prior eras of American Jews similarly adopted widespread ideas and practices found in American society. The emphasis that Libenson and Rofeberg place on the archive of tradition for the possibilities of creation, for instance, is common to many projects—not only religious projects—on the internet. As Heidi Campbell, drawing from new media theorist Lev Manovich, writes,

> While old media were based on a linear view of the world where technology was dependent on a fixed, sequential logic and hierarchy, new media are based on the logic of the database. While the cultural format of narrative or story "creates a cause and effect trajectory out of which seemingly unordered items and events find order," the database represents the "world as a list of items that it refused to put in a set order." In a database, each individual unit and its combination hold privilege over the overarching narrative structure they represent. Therefore, connections are primary and the complete entity is secondary. Database logic means individuals have the ability to easily change the content and the system or structures; they are not bound by one predetermined path. So while old media provide a "window on the world," or one person's view of reality, new media offer users a "control panel" of multiple possibilities to create new versions of the world.[29]

Manovich and Campbell's notion of a database that allows users a "control panel" of multiple possibilities to create new versions of the world" is exemplified by *Judaism Unbound*'s archive of Jewish traditions that are re-imagined toward the construction of new forms of Judaism,

---

[29] Campbell, *Digital Creatives*, 8. Campbell cites Lev Manovich, *The Language of New Media* (Cambridge, Mass.: MIT Press, 2002), 230.

as is the idea that new media/new Judaism rejects the claim of old media/old Judaism to a normative narrative of history and culture that gives order to the world.

Furthermore, *Judaism Unbound*'s emphasis on and utilization of modularization, iteration, and innovation reflect internet-era logics of constant experimentation and futurity. The promise of the internet, much like the promise of *Judaism Unbound*'s Judaism, is that it is never complete but always in a process of expansion, an endless space of possibility. As Campbell describes, new media "highlight a shift from a set, prescribed narrative to an interactive, changeable configuration. New media empower people to manipulate structures and meanings. This, some claim, teaches that nothing is ever final or complete; there is always room for improvement."[30] Libenson and Rofeberg's method toward the creation of new Judaisms, from this perspective, is not only hosted on the internet but is analogous to the internet. Judaism is, in the digital age, a digital Judaism with digital logics, digital methods, and digital forms. Although the general structure of *Judaism Unbound*'s religious logic is clearly tied to 20th-century American Jewish ideas of creativity, expansion, and non-normativity, the possibilities that Libenson and Rofeberg imagine in their podcast are only possible, both technologically and ideologically, with the advent of the internet.

For scholars of contemporary American religion, the internet provides a complicated and exciting new space for the study of religion. Not only can we track the spread of religious ideas and practices into online forms, but as I have argued here, we can also recognize internet-era logics and methods in contemporary religious thinking. While the ceaseless innovation, reinvention, and seeming democratization of the internet has appeared, to some scholars, in opposition to the emphasis that religious traditions place on long-lasting continuity in the face of cultural change, *Judaism Unbound* reveals an instance in which the internet is understood by religious practitioners as necessary to the ongoing creative tension of innovation and tradition, as well as to the internet's discursive possibilities. In *Judaism Unbound*, the internet is a powerful new tool for the age-old discursive methodology of tradition.

---

[30] Campbell, *Digital Creatives*, 7.

Acknowledgments

This book is obviously a collective effort, as it includes the words of more than two dozen of the leading Jewish thinkers, practitioners, and experimenters of the 21st century. We are grateful that they were willing to give of their time to be guests on the podcast in the first place (one behind-the-scenes secret of *Judaism Unbound* is that we record for about twice as long as the publicly released version of the podcast episode ends up), and we are grateful that they agreed to have their interviews published in book form and took the time to review the edited transcript of our conversation. We're also profoundly grateful to the hundreds of podcast guests whose interviews have not (yet) been published in book form; all these conversations have made *Judaism Unbound* what it is and what it is becoming.

Judaism Unbound would be pretty much nothing at all without our listeners. If a tree falls in the forest and no one is there to hear it, does it make a sound? Our gratitude goes to all of the people who listened to the early podcasts and saw our potential to catalyze a movement. And thanks to all the listeners who have joined us in the eight years since those early days. Thank you for reaching out to say, "Yes, I want more of this." All of your emails, whether kudos or critiques, were essential to our development. And thank you for the financial support you generously provided and continue to provide. We wouldn't have made it to this point without you.

To all of the supporters who donated to our Kickstarter campaign, please know this book would not exist without you. We appreciate your early support and encouragement for making *Judaism Unbound* podcast material accessible to a wider audience by putting it into written form. Thanks for your patience, as this project took longer than expected.

Several extraordinary individuals played critical roles in developing the book. The project would not have happened without Estee Solomon Gray, who believed in the idea and assembled a dream team to help us make it happen; Josh Joseph, who provided foundational financial support for the project; Esther Mack, who painstakingly and expertly transcribed the podcasts; Sara Saltee, who took on the brunt of the heavy lifting to edit down the transcripts and provide structure and connective tissue for the book; Kathryn Klibanoff and Daniel Spiro, who provided writing and editorial help at critical junctures; Greg Marcus, who managed the Kickstarter campaign; and Jim Stein, who has believed in the importance of a *Judaism Unbound* book from Day One and whose inspiration, persistence, and support made all the difference in bringing the book to across the finish line. Important elements of the book also bear the imprint of Katie Kaestner-Frenchman, who designed the cover and has been responsible for the visual aesthetic of *Judaism Unbound* for many years; Hillel Smith, who designed the jewishLIVE logo, which was refined into the new(ish) *Judaism Unbound* logo by David Grossman and Katie; Hannah Ruby and Micah Sandman, who provided critical administrative support; and Miriam Terlinchamp, who finally got the job done. And this material would not actually be a book without our very patient and encouraging publisher Larry Yudelson, who was insisting that *Judaism Unbound* was important Jewish journalism long before we saw it that way.

This book would not exist if *Judaism Unbound* did not exist, and *Judaism Unbound* wouldn't have existed for very long had it not been for Jim Heeger and Raymond Stern, who provided financial and moral support that made it possible for us to make it through our first year; Zack Bodner and Apryl Stern, who helped us keep going in those early years and turn challenges into opportunities; and Ed Hamburg and Sarah Abella who have been with us through thick and thin as our founding board members. We so are grateful to everyone who has offered their time or treasure to *Judaism Unbound* over the years.

Finally, thank you to our families, who have always been encouraging despite the challenges in explaining that their loved one is a Jewish podcaster. We love and appreciate our parents, Ruth Lebed, Peter Rofes, Eli Libenson, and Suzy Libenson; our spouses, Beth Niestat and Valerie Rofeberg; Dan's children, Sam Libenson and Miriam Niestat; and our non-human companions, Porty, Pointer, Mordy, Peeve, and Gandalf, who play a very important role when you work from home.

Kickstarter Supporters

Special Mention

Jim Stein, our Super Mensch,
for believing in this project and giving so generously.

Alitia Abrams * Cara Abrams-Simonton * Kara Agnetta * Meryl Ain * Hank Albert * Adam Allenberg * Gregg Alpert * Julie Alweis * Bill Anspach * Del Atwood * Susan Averbac * Gary Bass * Lori Bassman * Marissa Beck * SB Berman * Julie Bir * Michael Blackmore * Roger Blonder * Diana Bloom * Arielle Branitsky * Todd Brecher * Anne Bussler * Anna Caplan * Susan Carsen * Amber Caulkins * Ceceley Chambers * James Cherney * Ann Chernicoff * John Cook * Ella Cooperman * Rebecca Cynamon-Murphy * Bonnie Davis * Mia Diamond Padwa * Meig Dickson (A-Dinosaur-A-Day) * Garrett Dieckmann * Sue Donnelly * Michael Dorff * Michelle Driscoll * Kenneth Einstein * Robin Eiseman * Abby Eisenberg * Gerald Elgarten * Caroline Ellen * Alexander Emery * Brent Epstein * Loree Farrar * Len Feldman * Darlene Feldstein * Lauren Finkelstein * Mario Fleck * Lisa Friedman * Suri Friedman * Daniel Gelbtuch * Harold Geller * Andrew Geske * Gili Getz * Joshua Gewolb * Alanna Gibbs * Natalie Goldfein * Jill Goldstein Smith * Paul Golin * Rachel Gollay * Elizabeth Gossage * Gilad Gray * Asya Gribov * Nadya Gross * Rebecca Gross * Jordan Haar * Ethan Hammerman * Denise Handler * Andrea Haverkamp * James J. Heeger * Elizabeth Heineman * R'Lizzi Heydemann * Keith Highiet * Emily Holtzman * Daniel Horwitz *

Stefanie Jacob * Lauren Jacobson Spokane * Ann Jaffe * Josh Jeffreys * Zoe Jick * Jennifer Kahn * Rena Kaminsky * Lawrence Kaplan * Brian Kates * Debi & Steve Katzman * Jason Kaufman * Margery Dine Kessler * Cherie Kirschbaum * Darren & Debra Kleinberg * Aliza Kline * David Daniel Klipper * Binya Koatz * Bernie Kraatz * Casper Ter Kuile * Elisheva Kupferman * Jodi Kushins * Sidney Kushner * Raymond Laliberte * Arnold Landy * Simona Lang * Betty Langberg * Eric & Laura Langberg * Benay Lappe * Wendie Lash * Brian Lass * Noah Leavitt * Richard Lebed * Ruth Lebed * Irene Lehrer Sandalow * Stephen Leonardo Silva * Charlie Leppert * Seth Leslie * Jack Levy * Sarah Lewin Frasier * Daniel Libenson * Eli Libenson * Michael Libenson * Rachel Libenson * Avi Lichtenstein * David Lieberman * Brett Lockspeiser * Deanne Loonin * Susan Lubeck * Devorah Lynn * Sara Lynn * Sharon Madnek * Bryan Mann * Greg Marcus * Eric Marks * Deni Marshall * Nathan Martin * Shannon Mayes * Jacob C. McDonald * Keren McGinity * Mandie McGlynn * Dan Mendelsohn Aviv * Cynthia MinsterCheng * Evan Moffic * Dr. Jerid Morisco * Lisa Narodick Colton * River Navaille * Marshal Neal * Ed Nickow * Debi Niestat * Eleanor Niestat * Herbert Niestat * Liz Noteware * Vanessa Ochs * Schachar Orenstein * Katy Orr * Heather Paul * Amy Pessah * Genevieve Podleski * David Polacek * Fredric Price * Andrew Reichart * Barak Richman * Eric Robbins * Rabbi Stephen Roberts * Eric Robsky Huntley * Lara Rodin * Lex Rofeberg * Anne Rogal * Jamie Roitman * Ben Rosenthal * Caroline Rothstein * Michelle Rubel * Jeff Ruby * Nancy Rudin * Jill Sarkozi * Adam Schaffer * Zachary Schaffer * Josa Scheider * Jim Scheinman * Margalit Schindler * Bradley Schlesinger * Jordana Schmier * Miriam Schoeman * Brian Schwartz * Kathy Seidel * Debra Seltzer * Helaine Sheias * Jessica K. Shimberg * Tiffany Shlain * Aviv Siegel * Noam Sienna * Jane Silverman * Zoe Silverman * Becky Silverstein * Estee Solomon Gray * John Stein * Aaron Steinberg * Apryl Stern * Shira Stutman * Marc Swetlitz * Solange Tajchman * Mia Tavan * Miriam Taylor * Miriam Terlinchamp * Barbara Thiede * Dorothy Thursby * Adam Toobin * Amy Travis * Evan Traylor * Ellen Triebwasser * Luciana Turchick * A.P. Vague * Alexandra Wall * Nahum Wardlev * Gabriel Weinstein * David Weisberg * Leon Wiener Dow * Rachel Wilstein * SJ Wissows * Jeremy Wolfe * Laurie Yablon * Larry Yudelson * The Creative Fund by BackerKit *

About the Authors

DAN LIBENSON

Dan Libenson is the founder of *Judaism Unbound* and served as its first president from 2015-2023. Since 2023, Dan has been the president of Lippman Kanfer Foundation for Living Torah, while he continues to co-host the *Judaism Unbound* podcast and to teach in *Judaism Unbound*'s UnYeshiva digital center for Jewish learning and unlearning.

Prior to founding *Judaism Unbound*, Dan spent over a decade working with Jewish students at Harvard and at the University of Chicago. His innovative work on campus was recognized with Hillel International's highest honor, and he was awarded the prestigious AVI CHAI Fellowship in 2009.

Dan has served on the faculties of numerous Jewish leadership education programs, and he has translated the work of an acclaimed Israeli novelist. An honors graduate of both Harvard College and Harvard Law School, he was an editor of the *Harvard Law Review*, clerked for a federal appellate judge, and taught law for five years. Originally from New York, Dan now lives in Chicago, Illinois.

LEX ROFEBERG

Lex Rofeberg joined *Judaism Unbound* as Strategic Initiatives Coordinator soon after its founding and has co-hosted, produced, and edited the *Judaism Unbound* podcast since it launched in 2016. In 2021, Lex became Senior Jewish Educator, spearheading the launch of *Judaism Unbound*'s UnYeshiva, a digital center for Jewish learning and unlearning.

Passionate about digital Judaism, Lex has led numerous projects within *Judaism Unbound*, such as its annual ShavuotLIVE gatherings (online, 24-hour Jewish learning festivals), and he is well known for his engagement with Jewish questions on Facebook. His writing has been featured in publications including JTA, *Jewish Currents*, and MyJewishLearning.

Lex is a graduate of Brown University, was ordained as a rabbi through ALEPH: Alliance for Jewish Renewal, and holds a certificate in Interfaith Families Jewish Engagement from Hebrew College. He serves on the advisory board or board of directors for The Shalom Center, Tikkun Olam Productions, and Evolve: Groundbreaking Jewish Conversations. A native of Milwaukee, Wisconsin, Lex lives in (Divine) Providence, Rhode Island.

Recent books from *Ben Yehuda Press*

Just Jewish: How to Engage Millennials and Build a Vibrant Jewish Future by Rabbi Dan Horwitz. Drawing on his experience launching The Well, an inclusive Jewish community for young adults in Metro Detroit, Rabbi Horwitz shares proven techniques ready to be adopted by the Jewish world's myriad organizations, touching on everything from branding to fundraising to programmatic approaches to relationship development, and more. "This book will shape the conversation as to how we think about the Jewish future." —Rabbi Elliot Cosgrove, editor, *Jewish Theology in Our Time*..

Judaism Disrupted: A Spiritual Manifesto for the 21st Century by Rabbi Michael Strassfeld. "I can't remember the last time I felt pulled to underline a book constantly as I was reading it, but *Judaism Disrupted* is exactly that intellectual, spiritual and personal adventure. You will find yourself nodding, wrestling, and hoping to hold on to so many of its ideas and challenges. Rabbi Strassfeld reframes a Torah that demands breakage, reimagination, and ownership." —Abigail Pogrebin, author, *My Jewish Year: 18 Holidays, One Wondering Jew*

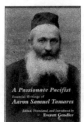

A Passionate Pacifist: Essential Writings of Aaron Samuel Tamares. Translated and edited by Rabbi Everett Gendler. Rabbi Aaron Samuel Tamares (1869-1931) addresses the timeless issues of ethics, morality, communal morale, and Judaism in relation to the world at large in these essays and sermons, written in Hebrew between 1904 and 1931. "For those who seek a Torah of compassion and pacifism, a Judaism not tied to 19th century political nationalism, and a vision of Jewish spirituality outside of political thinking this book will be essential." —Rabbi Dr. Alan Brill, author, *Thinking God: The Mysticism of Rabbi Zadok of Lublin*.

Seeking the Hiding God: A Personal Theological Essay by Arnold Eisen. "This generation's preeminent scholar of contemporary Jewry, Arnold Eisen has devoted his career to studying the spiritual strivings within the Jewish soul. In *Seeking the Hiding God*, Eisen provides a personal window into his own theological vision. Eisen's explorations will inspire readers to ask today's urgent questions of meaning and faith." —Rabbi Dr. Elliot Cosgrove, author of *For Such a Time as This: On Being Jewish Today*.

Embracing Auschwitz: Forging a Vibrant, Life-Affirming Judaism that Takes the Holocaust Seriously by Rabbi Joshua Hammerman. The Judaism of Sinai and the Judaism of Auschwitz are merging, resulting in new visions of Judaism that are only beginning to take shape. "Should be read by every Jew who cares about Judaism." —Rabbi Dr. Irving "Yitz" Greenberg

Put Your Money Where Your Soul Is: Jewish Wisdom to Transform Your Investments for Good by Rabbi Jacob Siegel. "An intellectual delight. It offers a cornucopia of good ideas, institutions, and advisers. These can ease the transition for institutions and individuals from pure profit nature investing to deploying one's capital to repair the world, lift up the poor, and aid the needy and vulnerable. The sources alone—ranging from the Bible, Talmud, and codes to contemporary economics and sophisticated financial reporting—are worth the price of admission." —Rabbi Irving "Yitz" Greenberg.

The Way of Torah and the Path of Dharma: Intersections between Judaism and the Religions of India by Rabbi Daniel Polish. "A whirlwind religious tourist visit to the diversity of Indian religions: Sikh, Jain, Buddhist, and Hindu, led by an experienced congregational rabbi with much experience in interfaith and in teaching world religions." —Rabbi Alan Brill, author of *Rabbi on the Ganges: A Jewish Hindu-Encounter*.

Recent books from *Ben Yehuda Press*

Burning Psalms: Confronting Adonai after Auschwitz by Menachem Rosensaft. "It's amazing that Menachem Z. Rosensaft's *Burning Psalms: Confronting Adonai after Auschwitz* doesn't burst into flames. This book of poetry — every poem in it a response or counterpoint to every one of the psalms in the biblical book — written by the son of Holocaust survivors and the brother of a murdered sibling he never knew, is composed with fire, fueled by a combination of rage, love, and despite-it-all faith that sears your eyes as you read it." —*New Jersey Jewish Standard*

Weaving Prayer: An Analytical and Spiritual Commentary on the Jewish Prayer Book by Rabbi Jeffrey Hoffman. "This engaging and erudite volume transforms the prayer experience. Not only is it of considerable intellectual interest to learn the history of prayers—how, when, and why they were composed—but this new knowledge will significantly help a person pray with intention (*kavanah*). I plan to keep this volume right next to my siddur." —Rabbi Judith Hauptman, author of *Rereading the Rabbis: A Woman's Voice*.

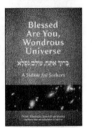

Blessed Are You, Wondrous Universe: A Siddur for Seekers. Non-theistic Jewish prayers by Herbert J. Levine. "Herb Levine has fashioned a sparkling collection of prayers for a thinking, feeling modern person who wants to express gratitude for the wonder of existence." —Daniel Matt, author, *The Essential Kabbalah*. "An exercise in holy audacity." —Dr. Shaul Magid, author, *The Necessity of Exile*

Siddur HaKohanot: A Hebrew Priestess Prayerbook by Jill Hammer and Taya Shere. Creative and traditional Jewish rituals and prayers that explore an earth-honoring, feminine-honoring spirituality with deep roots in Jewish tradition. "Far more than a prayerbook, this is a paradigm-shifting guidebook that radically expands our religious language, empowering us to reclaim what our souls have known for centuries: how to cook, season, and feast on our love of life, Spirit, and each other." —Rabbi Tirzah Firestone, author, *The Receiving: Reclaiming Jewish Women's Wisdom*

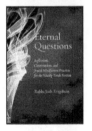

Eternal Questions by Rabbi Josh Feigelson. These essays on the weekly Torah portion guide readers on a journey that weaves together Torah, Talmud, Hasidic masters, and a diverse array of writers, poets, musicians, and thinkers. Each essay includes questions for reflection and suggestions for practices to help turn study into more mindful, intentional living. "This is the wisdom that we always need—but maybe particularly now, more than ever, during these turbulent times." —Rabbi Danya Ruttenberg, author, *On Repentance and Repair*.

Musar in Recovery: A Jewish Spiritual Path to Serenity & Joy by Hannah L. with Rabbi Harvey Winokur. "A process of recovery that is physically healing, morally redemptive, and spiritually transformative." —Rabbi Rami Shapiro, author of *Recovery: The Twelve Steps as Spiritual Practice*. "A lucid and practical guidebook to recovery." —Dr. Alan Morinis, author, *Everyday Holiness: The Jewish Spiritual Path of Mussar*.

Other Covenants: Alternate Histories of the Jewish People by Rabbi Andrea D. Lobel & Mark Shainblum. In *Other Covenants*, you'll meet Israeli astronauts trying to save a doomed space shuttle, a Jewish community's faith challenged by the unstoppable return of their own undead, a Jewish science fiction writer in a world of Zeppelins and magic, an adult Anne Frank, an entire genre of Jewish martial arts movies, a Nazi dystopia where Judaism refuses to die, and many more. Nominated for two Sidewise Awards for Alternate History.